ESCAPE FROM HITLER'S REICH

ESCAPE FROM HITLER'S REICH

AMAZING STORIES OF PoW ESCAPES BY ALLIED AIRMEN IN WW2

MARTIN W. BOWMAN

AIR WORLD

ESCAPE FROM HITLER'S REICH
Amazing Stories of PoW Escapes by Allied Airmen in WW2

First published in Great Britain in 2024 by
Air World
An imprint of
Pen & Sword Books Ltd
Yorkshire – Philadelphia

Copyright © Martin W. Bowman, 2024

ISBN 978 1 39907 320 2

The right of Martin W. Bowman to be identified as Author of this work has been asserted by him in accordance with the Copyright, Designs and Patents Act 1988.

A CIP catalogue record for this book is available from the British Library.

All rights reserved. No part of this book may be reproduced or transmitted in any form or by any means, electronic or mechanical including photocopying, recording or by any information storage and retrieval system, without permission from the Publisher in writing.

Typeset by SJmagic DESIGN SERVICES, India.

Printed and bound in the UK by CPI Group (UK) Ltd.

Pen & Sword Books Limited incorporates the imprints of After the Battle, Atlas, Archaeology, Aviation, Discovery, Family History, Fiction, History, Maritime, Military, Military Classics, Politics, Select, Transport, True Crime, Air World, Frontline Publishing, Leo Cooper, Remember When, Seaforth Publishing, The Praetorian Press, Wharncliffe Local History, Wharncliffe Transport, Wharncliffe True Crime and White Owl.

For a complete list of Pen & Sword titles please contact

PEN & SWORD BOOKS LIMITED
George House, Units 12 & 13, Beevor Street, Off Pontefract Road,
Barnsley, South Yorkshire, S71 1HN, England
E-mail: enquiries@pen-and-sword.co.uk
Website: www.pen-and-sword.co.uk

or

PEN AND SWORD BOOKS
1950 Lawrence Rd, Havertown, PA 19083, USA
E-mail: uspen-and-sword@casematepublishers.com
Website: www.penandswordbooks.com

Contents

Acknowledgements vi
Prologue viii

Chapter 1   Against the Wind 1
Chapter 2   My Escape Through Belgium and France 12
Chapter 3   Wingless Journey 28
Chapter 4   O'Leary Line to Freedom 45
Chapter 5   Heydekrug 65
Chapter 6   Comet Line Escape: Flight Sergeant
            Stanley Munns 76
Chapter 7   The Ides of March 94
Chapter 8   The Great Escape 103
Chapter 9   'Home by Christmas 1945?' 141

Postscript   The Legend that is Colditz 166
Index 189

Acknowledgements

I would like to offer my grateful thanks to the following British airmen and friends for the kind use of their stories and anecdotes used in this book, which they related to me in correspondence and fascinating interviews, some of which began more than forty-five years ago. I am indebted to the late Cyril Rofé; and the People's War site by Viv Foulds of Egerton Telecottage on behalf of Joe Pack. *RAF Evaders: The Comprehensive Story of Thousands of Escapers and their Escape Lines, Western Europe, 1940–1945* by Oliver Clutton-Brock (Grub Street, 2009; *Wingless Journey, Escape or Die: Authentic Stories of the RAF Escaping Society* by Paul Brickhill; the stories of the late Leslie Sidwell are adapted from his book *Wingless Journey* (Merlin Books, 1 April 1996) with the kind permission of James Sidwell, Leslie's grandson. I am indebted to Gordon Henry Francis Carter for his various accounts and other accounts in several books, and to the late Warrant Officer Kenneth Albert Goodchild and to the *WWII escape and evasion Information Exchange* website, part of the *Conscript Heroes* website; Geoff Parnell; accounts of the Wooden Horse escape recorded in the short book *Goon in the Block* by the late Eric Williams; *First Over Germany: A History of the 306th Bombardment Group* by Russell A. Strong (1982); the late Stanley Munns; *Footprints on the Sands of Time* by Oliver Clutton-Brock (Grub Street, 2003). *Journey to the Horizon: Escape and Evasion during World War II* by Hans Onderwater and Brian Lissette; *Free To Fight Again: RAF Escapes and Evasions 1940–1945* by Alan W. Cooper; *Behind the Wire: Allied Prisoners of War in Hitler's Germany* by Philip

ACKNOWLEDGEMENTS

Kaplan and Jack Currie. (Pen & Sword Aviation, 2012). *Lonesome Road* by George Harsh (Sphere Books London 1972). Lieutenant Colonel Clark's experiences are described in his memoir *33 Months as a PoW in Stalag Luft III: A World War II Airman Tells his Story*. *Final Flight* by Squadron Leader John Hartnell-Beavis DFC (Merlin Books Ltd, Braunton, 1985). Stories of the Great Escape come from many sources, including *The Life and Death of Roger Bushell Love, Betrayal, Big X and the Great Escape by Simon Pearson* (Hodder, 2013). *Home By Christmas 1945?* is adapted from the *Wingless Journey* by the late Leslie Sidwell (Merlin Books, 1 April 1996) with the kind permission of James Sidwell, Leslie's grandson. Stories relating to Colditz come from many sources including Airey Neave DSO OBE MC TD and *'Bush' Parker: An Australian Battle of Britain Pilot in Colditz* (2007) by Colin Burgess.

Prologue

There were literally hundreds of escapes from German PoW camps and their associated work camps during the Second World War but most escapers were recaptured (some several times). M.R.D. Foot and J.M. Langley in their *MI9: Escape and Evasion 1939–1945* quote a figure of 26,260 for the total number of British and Dominion escapers and evaders from all war theatres, of which 2,865 were RAF. For the Western Europe war theatres alone, there were a total of 3,631, of which 2,138 were Air Force.

Flying Officer Harry Burton, a Wellington pilot on 149 Squadron, is believed to be the first British PoW escapee of the Second World War to have successfully made a 'home run'. Born at Rutherglen in 1919, he was educated at Glasgow High School. He joined the Royal Air Force in 1937 and having graduated from No. 10 FTS was posted to No. 215 Squadron to fly Harrows. By the beginning of the war he was flying on operations in Wellingtons with 149 Squadron. He was forced to bail out near the Franco–Belgian border while returning from Germany in the early hours of 6 September 1940 when one of the engines seized. He evaded alone for two days until he was captured by a German soldier. Next morning, he was driven to Le Touquet and handed over to the Luftwaffe, who treated him to breakfast before taking him to Saint-Omer. That evening he was taken to Brussels, where he found several of his crew already in captivity. A few days later they were taken to Dulag Luft at Oberursel, 13km north-west of Frankfurt-am-Main (where Burton met Wing Commander Harry Day), and on about 16 September 1940, Burton, his crew and about sixty other men were transferred by troop train to Stalag Luft I (Barth)

PROLOGUE

near the Baltic coast. During the journey he availed himself of the railway maps conveniently left in the carriage compartments and these were to prove invaluable later.

Burton made several unsuccessful escape attempts from Barth. His first attempt to escape in May ended when he was caught installing air pumping gear in the getaway tunnel. As punishment he was sentenced to ten days' solitary confinement on reduced rations. Determined to escape, in the early hours of 23 May 1941 he set about loosening the bars of the cooler with a table knife that he had hidden and with this knife he was able to burrow out from beneath the perimeter fencing. Striking a railway line, he set off in the direction of one of the Baltic ports and walking by night and hiding during the day he eventually reached Sassnitz on the German island of Rügen on 31 May. Here he hoped to sneak aboard a ferry boat to Sweden. However, the vessel was heavily guarded so, noticing a freight train apparently waiting to be loaded, he crawled beneath it and clung to the underside of one of the wagons. Luck was with him here and the mail car, as it proved to be, was shortly shunted aboard. Once clear of German territorial waters he gave himself up to the Swedish police. He was taken to Trelleborg and the ordeal was over. He was flown overnight to Britain from Stockholm on 19 July to become the first escaped PoW to make a 'home run' to Britain in the war. For this and for the information that he was able to provide about methods of interrogation employed by the enemy Harry Burton was appointed to the Distinguished Service Order.

Escaping and evading airmen relied heavily upon various Resistance groups in Holland, Belgium and France. Patriots put their lives at risk organising escape routes to neutral Switzerland and Spain and some of the most highly organised were in Belgium. It all began towards the end of 1940 when some ex-officers of the Belgian Army who were not incarcerated in PoW camps formed groups called Mouvements de Résistance. The existence of such groups was later admitted by the Belgian government in exile in London. Some, like the Front de l'independence (FI), was very active but its members were predominantly communist. Their leader was Fernand Demany, a Belgian journalist, writer and prominent Resistance fighter. Two other large groups, the Milices Nationales Belges (MNB) and the Mouvement Nationaliste Royaliste (MNR) also gave the German occupation forces many headaches.

All these groups were known collectively as the Armée Belge Secrete (ABS). It was perhaps better known as the Armée Secrète (AS) or Secret Army. Its leader was Lieutenant General Jules-Joseph Pire, a Belgian career soldier born in Hannut in the province of Liège on 29 March 1878. His orders for sabotage and Resistance came from London via special radio contacts and coded BBC transmissions. With Belgium under German occupation, Pire had become involved in the Resistance. In 1941 he was involved in the creation of the Belgian Legion, a group in the Belgian Resistance with right-wing political sympathies. He became the group's commander in Wallonia. The Belgian Legion subsequently merged with other groups, eventually becoming the Secret Army in 1944. Following the arrest of Jules Bastin and his successor's escape to England, Pire became head of the Secret Army in January 1944.

Apart from carrying out acts of sabotage, the Resistance movement in Belgium had a very efficient escape line for downed Allied airmen. Collectively, the escape lines helped more than 5,000 Allied military personnel, mostly airmen, escape occupied France, Belgium and the Netherlands.

The Pat O'Leary Line[1] received financial assistance from MI9, a British intelligence agency, and exfiltrated more than 600 Allied

---

1. On 31 May 1940, a Belgian doctor, Albert-Marie Guérisse, had left the beaches of Dunkirk for England. On the capitulation of Belgium, he returned to France, but in the chaos that was taking place headed south again, to join other Belgians on their way to Gibraltar to continue the fight. Guérisse had been taken on by SOE and assumed the identity 'Pat O'Leary' (the alias of Patrick Albert 'Pat' O'Leary, purportedly the name of a peacetime Canadian friend) in order to protect his family in Belgium. Major General Count Albert-Marie Edmond Guérisse GC KBE DSO died on 26 March 1989.

PROLOGUE

soldiers and airmen from France to Spain. This line began in 1940 when stranded soldiers were 'helped' by French and Greek civilians in southern France. Following on from Dunkirk, Saint-Valery and Calais, the 'helpers' assisted Allied servicemen with their efforts to evade the Germans, and make their dangerous journey from northern France to Marseille; here they would be met by mountain guides and couriers who would take them over the Pyrenees into Spain and onward to Gibraltar. Although the line originally ran from northern France to Marseille, it later expanded its activities to assist those servicemen who had made their way to neutral Switzerland. As well as making their escape over the mountains, servicemen were also evacuated by sea, taking them from the beaches of southern France directly to Gibraltar. Many of the 'helpers' were arrested, and the line almost closed when enemy agents infiltrated the group in early 1943. Despite this setback, the line re-routed through Toulouse and ran until the end of the war. More than 100 volunteers or 'helpers' as they were often called, mostly French, working for the Pat Line were arrested and imprisoned by Vichy French or German authorities. Most were imprisoned for the remainder of the war and many were executed or died in concentration camps.

By July 1941 stricken RAF crews were parachuting over the Low Countries in ever increasing numbers. As a result, the Comet Line came into existence. Patriots set up safe houses along a route that led from Holland and Belgium through France to neutral Spain. Crews brought down in the Brussels area who were rescued by the Belgian Resistance were sent on to Paris, where they came under the wing of Frédéric De Jongh, born 13 December 1897. De Jongh and Walthère Dewé were responsible for the functioning of the Comet Line, originally called the 'Réseau (Network for Action) D-D' after Dewé and De Jongh. The British Secret Service referred to it as the Comet Line because of the speed needed to whisk stranded airmen through occupied France to safety.

Dewé, born on 26 July 1880, was a brilliant engineer in civilian life and had been a founder member of the Dewé-Blauche Resistance movement during the First World War. In the months preceding 1940 he was in charge of a special information service called 'Cleveland'. After the Belgian surrender in 1940, General Dewé was removed to Germany and made a prisoner of war. But he was soon released when the Germans discovered that he held high technical qualifications. At the end of 1940 he joined the German-controlled Telegraph and Telephone Service. Dewé operated Clarence Réseau at this time, trying, unsuccessfully, to make contact with the British. It was not until 29 January 1941, when a British parachutist was dropped into Belgium, that contact was finally established. During this period Dewé left his job and devoted all his time to the Clarence operation. On 7 January Dewé's wife and two daughters were arrested by the Geheime Feldpolizei (GFP). Seven days later Dewé was killed by a Luftwaffe officer during a pursuit. His death effectively ended the Comet Line but Marathon took over and the flow of evaders through Belgium and France was maintained. Secret camps set up in the forests of the Ardennes collected groups of airmen ready for transit across France to the Pyrenees and into Spain for safe passage to England via Gibraltar.

Chapter 1

Against the Wind

Cyril Rofé was born in Cairo of Jewish parents on 11 April 1916. He was educated at Clifton College, Bristol, and Chillon College in Switzerland, trained for the hotel business at the Swiss Hotel School in Lausanne and, after a period at the Mayfair Hotel in London, went to the Bristol, in Vienna, where he acquired a love of opera and skiing. He got out ten days after Hitler marched into Austria and on the outbreak of war volunteered for aircrew. While waiting for training he joined the Scots Guards' special ski battalion, which was intended for Norway, and when this was disbanded went into the Royal Air Force and trained as an observer (navigator and bomb aimer). Short, wiry and always determined, he was on the crew of a Wellington bomber on 40 Squadron that was shot down into the Maas Estuary on 11–12 June 1941.

On the night of 11–12 June 1941 attacks were made on Duisburg and Boulogne and Düsseldorf, which despite a dense fog en route, was attacked by ninety-two Wellingtons and six Stirlings. Six Wellingtons were lost on the operation on Düsseldorf. One of these was Wellington IC R1323 on 40 Squadron at Alconbury piloted by Squadron Leader Mark Evelyn Redgrave, which was shot down by Kriegsmarine flak-ships and crashed in the Haringvliet, a large inlet of the North Sea, in the province of South Holland Estuary near Hellevoetsluis. After the crash Sergeant Cyril Rofé woke up in a half-filled dinghy. The crew had put him in it while the tail gunner, Sergeant James Alexander Stephen Abernethy was still trapped in the wreck of the Wellington. Rofé had a badly injured right arm. It was a miracle that all crew members had survived the crash because the bomb bay was still loaded with bombs. When a ship eventually arrived with the rising tide, they were helped aboard, where Rofé again lost consciousness. He was taken to Vlaardingen hospital, where he also found the second pilot, Sergeant Alan Frank Potter RNZAF and two gunners, Sergeant Phillip Rockingham and Sergeant Robert Alldrick RCAF. Redgrave and Abernethy were brought to the local flak post. Potter and Abernethy were considered 'walking patients' and were transported to the hospital in Amsterdam, where they would be treated for their injuries and then travel further. Rofé and Rockingham were taken to hospital in Rotterdam. However, the hospital was completely full and they too had to travel to Amsterdam. Rofé had a complicated fracture of the right arm that was set neatly. Even here he found another RAF airman, with whom he had completed training. Both were shot down on the same night.

In this hospital room with primarily German wounded, Rofé first announced his Jewish background but since he was a prisoner of war this did not really matter to most Germans. Jewish PoWs in most cases received the same treatment as any others. Only at the end of the war was there some change. After his wounds had healed Rofé was moved to a hospital in Frankfurt. Then he was sent to Dulag Luft and eventually he ended up in Stalag Luft VIIIB Lamsdorf in Silesia. Many other camps would follow. The Geneva Convention stipulated that officers and NCOs could not be made to work during captivity. All other prisoners of war, however, had to join work shifts. Security was very limited and sometimes completely absent. This offered an easy chance to escape and one that Rofé did not want to ignore. The life of officers and NCOs was much better and that in turn attracted some ordinary soldiers. The result was a lively exchange of identities, which was later complicated by identity cards with photos but in the beginning only officers carried such identity cards. The photos were not very good and as long as the person you swapped with looked vaguely like you did not run too many risks. Rofé decided to switch identities and went looking for a good candidate. The change would take place during a football match between enlisted men and officer teams. That was not easy because such events did not happen every week and prisoners were constantly transferred to other camps. Some transfers were therefore cancelled at the last minute because one of the people had moved.

Eventually Rofé changed identity with Vienna-born Simon Kacenelenbeigen, a Jewish-British soldier who felt the risks of escape were too high. For Rofé this was an unpronounceable name but a chance to leave the camp. He had to learn all the details of Kacenelenbeigen's life by heart because trick questions were regularly asked to confirm the identities.

The first time Rofé undertook an escape attempt he tried to reach Switzerland on foot. His mother still lived there but after having walked for ten days through the woods towards Czechoslovakia he was discovered by blackberry pickers and reported to a forester armed with a shotgun, who promptly apprehended him. Back in Lamsdorf, Rofé was welcomed with a couple of days' solitary confinement and was again working with the other prisoners of war. This time he was assigned to a group in Poland in the coal mines. That pleased him not at all and soon he was again walking the roads to freedom, heading to Danzig to try to board a Swedish freighter. Halfway to Danzig he was betrayed by a Polish collaborator and returned to be told that the next time he tried to escape he would be sent to a 'special' camp for Jews. In the prison camps there were stories told of these places and Rofé knew this was no idle threat. During various operations they had already met groups of Jewish slave labourers. These prisoners of Auschwitz were spared because they still could be useful to the Germans. These groups were treated much worse than other prisoners of war and it was terrible to hear what took place in the concentration camps. Rofé and the other PoWs helped such groups as much as possible with what food was available. Such groups provided prisoners with the civilian clothes they needed for their escape. Rofé did not see the threat of a one-way trip to a concentration camp as any reason to stop, especially since some of the guards had indicated that all Jewish prisoners would end up there eventually anyway. The winter stopped escape activities for a while and in the spring of 1944 Rofé often suffered from the arm that was injured during the crash. During the various activities outside the camps he also once came across a group of Dutch volunteers for the Eastern Front. Rofé remembered the encounter well because this group oddly appeared to have great sympathy for the RAF.

In the summer of 1944 Rofé was building barracks at Schömberg and Katowice in the far east of what was then Germany, on the border with Poland and Czechoslovakia. This was hundreds of miles from Switzerland and Sweden but Rofé quickly realised that just 250km to the east the Russian troops were approaching. Russia meant escaping through perhaps the longest detour to England but also in the end maybe the fastest. He asked his fellow Jewish prisoner on the working party, Karl Hillebrand, a thin, studious-looking Palestinian corporal in the British Army who was born in Vienna, if he wanted to go along.

'If we get caught, it can mean Auschwitz,' Rofé said. 'Maybe it will be Auschwitz anyway so let's just try,' replied Hillebrand. 'The only way to avoid Auschwitz is to outsmart the Germans.' They decided to escape towards the Russians and break through the front line or simply wait until the Russians arrived; a plan that later proved more difficult than it seemed. By 20 August they had received a hundred German marks, a small amount of food consisting of chocolate, biscuits and cigarettes and the necessary forged papers from the local escape committee showing them to be Belgian electrical workers with permits to travel to Saybusch. Rofé had an old grey suit, a grey trilby and a briefcase, and Hillebrand had a black jacket, grey trousers and also a trilby. At 0530 hours they were woken by the familiar '*Raus! Raus!*' and were quickly led to the construction site. The other members of the group took care of the distraction so that the two escapers could swap their clothes and were able to slip away from the site while the guards were busy with other things.

AGAINST THE WIND

Waiting for the tram from Schömberg to Beuthen in Upper Silesia, Hillebrand recognised a man that had visited the camp. Hillebrand quietly swore, grabbed Rofé's arm and swung him so that they both faced away. 'He was working on the wiring at the huts the other day,' Hillebrand hissed. 'He would remember me.' The man stopped just behind them, and they stayed looking nervously and self-consciously the other way until the tram arrived and the man climbed into the front compartment. Hillebrand and Rofé got into the rear, and the man never glanced round all the way to Beuthen, but luckily for them he seemed not to recognise them.

In Beuthen, waiting for the connection to Katowice, they were approached by a policeman. Fortunately for them this was a Ukrainian who spoke German worse than them and was only interested in finding out the time. At first Rofé did not understand and looked at him dumbly. The German spoke again, more slowly. Rofé looked at his watch and said with an attempt at a smile, 'Sechs Uhr and Halb'. Hillebrand, whose German was faultless, had moved to the rescue and was telling the policeman kindly that everyone could not be German. They chatted amiably until the tram arrived and the policeman got in with them and talked all the way to Katowice, which was reassuring when two more police got in at a little village and looked arrogantly round the tram. No one asked 'difficult' questions. Everything seemed to go well until at Katowice a railway police officer took their papers during an inspection. They heard him explain to other people that 'this was the kind of paper they needed!' And then Rofé and Hillebrand were returned their papers with a smile. They boarded a train for Saybusch, and a woman in the opposite seat insisted on telling them about the time she was bombed out of Berlin and what she would do to any RAF airman she got her hands on. Rofé left most of the talking to Hillebrand, bracing himself to agree with the woman now and then. From Saybusch they moved towards the east on foot, sleeping in the woods by day and walking through the vast fields that were occasionally worked on by farmers. Near Rabingora the border between Germany and Czechoslovakia could be found but their handmade map was not exactly accurate. Eventually they roamed the area for several days and several times crossed the border without knowing it. Finally, they managed to dodge the various German patrols and found their original route. This led them through the Tatra Mountains, where they tried to avoid the main roads as much as possible. The local population was generally anti-German and it was not difficult to find food and shelter, especially after Rofé announced that he was RAF. That same population was worried about how they would fare after the 'liberation' by the Russians. Rofé had never seen such poor people. They lived in simple houses, walked barefoot and only had home-made clothes. Yet they helped Rofé and Hillebrand where they could.

In the market town of Markowa in south-eastern Poland they decided to walk as fast as possible through the crowds. However, they found several Germans on their way, and among them some SS. It was too late to turn back so they just walked on. For a moment it seemed that their attempt to escape had failed but thankfully and to their surprise they were not approached and nobody spoke to them. On the other side of the village they found Polish workers guarded by Germans who were building fortifications, the first sign that the front was approaching. Rofé had never seen such poor people. Their houses were of baked mud, brick and thatch, usually divided into two rooms with hard earth floors, and the women went barefoot, dressed in shawls and simple homespun dresses that hung on them like sugar bags.

On the eighth day, as they walked through the woods, they came across three uniformed and armed figures. It was too late to flee and a hiding place at such a moment was nowhere to be found but Hillenbrand recognised them. They were Polish partisans! The men took the two escapers to their accommodation and said they would help them. Rofé and Hillebrand did have concerns about their plan to cross the front line but, rather than wait for the arrival of the Russians, decided to go on. The partisans helped them across the

Poprad river and gave them the direction they should follow. These Polish partisans were no friends of the Russians and hoped that in the confusion after a Russian victory they could create their own Polish state. Their leader, however, would later be killed by the Soviets because of his 'fascist' sympathies!

Rofé and Hillebrand tried to move from one group to another to get closer to the front. In between they again came across a German patrol, but miraculously managed to talk themselves out of the situation. Their falsified papers and their excuses were obviously of very good quality.

After several days on a mountain named Jaworze they came across a partisan band led by a man called Kmicic, an elusive, blue-eyed, dynamic young man who was the hero of the district, who told them that the Germans and Russians were preparing a major battle in the north near Tarnów. In the east, the front was more dynamic and offered better opportunities to cross the front line. The group contained an escaped Russian soldier named Achmetow, a cherubic little man in remnants of tattered Russian uniform, who wanted to cross the front as well and could help them do so. Achmetow spoke a few words of German and liked their plans. Kmicic drew a simple map with the route to the front and on 17 September they left the partisans. In the night they could hear the thunder of the Soviet artillery in the distance. The farmers were vague about the Russians until they met one who had lived in America for years and spoke English well. He stated that there was no clear front and some Russian units not far away had broken through. Two days earlier Russians had been seen just 3km away. They decided to go on in the direction of the cannon. Suddenly three men stepped from behind some trees. Achmetow shouted '*Russki! Russki!*' He was running madly ahead. They watched him talking excitedly to the three men and then he turned and beckoned wildly. Rofé thought they could not be Russians but as he went cautiously forward, he could see that the three men had medals on both sides of their chests, black fur caps and dark uniforms with rather full-cut trousers tucked into riding boots. 'My God, they are Russians,' Rofé yelled and broke into a run. He could make out the officers' tabs on their shoulders and as he came up to them one of them, a middle-aged man, said in German: 'You are British?' 'Royal Air Force,' Rofe announced. 'We are the Red Army,' declared the officer and Rofé said breathlessly, '*Deutschland kaput! Deutschland kaput!*' It was all he could think of to say. Rofé and Hillebrand could not believe these were the first real Russian troops they had met and that they themselves had crossed the front. They had seen no Germans! These Russians were part of Cossack units consisting of hundreds of men who were cut off from other units but who continued fighting behind German lines. The Germans were afraid they were being surrounded and did everything possible to eliminate these units.

When in 1917 after the revolution civil war broke out between the Mensheviks and Bolsheviks, most Cossacks fought against the Red Army. After its triumph the Soviets obviously retaliated. Many wealthy Cossacks lost everything they owned. They also lost all their military and police powers and their cavalry units were disbanded. Many Cossacks were exiled to Kazakhstan and Siberia. However, in 1936 the Soviets decided to re-establish Cossack units and from 1939 to 1945 they were used during the war. There were also large groups of Cossacks who joined the Germans in the hope of regaining their former status, and the Italians also had Cossack regiments. The tragedy of a proud people was that eventually they fought each other and were abused and crushed by the great powers.

Rofé and Hillebrand were staggered by the sight of thousands of Russians camped in the fields. They looked so peaceful, as though no war existed and no enemy encircled them. The two escapers were greeted warmly by the Cossacks, who belonged to Division 'P' of the Fourth Cossack Corps, and after questioning them about their escape, the route they had followed, the partisans and the lack of Germans in the territories they crossed, they were invited for dinner. At a field kitchen a grinning Russian soldier with a three days' beard stubble gave them hunks of bread and a plate of meat. It occurred to Rofé that he, himself, must look even worse. He suggested to Hillebrand that they freshen up to meet the colonel and a little later, when they came to a stream, he made Achmetow wait while they stripped and then swam and shaved. They wondered about the Russian troops, their equipment and the female Russian soldiers. They usually slept under the open sky. The Cossacks were supplied by air and had enough food and ammunition. One night when dusk settled over the fields they heard the drone of aircraft, growing louder. The dark shape of what looked like a Dakota slid over the trees towards them and over the field a cloud of parachutes broke from the aircraft and floated down. A dozen more aircraft came over and dropped more supplies and then several antiquated single-engined biplanes puttered over the field. Someone flashed a torch at them and one by one they switched on their landing lights, side-slipped steeply and made miraculous uphill landings in the field. Under the wings on each side were little nacelles like overload tanks and Cossacks went up with stretchers of wounded men and loaded them into the nacelles like mummies. One by one the planes turned, roared over the field and lifted into the darkness on their way back to their own lines and hospital treatment. It was unbelievably quick and efficient.

Over the next days, Rofé and Hillebrand went along with the Cossacks and had several encounters with German units. Several times they were shot at and had to dive for cover as bullets flew over their heads. After a few days the Russians decided to break out and cross the front line back to the other Russian units. The units had large numbers of horse-drawn wagons that transported supplies for the Cossacks. The two escapers were initially assigned to one of these. At some point Rofé and Hillebrand were separated but on 26 September continued with the Cossacks to the Russian lines in the border country between Polish Galicia and Slovakia. Rofé searched for Hillebrand and ended up in the rear. As Rofé could ride he was assigned a horse. The rear was the last part of the Cossack unit to cross open ground to the Russian lines.

ESCAPE FROM HITLER'S REICH

The Cossacks and other Russians kept the Germans at a distance but by the time the rear started to cross the whole area was under fire. There remained nothing for the rearguard to do but carry out a charge across the open field in a howling mad gallop towards the secure Russian lines. Cossacks were good at what they were trained to do. Having gathered in the woods, the officers drew their swords and dozens of shouting Cossacks gave their horses the spurs. The horses sprang forward from the forest cover and the Cossack cavalry appeared in the open. The Germans were alerted by the retreat of the previous units and began a deadly barrage across the plain. Left and right of Rofé Cossacks were hit and fell off their horses, but the horses continued without riders in their mad charge.

The head of a Cossack in front seemed to split and his hat spun crazily back. A fleeting glimpse. Bullet or shell. He rolled sideways off the horse and it carried on galloping riderless with them. Two more horses went down and Rofé crazily thought he was part of a film again; they were Red Indians, the Light Brigade, the gallant Six Hundred charging into the cannon and the cameras. And yet the taste of reality was like iron on the tongue: an RAF sergeant in a Cossack cavalry charge. All was confusion, but it was madly exciting. Something buzzed sharply by Rofé's ear; another horse and rider were down. The earth rumbled beneath the beat of hundreds of horses along with the screams of raging Cossacks, the whizzing of bullets flying past, the impacts and the roar of guns. This resulted in an unrealistic atmosphere filled with adrenaline. Cossack officers waving their swords over their heads raged on in a trance and continued to urge the horses and men. Rofé's beret fell off. He had no sword, but waved his arms during the charge.

When passing through the Russian lines, they were loudly hailed from the advancing tanks and from the trenches filled with troops. These were the most anxious minutes in Rofé's life, something he would not like to repeat but it gave him a huge kick. By his participation in this charge Rofé was officially the last British soldier in the history of the British Army to participate in such an old-fashioned cavalry charge.

AGAINST THE WIND

They were on the Russian side of the front but that did not mean there was an end to the escapers' adventures. A few days later Rofé found Hillebrand, who had crossed the front line on his trusted horse and cart before the Germans laid a barrage across the plain. It would be weeks before they could leave the front area and they were then taken to Moscow. After only five days they were brought into contact with the British Embassy, after which they were quickly taken to Murmansk. Rofé and Hillebrand returned to England in early 1945 by means of a regular North Atlantic convoy. However, this was attacked immediately by U-boats after leaving Murmansk and Rofé and Hillenbrand had to fear for their lives again. Fortunately, a North Atlantic storm broke out that made it impossible for the U-boats to carry out further attacks but it also caused the two escapers to suffer from seasickness for the rest of their journey. On Christmas Eve, Rofé reached London and an intelligence officer, welcoming him with admirable detachment and no interest whatsoever, asked, 'Have you come from the other side?' Rofé answered dryly, 'Yes, I feel in a way I have.'

Sergeant Rofé was awarded the Military Medal for his escape and also commissioned. He joined Transport Command as a navigator, flying the Middle East routes on 216 Squadron, and it was during this period that he took some leave in Palestine after the war and met Hillebrand again, still almost as thin as ever and now a lieutenant in the Israeli Army. On this leave he again met Kacenelenbeigen, the Jewish soldier with whom he first exchanged places at Lamsdorf, and Joseph Luxenburg, his partner on his first abortive escape. Rofé later left the RAF, married and started a restaurant called The Escaper in South Kensington. Cyril Rofé described his adventures in 1956 in the book *Against the Wind.* He died on 20 September 1977 in Northwood, Middlesex, aged 61.[1]

---

1. See also *Escape or Die: Authentic Stories of the RAF Escaping Society* by Paul Brickhill.

Chapter 2

My Escape Through Belgium and France

Joseph Thomas 'Joe' Pack was born in 1918 to Delia and Jeffrey Pack, a builder. He was the third of four children and later wrote an entertaining account of his rural childhood in the Kent village of Egerton. Keen on bell ringing, at 15 he became apprenticed to a bell foundry but later felt that there was a better future for him in civil engineering. By 1940, when he joined the RAF, he was working in the Dagenham Borough Surveyor's office. After twelve months' training Joe was assigned as a Halifax bomber pilot. On the night of 8–9 June 1942, during his eighteenth operational flight on 35 Squadron, he was shot down on the German–Dutch border and found himself 'swinging across the skies on my parachute, like a huge pendulum'. His adventures involved the men and women of the Resistance, who risked their lives to take him through Belgium and France and across the Pyrenees.

'In September 1939 life was going on as usual in our small village of Egerton in the Weald of Kent but for several weeks we had been aware of lots of activity in the air. Hurricanes and Spitfires were flying in formation or having dogfights with one another high above us, over the Weald. In 1940, the weekend that our soldiers were brought back from Dunkirk, my friends and I cycled to the main road between Dover and London to witness an endless line of coaches brought from all parts of the south of England, filled with dispirited soldiers. Some were only partly clothed. There was no joy on their faces. They were dazed and dejected after their escape from Dunkirk and were still living the terror they had experienced during the past few days. Yes, the war "proper" had arrived.

'One or two of the lads from the village had been called up. I was aged about twenty and although my age group had yet not been called up, I felt guilty about still being out of uniform. When I told my mother that I intended to volunteer as aircrew in the RAF she took it well, as I had expected. The following day I drove to a Recruiting Office in Chatham to volunteer for the RAF. I felt a little foolish volunteering as aircrew as the RAF had suffered severe losses at the time. Ten days after "signing on" I travelled to RAF Cardington. This was my last day in my own "civvy" clothes for several years. After drill training in the huge hangars there – which had once held the ill-fated R100 airship – our squad was moved to Blackpool to continue drilling. This was usually at the end of the pier, which gave the holidaymakers something to interest them as the usual Blackpool attractions had long since closed down. From Blackpool we transferred to Emmanuel College at Cambridge even though many of the students were still in residence. We stayed in the comfortable quarters of the college and ate in the dining hall served by the College retainers. We felt quite important.

'After experiencing the joys of Cambridgeshire, we were sent for a few weeks' further training as pilots at Babbacombe in Devon. So far being in the RAF had been most enjoyable and I looked forward to flying an aeroplane for the first time! Most of the lads on our course were posted to Canada for their Elementary Flying Training. My RAF friend and I were posted to Luton for training to fly the Miles Magister trainers, a single-engined solo plane. We found ourselves part of a course of New Zealand Navy volunteers. Not being sailors, we were excused all kinds of drills and unpleasant duties so one day I found myself taking to the air for the first time in my life in the rear of a Magister trainer with my instructor in the front seat. After a week or so of shouting and bullying from my instructor and eight hours' instruction, I was able to fly solo.

'On one occasion I was sent up to practise "looping the loop" as part of my solo training. It was a bumpy day and I felt a little sick so I flew out of sight of the aerodrome and did a few steep turns to waste time, but did not practise any loops. On landing at base, I taxied to dispersal and attempted to unfasten my straps. To my horror I found the chute I had been sitting on (which formed part of my seat) was not attached to me and I was not strapped in the aircraft! My loops were never good. I would invariably hang on to my straps at the top of the loop: I nearly became a corpse on that day! After that I moved from Luton to Brize Norton to convert to twin-engine Oxford trainers. This time I was flying at night as well as during the day. I found Oxfords easy to handle and went solo night and day after a few hours' instruction. From there I transferred to an operational training unit in Kinloss in Scotland and converted to antiquated Whitley bombers, a twin-engined aircraft with a huge wingspan. After a month or so, twelve months after joining the RAF, I was posted to an operational squadron (35) flying Halifaxes at Linton-on-Ouse in Yorkshire.

'Learning to fly a four-engined bomber was very different from the previous planes I had flown, but I was soon taking off and landing the Halifax without too many problems. Flying at night was rather more difficult. The instructor who sat in the 2nd pilot's seat was on "rest" after completing a tour of operations, which took 30 trips at that time. Some rest! I was eventually teamed up as 2nd pilot with Flight Sergeant George Henry Steinhauer, a Canadian, born on 13 November 1919 in Morse, Saskatchewan. Although most of the Canadian aircrew was commissioned, George was quite sure he could not get a commission because of his German surname – and it seems he was right.

'Our first operational trip was on 18 December 1941' [when forty-seven aircraft – eighteen Stirlings, eleven Manchesters and eighteen Halifaxes (six on 35 Squadron, seven on 10 Squadron and six on 76 Squadron) attempted a daylight raid on Brest to attack the German battleships *Scharnhorst* and *Gneisenau*, which had sheltered in the port]. 'We flew down from Linton-on-Ouse over a darkened

MY ESCAPE THROUGH BELGIUM AND FRANCE

England, climbing slowly with full petrol and bomb load and crossed our coast at a "safe" point, clear of our coastal defences. We crossed the French coast at about 12,000 feet and all was quiet as we set course for Brest. Within ten minutes of our ETA to arrive at Brest, the skies ahead suddenly lit up with searchlights and enemy shells. The first of our aircraft had arrived ahead of us. Still some miles from the target area, we slowly nosed our way into the medley of bursting shells and searchlights which were trying to home in on us with the enemy radar. It was a relief to hear the words, "bomb doors open" over the intercom as the bomb aimer guided us onto the target and later "bombs gone" when the aircraft lifted vertically having shed its load. Turning slowly onto a course for our return, peace eventually reigned again as we scanned the skies for enemy night fighters.

'On the night of 5–6 January 1942 we flew to Brest on 35 Squadron to attack the *Scharnhorst*, a potential menace to shipping in the Atlantic. There was a large concentration of ack-ack guns in the target area and the coloured shells joined together. It was weird, they would come up in an almost leisurely fashion, yet they were obviously lethal – we called them "Flaming Onions". On 8–9 January we were back again. This time our Halifax was hit with shrapnel. With one engine out of action, we landed at Abingdon, returning to Linton-on-Ouse the following day. Later we bombed Wilhelmshaven,[1] Hamburg and Kiel, followed by a daylight trip, again in search of the elusive *Scharnhorst*, which had cheekily slipped into the English Channel

---

1. On the night of 10–11 January Steinhauer succeeded in reaching the mainland but shortly after doing so his rear gunner's oxygen mask froze up and the rear gunner contracted frostbite and passed out, their height being 19,000ft and the temperature -35°. The flight engineer was despatched to render first aid, but having omitted to take his portable oxygen supply with him, failed to reach the rear turret and was only brought back to life after the captain had executed a rapid dive to 12,000ft. Steinhauer, with an unserviceable hydraulic system, accidentally hit a mobile floodlight (at Mildenhall) on landing, damaging a starboard flap and the lower half of a rudder.

during bad weather. This was my last trip as 2nd pilot with George Steinhauer. He flew up to Kinloss with a new second pilot to attack the *Tirpitz* [on 30–31 March], which had gone into Trondheim. More than half the squadron was lost that night. George and his crew did not return.'[2]

During the following weeks and months Joe's new crew attacked Essen and Cologne ('several times') the Renault works at Paris, Saint-Nazaire, Bremen and Emden. 'The trip to Cologne on 13–14 March was less than comfortable. We were shot up badly over the target area, lost an engine, iced up on the return journey and crossed over Dunkirk at 1,500 feet. We landed at Manston without an air speed indicator. Although we lost an engine on several occasions, it was sometimes due to overheating, i.e., glycol leaks. As a crew we regarded ourselves as reasonably lucky – until the night of 8–9 June at Essen.' That was when W7701 was one of four Halifaxes from the ten dispatched by 35 Squadron that failed to return.

'We had got ourselves boxed in with searchlights and ack-ack. Diving and climbing and turning steeply would not free us. I could smell cordite and hear the sound of exploding shells. It was all very unpleasant. We eventually cleared the Ruhr at 21,000 ft. No one saw the fighter which shot us down. Within seconds it seemed there was a large burning hole where my instrument panel had been. The plane was on fire and five of the crew were killed.[3] A little later I was

---

2. Flight Sergeant George Henry Steinhauer RCAF and crew were laid to rest in Trondheim (Stavne) Cemetery.
3. Halifax II W7701 TL-U crashed north-north-east of Genk in Belgium. The remains of 29-year-old Flight Lieutenant Roy Blackwell Chadwick, observer; Flight Sergeant William Edgar Pilborough RCAF, the 30-year-old WOp/AG, and Sergeants John Ralph Storey, the 21-year-old flight engineer, John McKinstry (24), air gunner and William John Hopkins, the 22-year-old air gunner, were located at Brusthem airfield (St-Trond). On 31 January 1947 their bodies were exhumed, identified and reinterred at Heverlee War Cemetery. Sergeant John Andre Catley bailed out at just 500ft yet landed safely 15km north-north-east of Genk and was taken into captivity.

swinging across the skies on my parachute, like a huge pendulum. Twenty to thirty minutes later I hit the ground. I expected to be immediately arrested, but there was complete silence. I discovered later that I had landed to the west of Aachen [in a marshy field near Kirchhoven, a northern suburb of Heinsberg].[4] I did the only thing which occurred to me; I hid my parachute in a deep field drain and finding my small issue compass to be of little use, set off in a westerly direction by taking a bead on the North Star. I ran as fast as I could in a south-westerly direction. Forced to head north-west for an hour or so, I then walked unchallenged through a hamlet, but soon after dawn began to meet workmen on bicycles. I hid from the first few but no one who saw me showed any interest so I walked along the road.

'Come the dawn I hid in a wood, sleeping most of the time. The following night I continued my progress. By dawn I was near a village and very wet as it had been raining. [Without realising it, Pack was only three or four kilometres from the Dutch border and he had crossed into that part of Holland that forms a narrow corridor between Germany and Belgium.] After a further three hours or so I was confronted by the Juliana Kanaal, which runs parallel to and only a couple of hundred metres east of the Maas (the Meuse in Belgium and France). Unable to cross the canal, I hid in a small patch of fern and firs as there were many people about. Trying to sleep, I was interrupted by three men who appeared to be surveying the canal. Plucking up the courage to speak to the men, I went up to the youngest; a man of about 24 [Albert Bidelot] and spoke to him in English. He made a rush towards me, pointed to the sky and asked if I was an aviator. When I said I was, he shook hands with me and called to the two others, one of whom was his father. After they had told me I was near Maeseyck they hid me in deeper shrubbery. Having gone for help, the young man returned with a friend, a man

---

4. The Halifax crashed at 0150 hours between Meeuwen and Gruitrode (Limburg) 15km north-north-east of Genk, Belgium.

of about 50 [Mathieu Tras-nys], who claimed to be in the Belgian Secret Service and said he would take me to Switzerland on the back of his bicycle. After the younger one had produced a change of clothes, I discarded my uniform and flying boots, exchanging them for rough civilian clothes. With the help of these men, I was able to avoid the border guards. I was passed from one patriot to another by foot, bicycles and train. At Maastricht it was a bit of a shock to find the town full of the German military.'

Joe's travels on the bicycle with the older man was only 'across the canal and river and round Ophoven', a small village in Limburg, approximately 54 miles north-east of Brussels. He was taken to a house near the village where there were two elderly ladies. 'I was given a good meal and champagne and shelter for the night,' Joe recalled. On the afternoon of 10 June, a woman of about 25 brought him some better clothes and she, together with her fiancé, took him by bicycle that evening to the mill at Dilsen, home of Gertrude Moors, a courier for the Comet escape line who personally took evading airmen and escaped French prisoners of war to Liège by tram. Gertrude-Maria Hubertina Moors was born in Dilsen on 16 August 1902. The windmill was a reference point for shot down Allied pilots and for escaped French prisoners of war. After her father's death, Gertrude's mother remarried, but she too died in 1932, after which Gertrude took care of the family.[5]

---

5. As a result of infiltration of the Comet Line, Gertrude was captured by the secret Feldpolixei in Paris on 18 June 1943. Severely tortured in the prison of St-Gilles and in the Bergynestraat in Antwerp, Gertrude was condemned to death on 2 July 1944. Eventually she was sent to Ravensbrück concentration camp, where she performed forced labour until her death. In 1948 there was still no news of Gertrude. It was only in 2012 that an exact date of her death was discovered as 31 March 1945. According to the Comet source, the number of airmen who she returned to England was twenty-five. The L100 network of Liège (which was already active before the war and was part of the state security) is said to have helped at least 1,100 downed airmen in total.

MY ESCAPE THROUGH BELGIUM AND FRANCE

Doctor Michel Groenen, an English-speaking doctor, arrived to ask Joe various questions to prove his identity. Finally, at one o'clock on the morning of 11 June, satisfied that Pack was genuine, the interrogation ended. At 4.30 am a young man arrived to take Pack by tram on a six-hour tram journey to the cathedral at Liège (60km to the south). On arrival he handed Joe a rosary and left him kneeling. He was soon joined by a man who interrogated him in broken English for a while. Later he met Joe outside in the street and took him to visit his friends, the butcher, the baker and others. On being introduced they produced a bottle of cognac and toasted one another. In his tipsy state they boarded a tram together with a bunch of German soldiers and Joe pushed them to make room for him, without a care in the world!

Taken to the church of Saint-Denis, Joe was handed over to an elderly man, who turned out to be Maurice Cullignon, the chief of police in Louvain. He was saluted by all the policemen they passed. (Later in the war he was apprehended and shot.) Joe was hidden in a room about 10ft × 8ft at 30 Rue de Waroux, the house of two elderly ladies, Jenny and Mathilde Ritschdorff, for about fourteen days, during which time he was provided with another suit of clothes and then with English books (by a British lady). On 20 June he was taken to Louvain by train by the head of the organisation, Paul Schoenmecker, an ex-Belgian Army officer. After the train journey to Louvain – which had its moments – Joe was taken to Brussels, to Schoenmecker's apartment at the Ministry of Justice, by tram. Brussels was full of armed troops. Occasionally he would see a man or woman with the yellow Star of David stitched to their backs to distinguish Jews for transporting to the extermination camps of Poland. That night a young Belgian took Joe to his flat at the gatehouse serving the entrance to the Palace of Justice. The family living there was employed to open and close the large metal gates for the German limousines with swastika pennants that drove in and out of the palace. That night the family invited friends to a party at the gatehouse in Joe's honour. Joe seemed to be the only one present worried for their safety. They photographed him and days afterwards produced a passport and work pass. The father of the young Belgian then took him to stay with friends Roger and Stéphanie LeBlois about 20 miles out of the capital in Hoeilaart. Stéphanie was a secretary at the Ministry of Justice and she would smuggle out copies of her typing to the Resistance – how she hated her employers! Her husband was a racehorse trainer and had six or eight loose boxes where he hid with his horses. 'He was very frightened (can you blame him?)' recalled Joe, 'but after two or three days he moved me into his house.' (Before the year was out the couple and their three teenage children disappeared. Only Stéphanie appeared again – after the war.)

On 4 July Joe was taken back to Brussels and given an identity card and German pass for the frontier. Next day, accompanied by Andrée Dumon, 'a 21-year-old Belgian girl otherwise known as 'Nadine' or Dédée ('little mother'), he and two other RAF airmen set off for Louvain.[6] Flight Sergeant Bernard Evans DFM of 15 OTU had been shot down aboard a Wellington on the Thousand Bomber raid on Cologne on 30 May 1942 by a Bf 110E-2 crewed by Leutnant Helmut Niklas and Unteroffizier Heinz Wenning of 6./NJG 1.[7] Pilot Officer John Henry Watson was the navigator on Wellington X3359 on 419 Squadron RCAF, which was shot down returning from Essen on 16–17 June 1942. Watson's 19-year-old Canadian Flight Sergeant Charles Emile

---

6. In October 1940 Andrée Dumon had met Frédéric De Jongh (aka 'Kiki'), who originated the Comet escape line with his daughter Andrée De Jongh, also known as Dédée. Frédéric invited Andrée Dumon to work for him and she had immediately accepted with enthusiasm, operating as 'Nadine' to avoid any confusion with Frédéric's daughter. During 1942 she alone guided eleven airmen from Brussels to Paris.

7. His pilot, Sergeant D. J. Paul DFM, was taken prisoner. The three other crew members were killed.

Leblanc, affectionately known as 'Little Bomber' and 'Pee Wee' by the crew, who stayed at the controls of the aircraft too long to safely bail out, was killed.

The party boarded a crowded train heading for Paris. Arriving in Brussels, they were lucky not to be taken off. And then, at the French border the passengers thinned out. German officers searched everything and everyone. Watson repeatedly said the wrong thing in reply to the official's questions. Andrée was in tears, but passed them off to the officials as deaf mutes. Fifteen hours after boarding the train, standing in crowded corridors, they arrived at the Gare du Nord in Paris. On leaving the train the party split up. There were military personnel everywhere. At the barriers German soldiers going on leave would show their credentials and salute with the word *Heil*! Joe crept through on the other side. As he crossed the road outside the station he was confronted by a German officer with yellow lapels. Joe put his hands up, the officer searched him and his bundle of clothes, razor etc, dumped them on the road and then left him. 'I had been searched by the Gestapo!' Joe recalled.

In Paris the three airmen were taken to the Hotel Luxembourg in the Latin Quarter where Frédéric de Jongh kept a room. Later that morning Andrée Dumon returned to Brussels. In August 1942 the Germans mistook her for Andrée de Jongh, arrested and then sent her to Germany.[8] 'Nadine' passed through the Ravensbrück and Mauthausen camps and returned to Belgium in May 1945 in a precarious state of health. She gradually recovered.

The RAF men were joined by Andrée de Jongh and her father, who, together with her sister, laid the foundations for many Allied

---

8. Between August 1941 and December 1942 Andrée Eugénie Adrienne de Jongh escorted 118 people, including more than eighty airmen, from Belgium to neutral Spain, from where they were transported to the United Kingdom. Arrested by the Nazis in January 1943, she was incarcerated for the remainder of the war and after it worked in leper hospitals in Africa.

airmen to escape to freedom using the Comet Line. Here Evans and Watson left with the de Jonghs for Frederic's apartment. There they met Sergeant Joseph Arthur Angus Bruneau Angers RCAF (Charles LeBlanc's rear gunner) and Sergeant Marian Henryck Zawodny of the Polish Air Force (who was shot down on a 301 Squadron Wellington on 10 April 1942) and Private William MacFarlane of the 7th Argyll & Sutherland Highlanders.[9]

The following day MacFarlane was moved to the Coache's house at Asnières-sur-Seine. On 16 July the four airmen were escorted by train by Andrée de Jongh and Elvire Morelle to Bayonne, where, in Anglet, they were met by Elvire De Greef, code-named 'Tante Go' or 'Auntie Go', who after leaving Brussels to escape the Germans, set up home at the Villa Voisin (less than 1km from the house where the German military commander lived), the last safe house before the crossing of the Pyrenees, where she lived with her husband Fernand (code name 'Uncle'), daughter Jeanine, son Freddy and the dog Gogo. When the Germans had occupied the area in June 1940, Fernand had got a job with the city government. As a translator and interpreter for the French with the German army, he had the opportunity to gather intelligence and steal and falsify documents, stamps, and identification cards, and was assisted by his son, Frederick. Elvire became involved in the black market and smuggling, a time-honoured occupation of people on the Franco–Spanish border. The German occupiers were among her customers,

---

9. Who on the night of 21–22 March 1942 with Private James M. L. Goldie, also of the 7th Argyll & Sutherland Highlanders, had escaped from Arbeitskommando 147 (the salt mines at Unterbreizbach, near Hersfeld in Germany). Travelling by rail in a salt wagon, they arrived on 3 April at Hasselt, Belgium, and then spent two days in a wagon marked 'Antwerp' waiting for it to leave. At the end of this period, they left the wagon and started walking towards Louvain, before eventually being put in touch with Comet. MacFarlane crossed the Pyrenees in July and Goldie followed in August. *RAF Evaders: The Comprehensive Story of Thousands of Escapers and their Escape Lines, Western Europe, 1940–1945* by Oliver Clutton-Brock (Grub Street, 2009).

relationships that she would rely on later. Her well-known black market activities gave her an excuse to be seen at odd times and odd places. 'Jonion', who ostensibly was her gardener-handyman, was in fact Albert Johnson, originally from Grantham in Lincolnshire. Johnson was a skilled motor mechanic who in 1928 had become chauffeur and travel secretary to the President of the International Olympic Committee in Brussels. In May 1940 all British subjects were advised to leave Belgium and he and other personnel travelled to the south of France, only to discover the Spanish border was closed. Unable to escape, Johnson stayed on and, code-named 'B', made a total of thirteen trips with a total of 122 men to freedom between June 1941 and March 1943. (Finally arrested by the Germans, Elvire de Greef used her husband Fernand's knowledge of the black market dealings of the Germans and a threat to expose them resulted in his release after only one day. It was too dangerous for 'B' to stay in France so he left for Spain and worked for MI9.)

Continuing to St-Jean-de-Luz, the four airmen found the station crowded with Germans, as a number of searchlights had just arrived. It was, therefore, impossible to leave by the workmen's passage as was usually done and they all had to walk through the Customs. Fortunately, they were neither stopped nor questioned. The group split up and all made their way to the house of Ambrosio San Vicente, at 7 Rue Salagoity (not even ten minutes away from the station) which was used regularly to house evaders from 6 June 1942 until 13 January 1943. The airmen stayed for two days. On 19 July, with Andrée de Jongh and two guides, 'Florentin' and 'Thomas' (Florentino Goïcoechea Beobide, a 44-year-old Basque, a smuggler by profession, and 30-year-old Tomás Anabitarte Zapirain), they 'walked to a farmhouse about 10km away'. They left the farm at around 2130 and were walking through a defile at midnight 'in pitch darkness and pouring rain, when suddenly from some bushes in the bracken, about three yards from the path, two German soldiers leapt out, shouting wildly, into the midst of the party, which split up in confusion.'

While the others dashed forwards, Zawodny ran back down the path and Evans threw himself behind a bush. The Germans were clearly scared and one of them fired off a shot before they engaged in a heated discussion for some twenty minutes. Only Evans was left near them, the rest having made good their escape, but he was able to slip away, too, when it began to rain even harder, covering the noise as he 'crawled up the mountainside' in the beating rain. Watson made a solo crossing to Spain. He was arrested and was not to return to England until 15–16 October 1942. The others, meanwhile, returned eventually to either San Vicente's house or to the farmhouse. They rested for a day, during which time Evans was treated for a twisted knee, 'the result of my wanderings in the mountains', before setting off once more, on 20 July. This time the crossing to Oyazun was uneventful and the airmen were collected from San Sebastián by a car from Madrid that 'had been waiting for us for about four days'. Evans, Angers and Zawodny were flown home from Gibraltar on 18–19 August aboard a BOAC Dakota to Whitchurch.

After he had split up with Evans and Watson, Joe Pack had spent two or three weeks hiding in the outskirts of Paris, spending most of the time with 'a wonderful French couple'. He went to the Coache family at Asnières for a fortnight, before spending a second fortnight with Frédéric de Jongh. 'There were two Scottish soldiers [Private William MacFarlane and Private James M. L. Goldie] hiding with me,' he wrote. 'Madame Raymonde Coache would take the three of us on to the Metro to Paris. On Bastille Day, 14 July, even though it was strictly forbidden by the Germans, we displayed blue, white and red ribbons in our buttonholes and Madame wore her national scarf. On another occasion she took us to see the German ack-ack gun, positioned over one of the Seine bridges. A few weeks previously the same gun had been firing at

MY ESCAPE THROUGH BELGIUM AND FRANCE

us as we bombed the Renault works. Madame Coache was taken by the Gestapo early in 1943 – her husband René escaped to England. Raymonde survived two concentration camps and lived with her daughter in the Seine area of Paris, in the flat where she hid us. Her exploits were acknowledged by both Governments – the medals she has she referred to as her "souvenirs".

'The events leading to our eventual train journey south are too detailed to enumerate. The masterminding of our eventual escape was all due to Andrée de Jongh and the people of the Comet Line.'

With Andrée de Jongh as guide, Joe Pack left for Paris and the Pyrenees on 30 and 31 July with Private William MacFarlane and Sergeants William Joseph Norfolk and Peter Wright. The latter two airmen were crew members on a 76 Squadron Halifax piloted by Sergeant Thomas Robert Augustus West that was shot down on the second Thousand Bomber raid on Essen on 1–2 June, probably by Heinz-Wolfgang Schnaufer.[10]

'At the Gare d'Austerlitz, after having bribed the railway officials, we occupied the compartment of a carriage reserved for German officers and collaborators. There were eight of us: Andrée de Jongh, a lady and her two daughters from Biarritz and four of us British.[11] Whenever our compartment door was opened, for one reason or another, the girl would talk across us, we would say *oui* or *non* according to a slight nod or shake of the head given by either of the girls – there was always a German in the corridor.

'On arriving at Biarritz station there was panic. Several of the "safe" houses had been visited by the Gestapo. We took a local train to Saint-Jean de Luz. Here we hid in a café.' The following night, Florentino Goïcoechea, who was to take us over the Pyrenees, was blind drunk. He was paid £100 for each person he delivered

---

10. West and one of his crew were killed, two being taken prisoner.
11. 'Bee' Johnson and Tante Go joined them en route.

safely.[12] Over the next fifteen or so exhausting and gruelling hours MacFarlane and I crossed the swiftly flowing Biddassoa river [with Goïcoechea and 'Bee' Johnson] and climbed the mountains in rope-soled espadrilles. We arrived at about 1000 the following morning at a farm in the Spanish Pyrenees, where we lay on the floor and drank goat's milk. A further ten miles' walk took us to the outskirts of San Sebastián, where there were plenty of Germans – on leave I suppose.

'After a couple of nights at San Sebastián [on the second floor of 3 Calle de la Marina, near La Concha-beach] we made a rendezvous with a British Embassy car in which we drove to Madrid. We stayed in wooden huts in the Embassy grounds with about sixty others of various nationalities, until it was decided that we would either be taking the train to Gibraltar or going to a Spanish prison. I was fortunate and took the train to Gibraltar where I sent a telegram to my family on 13 August. Walking over the causeway, seeing British soldiers and hearing British voices, was an experience I never really expected to happen.

'After a couple of days, the RAF got me into a uniform again; I flew circuits for the experience in both a Sunderland and a Catalina. Then the Gibraltar authorities in their wisdom got me a passage in a destroyer, which was detailed with two others to guard a large slow convoy, travelling at five knots. We had to sail out into the Atlantic [on 19 August 1942] before going north to (hopefully) avoid subs. We only had one scare and dashed around the convoy at thirty knots

---

12. Florentino guided more than 200 Allied airmen shot down in occupied Belgium and France over the Pyrenees to neutral Spain. On 26 July 1944, Florentino was shot four times by German border guards, although he managed to hide the documents he was carrying before being captured. His leg was shattered. The Germans took him to a hospital in Bayonne, where he was rescued by local Comet Line helpers on 27 July. He remained in hiding until the Nazis abandoned south-western France a month later. He was honoured with the George Medal by the United Kingdom and the Légion d'honneur by France. In the ceremony at Buckingham Palace, the old smuggler said in broken English that he was in the 'import-export business'.

MY ESCAPE THROUGH BELGIUM AND FRANCE

throwing off depth charges from the sides. However, nothing was sighted – who would be a sailor!?

'It was six days before we arrived at Londonderry, Northern Ireland, just three months after I had left Yorkshire. The ferry took them from Larne to Stranraer, Scotland, and a train to London, where they had strict orders to report immediately to the Air Ministry. 'It was a Sunday morning when I arrived at Euston station in London. The Air Ministry was closed so I took a train to Charing in Kent and got a lift to Egerton, my home village. My knock at the front door was answered by my mother. She had received a telegram from the Air Ministry the previous day – "Missing, believed killed on active Service". I would always shed a tear to think of that meeting.'[13]

Joe Pack was debriefed by MI9 services in London on the 26th. He received a Mention in Dispatches and was reassigned to flying boats, which was when he first met Margaret Dillon, a WAAF Officer (his senior in rank) serving at RAF Oban. During his action-packed posting on patrol in the Indian Ocean they began an air mail courtship, marrying only five weeks after their second meeting in a pub at Euston Station in 1945.[14]

---

13. People's War site by Viv Foulds of Egerton Telecottage on behalf of Joe Pack. See also, *RAF Evaders: The Comprehensive Story of Thousands of Escapers and their Escape Lines, Western Europe, 1940–1945* by Oliver Clutton-Brock (Grub Street, 2009).
14. The Brentham Society Archive. Margaret died in 2002 and Joe in 2004. *'Love is in the Air'* edited by Jeff Pack, Joe's son tells the story of Joe's early life, wartime exploits and the letters of Joe and Margaret and is available from www.woodfieldpublishing.com.

Chapter 3

Wingless Journey[1]

Hamburg suffered its most severe air raid to date on 26–27 July 1942 and widespread damage was caused, mostly in the housing and semi-commercial districts. The fire department was overwhelmed and forced to seek outside assistance for the first time. Some 337 people lost their lives, 1,027 were injured and 14,000 people were made homeless. Damage amounted to the equivalent of £25 million. Bomber Command was stood down on the night of 27–28 July but this was the full moon period, and on the night following, a return to Hamburg was announced at briefings when crews were told that the raid would be on a far bigger scale than two nights before. Nearly 800 aircraft were allocated to bomb the devastated town. Bad weather over the stations in 1, 4 and 5 Groups, however, prevented their participation and ultimately only 256 aircraft took part: 165 in 3 Group and 91 OTU, totalling 161 Wellingtons, 71 Stirlings and 24 Whitleys.

At Oakington, Cambridgeshire, Pilot Officer Leslie Raymond Sidwell, the rear gunner on Stirling I W7565 'B-Beer' on 7 Squadron, made a note that said it was another 'Thousand Raid'. Sidwell, who was born and bred in Coventry, where he worked for Courtaulds silk works, surmised, correctly, that the number was again being made up with OTU crews. His skipper, Flight Lieutenant Douglas Weston Whiteman, was born on 24 September 1918 in Bengal, India, where

---

1. Adapted from the book of the same name by Leslie Sidwell (Merlin Books, 1 April 1996) with the kind permission of James Sidwell, Leslie's grandson.

his father was serving as a lieutenant in the Royal Artillery. By 1932 his family had returned to London. After schooling at Brighton College, in January 1939 Douglas joined the RAF. Warrant Officer W. F. Carter the flight engineer and Sergeant Alfred Leslie Crockford, a new pilot on the squadron, who joined the crew late on to fly as 'second dickey' for experience, were the other regular members on Whiteman's crew. Twenty-six-year-old Sergeant Albert Henry Charles Bates, RAAF, of Enfield, New South Wales, where his wife Lorna Ethel Bates lived, was a replacement for Sergeant 'Paddy' Leathem, the mid-upper gunner who had reported sick late on. Two other Aussie replacements, Sergeant John Boyle of Ipswich, Queensland, who was also 26 years old, and 30-year-old Sergeant Frank Lethbridge McIntyre made up the rest of the crew as WOp/AG and observer respectively. Bates and Boyle had been drawn from 1651 Conversion Unit at Oakington. McIntyre, born in Birmingham on 13 January 1912, had enlisted in the RAAF on 2 February 1941 at Melbourne. He was married, to Rosemary Emily McIntyre, of Chelsea, Victoria.

'Out at dispersal,' wrote Sidwell, 'we got everything finally checked and ready in the sweltering heat inside the aircraft before climbing out into the oh-so-welcome cool night air. It was lovely to relax outside on the grass and smoke casually before reluctantly putting on the flying kit, which I knew would be badly needed for the cold later on, after the muck-sweat had gone. I donned flying kit, regretfully and, knowing full well it would be freezing at height, was soon in another sweat in the aircraft. We took off at 2229 hours. The weather was good. We passed over Cromer and out over the North Sea. I spent the time taking the usual sightings from my rear turret on flame-floats we'd dropped to check drift for the navigator. We'd been briefed to cross the German coast north of the Elbe estuary, then to turn south 20 miles north of Hamburg to run up to the target.

'There was heavy flak and we were hit [by anti-aircraft fire that wrecked the starboard inner engine] just before the run up. Just after we'd bombed, someone on the intercom reported tracer coming up from below and we were finished off by night-fighter attack from underneath [reputedly by Leutnant Rolf Bussmann of 9./NJG 2, who was flying a Ju 88C-6]. I reported a decoy headlight out on the starboard quarter and searched around for other fighters. I reported one coming in from above on the port side and told the Skipper to turn to port. I think I hit him with a burst before my power went off. A fighter came in again from the rear and continued firing. My turret was shattered and we seemed to be in a steady dive. The Skipper gave the emergency bail-out order, quickly followed by what sounded like his cries of pain. Then the intercom abruptly cut off and we were on fire.'

Whiteman gave orders for the crew to bail out. He and the navigator remained in the aircraft to try to get the badly wounded wireless operator out but they did not make it before it crashed. It was even more of a tragedy as Whiteman was due to return home the next day to marry. It would take two years for his family to learn that he had been killed.

'When my turret power had failed,' said Sidwell. 'I'd been left partly on the beam. I started to operate the dead man's handle (emergency winding gear) to centralise my turret so that I could get back into the fuselage to grab my parachute and bail out. ('Chutes could not be stored in the rear turret as one did in earlier two-engined jobs, which were dead easy for rear gunners to quit in a hurry.) I wound away like mad at the hand-winding gear behind me, very conscious that we were losing precious height. As if in a dream, I saw a Me 110 closing in from astern with his guns blazing away. I wound away as I watched him through the shattered Perspex. My painfully slow progress was like a nightmare. I was conscious of the EBO order given in what seemed some time ago ... Would I be in time? He was extremely close to me when he eventually broke away and I finally managed to move the turret sufficiently to fall back hurriedly into the fuselage. I grabbed my 'chute from the stowage outside the turret doors, forced open the nearby emergency exit door and as quickly as I could, jumped out into space. In those seconds I was conscious of flame and smoke up front in the fuselage. I gave no thought at all to any dangers of bailing out, or that I'd had no practice in jumping. I just concentrated in getting out of a doomed aircraft. In my haste to get out I banged my head on something as I quit poor old "B-Beer", partly knocking myself out. I pulled the ripcord without counting as you were normally told to do. I must have done the right thing because I came to swinging in the air. I could see the waters of the Elbe shining below, with the full moon bright towards the south.

'After all the turmoil I was now swinging gently in a strangely contrasting silence, floating down and rather higher than I'd expected. This peace was suddenly interrupted by a dazzling searchlight, which probed around as if looking for me. It held me in its blinding beam. I felt naked, vulnerable and powerless hanging there, not knowing what to expect. I raised my arms and wondered, 'Is this It?' But it soon switched off, as if satisfied that I'd been located and I was left to watch the Elbe more clearly as I lost height and to worry about landing in the wide waters. I'd never fancied coming down in the water and I pulled the rigging lines as instructed, hoping to spill air from the 'chute to alter my course. Probably more by luck than anything else, the Elbe disappeared and I braced myself for a landing, south of the river. The ground seemed to loom up very quickly in the moonlight and it wasn't possible to judge my first parachute landing expertly. I landed rather clumsily and hurt my right ankle on the hard ground but tall growing crops helped to cushion me. My watch showed 0110 hours just after landing. I remembered that my first duty was to hide my 'chute. As I struggled to gather it all up, I thought I'd have a good view of a big "Thousand Raid" but I was surprised. Little was seen or heard and I wondered, "Where are they?"

'The sheer bulk of the parachute amazed me, first in trying to gather it together and then finding a hiding place for it. I seemed to be in the midst of waist-high wheat or barley. Loaded up with the parachute bulk, I set out to find a hiding place, but I couldn't make much progress through the waist-high crops. I found a few bushes and scrabbled away with my hands on the parched ground to hide everything. In addition to my life-saving parachute (how I offered grateful thanks up to the trusty WAAF who'd packed it properly so that it functioned when needed), my Mae West, Irvin suit and parachute harness all had to be disposed of. It was an impossible job with the baked ground. My fingers and nails were damaged and torn. I did the best I could, then set out SW by my little compass. I was dazed with the bang on my head and there was blood on my left leg. On inspection, it was only a graze on the shin – probably caused when the turret was first shattered. My clothing seemed to have bullet holes in it from this and I realised how lucky I was to be alive. It seemed as if the others had "bought it".

'I had to keep resting and every time I did so I heard constant swishing sounds and would jump up in alarm. Remembering the significance of the searchlight picking me up in its beam and switching off, I felt that my tracks through the crops were being followed and I tried to push on harder. After some time, the truth dawned on me. The swishing noises were not pursuers; it was the breeze rustling the crops and I could relax a bit.

'I knew I was south of the Elbe and tried to continue south-west, thinking my best bet was Holland, over 100 miles away. I probably travelled in circles as my head reeled, my ankle was painful, my shin was bleeding and my fingertips were raw. Then I must have passed out. I woke up in sunlight with civilians bending over me, talking excitedly. They motioned me to follow them towards a nearby village. The atmosphere was quite amicable and after exchanging family snapshots with each other, I was locked in a barn.

'Although pretty exhausted, I awoke from a short doze to check my position and I soon forced a window and tiptoed quietly round the farm buildings, but the alarm was raised and I ran straight into a group of men as I rounded a corner. I was put into the barn again and this time I was told that troops would soon arrive for me and searched. Everything continued to be pretty friendly. I was given some black bread and a sort of sausage to eat, which I found quite unpalatable, but I gratefully drank from a jug of water.

'About midday a Luftwaffe oberleutnant arrived with three guards. I had to strip for a more thorough search than the cursory frisk for weapons I'd had before. In the search they'd taken my "escape pack" and had rumbled my tiny escape compass concealed very cunningly in my short stud, but they hadn't discovered that my pipe held another tiny compass and that my tobacco pouch contained silk escape maps in the lining.

'I was taken by truck towards the direction of Hamburg. I tried to keep a watch on the journey for anything interesting and after a short time we passed close to an aerodrome on our left where much activity was going on. I saw Me 110s and Do 217s. I think one of the guards tried to indicate to me by gestures that night fighters from this airfield had finished us off and I sought some way of identifying this place. Our road was running alongside a railway line on the aerodrome side and as a small station came up, I managed to read the name: "Agathenburg".

'Somewhere along the road towards Hamburg we entered a camp. I was escorted upstairs into an office where a middle-aged hauptmann sat at a desk. He spoke briefly to my escorting officer, then the latter departed. The hauptmann motioned me to a camp bed at the far end of the office. He completely ignored my presence as he went on with his deskwork. I stretched out and fell asleep while I was trying to recall all the German words I thought I knew. I woke up later and a row was going on. The officer was playing merry hell with three scruffy-looking rankers who were obviously in some trouble. He continued to shout loudly at them before curtly dismissing them. Then he became aware that I'd been watching. In excellent English, smiling, he said, "You've got to keep these bloody swine down!" Then he asked if I was hungry and a tray soon followed. The coffee tasted bitter but I drank it. There was a plate of some kind of biscuits and these went down well, but more black bread with margarine made me think. I could never take to it.

'Afterwards the officer beckoned me to his desk and I sat down facing him. He asked me how I was and got a medical orderly in to dress the slight wound on my left leg, which had continued bleeding. They examined the bullet holes in my trouser legs. The hauptmann then started a mild interrogation, but nothing was pressed home when I replied that I could only give my name, rank and serial number. I think I was quite amazed (although I tried not to show it) that this didn't seem to surprise or perturb him at all. He said something about my friends, which I didn't understand properly. After a pause, he said that some of my comrades had been captured and would be joining me soon. I wondered who'd survived from "B-Beer".

'I slept again and woke up when two RAF aircrew walked in. They were Carter, our flight engineer, and Crockford, the last-minute "second dickey". Crockford was slightly wounded and both had lost flying boots in the process of bailing out. Carter told me that the skipper and the three Australians had been killed and that no one else had got out. It confirmed the death cries I thought I'd heard just before the intercom had failed.

'Transport arrived and we went south to Frankfurt, travelling through Buxtehude to Harburg railway station under charge of a leutnant and guards for our rail journey. It was cooler now after the heat of the day, but I was hardly aware of things like the passing of time. I was dazedly wondering about things back in England. Had my wife heard anything yet? I thought of the inevitable "Missing" telegram she'd get. Had the Committee of Adjustment sealed off my room and possessions at Oakington yet? It was the usual routine for missing blokes. "B-Beer" must have made an awful mess when it crashed.

'Harburg station was big and very busy. Our entrance caused some attention, mostly mild in the crowds. I learnt we were going to the interrogation camp near Frankfurt. No more details. There was an hour or two to wait for our train. The officer said in good English that we must not converse with each other. We had nevertheless managed to discuss escape possibilities. The leutnant and guards seemed pretty decent and we sat down in a refreshment room where the guards fetched us some soup, with glasses of rather weak beer. They only spoke a few odd words of English. We all exchanged family photos and things were quite friendly. A few onlookers made rude comments and were a bit hostile about the RAF, but the leutnant kept a grip on things and sometimes snapped back sharply. I couldn't help thinking back to the pictures of captured Luftwaffe types that appeared in our papers in 1940. Perhaps our very grubby and unshaven faces would be splashed in German papers to sustain civilian morale?

'In the early hours of 30 July, we entrained and left Harburg. Although well south of Hamburg, I thought and hoped that we'd see more signs of bomb damage but it was disappointing. Our route was via Bremen, Diepholz, Osnabrück and Münster. I half dozed but was always hopeful that our escorts might nod off when we slowed down or stopped, but no chance of escape arose. The many lavatory requests were always closely accompanied and they took it in turns to sleep. We tried to spot bomb damage whenever we stopped anywhere in the night, but little could be seen in the dark. It was a slow journey, with many hold-ups. I roused the others when we passed through the Ruhr. The visibility was bad. As we crawled through the murk, we saw little of Essen. Our escorts shared their rations with us and the guards got out at stations to fetch us hot drinks. We saw bomb damage around the Essen area but it was depressing to see much of the city remaining untouched.

'We had time to stretch our legs briefly at Düsseldorf before we ran into Cologne, where we had a long wait in the station. It was time for more food and drinks. Life in the station seemed busy in the night. Some damage to Cologne station had been patched up and I thought back to my first op, which had been to Cologne. I thought that this route down to Frankfurt was a real "Cook's Tour" for RAF targets that had become so well known. When I peeped outside the station all I got was a view of mainly undamaged property around the cathedral nearby. I tried to draw the leutnant out about RAF bombing damage, but he just shrugged his shoulders. I don't think he was really interested in local problems. He lived in Berlin. We followed the Rhine with stops, some of them lengthy, at Bonn, Koblenz and Mainz. We left the train at Frankfurt-am-Main and walked through the crowds out of the station to a nearby tram stop, where we joined the queue for Oberursel, our destination. The light was going when we left the tram. We struck off along a well-worn track to the left. Lights became visible and the wire of my first PoW camp appeared: Dulag Luft Interrogation Centre, before movement to Stalag Luft III, Sagan.'

Stammlager Luft III, literally 'Main Camp, Air, III' was a Luftwaffe-run prisoner of war camp for RAF and USAAF officers. It was established in March 1942 in Lower Silesia near the town of Sagan (now Żagań, Poland), 100 miles south-east of Berlin. The site was selected because its sandy soil made it difficult for prisoners to escape by tunnelling. The first compound (East Compound) of the camp was completed and opened on 21 March 1942. The first PoWs, or 'Kriegies' as they called themselves (from Kriegsgefangenen), to be housed at Stalag Luft III were British and other Commonwealth officers, arriving in April 1942. The Centre compound was opened on 11 April 1942 and originally held British and other Commonwealth NCOs; by the end of 1942, however, they were replaced by USAAF personnel. The North Compound for British airmen opened on 29 March 1943. A South Compound for Americans was opened in September 1943 and USAAF prisoners began arriving at the camp in significant numbers the following month, with the West Compound opened in July 1944 for US officers. Each compound consisted of fifteen single-storey huts, sleeping fifteen men in five triple-deck bunks, which were raised about 2ft off the ground to make it easier for the guards (called 'goons') to detect tunnelling. Eventually the camp housed about 2,500 RAF officers, about 7,500 US Army Air Forces and about 900 officers from other Allied air forces, for a total of 10,949 inmates, including some support officers.

It just so happened that Leslie Sidwell, 23-year-old Second Lieutenant Richard Michael Clinton Codner MC and Flight Lieutenant Eric Williams occupied the same hut. Each 10-by-12ft bunkroom slept fifteen men in five triple-deck bunks. Codner and Sidwell shared the bunk nearest the stove. Codner was born in Malaya on 29 September 1920, educated at Bedford School and Exeter College, Oxford, and commissioned as a second lieutenant into the Royal Artillery on 2 August 1941. The bronzed undergraduate with a mop of black hair and a sensitive, mischievous face, served in North Africa and was returning by motorcycle from a patrol when he was captured near Medjaz-el-Bad in Tunisia on 14 December 1942. He was flown to Sicily, then Naples and then, in error, sent to Dulag Luft at Oberursel. On 15 January 1943 he was taken to Oflag XXI-B (Schubin) in Poland, where he quickly formed a friendship with Williams, a Londoner, born on 13 July 1911. As a navigator on 75 Squadron, he was shot down on Short Stirling (BK620) on a bombing raid on the Opel Works at Fallersleben on 17–18 December 1942. Williams had evaded capture for three days, but was eventually caught. At Oflag XXI-B Codner, who spoke French, and Williams, planned and executed an escape through a tunnel. However, they were quickly recaptured and, as punishment, on 4 April were sent to Stalag Luft III.

Sidwell would often annoy the other prisoners, lying on his back in the upper bunk, his right arm curled round the top of head, his right hand gently stroking the left-hand side of his moustache and a blissful expression on his face. 'Why the hell do you keep doing that?' Williams asked. 'I like it old boy. Feels as though someone else is doing it.' Williams told him he was crazy. Sidwell replied, 'I know, it's nice.' Probably to ease the boredom, Sidwell specialised in translating air force slang literally into German and he sometimes used this on the guards and was genuinely surprised when they didn't understand. Ever innovative, he once made a golf ball from a round stone covered in wool from the top of a pair of woollen socks, which enabled the golfer to drive it 50 or 60 yards. He had cut down a pair of issue boots to make shoes and saved the soft leather of the uppers to make the cover of the ball. His latest invention was a cocoa tin suspended by a harness of string hung just above Codner's head. Through a hole in the top of the tin ran another string suspended, on the end of which was a bunch of bent and rusty nails. By pulling rapidly on the centre string Sidwell could conjure forth a most satisfactory noise. After Appell (roll call) one day, Sidwell returned to his bunk. He was plotting his post-war career. He had already decided to be a doctor, a game warden, a gold prospector, a holiday camp proprietor, a farmer, a big game hunter and a book-maker. He took one course of study after another, dropping each one as another more attractive career caught his fancy. He lived in a frenzy of enthusiasm – but nothing lasted for long with him. That though was about to change.

When Sidwell had arrived in the camp there had been no successful escapes. The prisoners were faced with the problem of digging an escape tunnel despite the accommodation huts, within which the tunnel entrance might be concealed, being a considerable distance from the perimeter fence. By early 1943 Codner, who was known around the camp as 'a classical fellow, always reading Latin and could spout it by the yard', with his knowledge of the Classics and hence pondering the story of the Trojan Horse, developed the idea of employing a gymnastic vaulting horse largely made of plywood from Canadian Red Cross parcels to conceal men, tools and containers of soil. Each day the horse would be carried out to the same spot relatively near the perimeter fence and while the undernourished prisoners conducted exhausting gymnastic exercises above, a tunnel would be dug by the two men inside. Tunnelling, too, was exhausting work. At the end of each working day, a wooden board would be placed over the tunnel entrance and recovered with surface soil. The gymnastics would disguise the real purpose of the vaulting horse and keep the sound of the digging from being detected by the Seismograph microphones placed around the perimeter of the camp. Codner approached Eric Williams and they developed the idea together.

Leslie Sidwell was also one of the 'Kriegies' who was involved in the scheme and one day his quick thinking probably saved the whole enterprise. There was a fall of sand in the tunnel near the horse and Codner was trapped. There were no air holes in the tunnel and he would quickly suffocate. With the guards in their towers watching the activity below them, Sidwell quickly pretended to hurt his leg as he vaulted the horse and lay on top of the hole. A stretcher was sent and Sidwell was rolled over onto it and a fellow prisoner pretended to attend to his leg while Codner summoned up his last reserves of strength and unblocked the tunnel.

The long list of prisoners who were needed for any escape attempt included everything from forgers to security officers,[2] as well as the vaulters and stooges – look-out men, or watchers, whose job it was to keep tabs on the ferrets (the latter term applied to the half-dozen or so 'goons' permanently wandering around in the camp tasked with detecting tunnels and looking for nefarious activities).

Canadian Flight Lieutenant Gordon 'Moose' Miller, who was awarded the DFC for repairing his damaged Wellington in flight and allowing the crew to parachute to safety, was one of the helpers who carried the wooden horse in and out each day under the German guns without faltering with the weight of two concealed diggers and a day's worth of earth. Members of the prisoners' orchestra also played an important role in the proceedings. Pilot Officer Thomas William Spencer Wilson, born in Birmingham on 12 December 1920, the son of a senior research engineer, played the violin to cover the noise of sand dispersal. An RAF navigator, he had flown on Beaufighters before joining 192 (Special Duties) Squadron operating modified Wellington bombers and was shot down on 25–26 May 1943. A precociously clever child, he was educated at Bishop Vesey's

---

2. The 'Y' Organisation was a group of forgers and tailors who supplied escape attempts. The 'Z' Organisation was the PoW Intelligence team responsible for outside communication.

Grammar School, Sutton Coldfield, where he excelled in science and languages and became an enthusiastic violinist. His renditions of Handel sonatas were from memory and he crushed almonds for oil to clean his prized violin.

For three months Codner and Williams, in shifts of one or two diggers at a time, dug more than 100ft of tunnel, using bowls as shovels and metal rods to poke through the surface of the ground to create air holes. No shoring was used except near the entrance. They would mole the last 10 or 15ft in October and do it in one go. After they had dug about 40ft of tunnel and the horse had been accepted as a camp institution, Codner said they needed a third man to help dig the tunnel from inside the horse and it was only fair to give him the chance to escape with him and Williams, who agreed. But the prisoner they approached turned the offer down because he didn't think they had an earthly chance of getting out. Williams said he would like to ask Leslie Sidwell but said that his leg was so 'dickey' he didn't think he would make it. Codner said, 'We shouldn't have let him do so much vaulting. With a wounded leg it was asking for trouble. He can hardly walk now and yet he comes out every day and hops round the horse – just to make it look like a crowd. He ought to go into hospital. They assumed that Sidwell had been wounded when a German soldier had taken a shot at him coming down after bailing out of the Stirling and that a doctor had patched him up badly.

In June 1943 Codner and Williams approached Flight Lieutenant Oliver Philpot to 'register' their escape scheme with the escape committee, as Philpot was the escape co-ordinator for the hut in which the three of them lived. Oliver Lawrence Spurling Philpot MC DFC was born in Vancouver, British Columbia, on 6 March 1913, the son of an expatriate London engineer. Holding both British and Canadian citizenships, he returned to England as a child. He was educated first at Aymestrey School near Worcester, then at Radley College between 1927 and 1932 and then studied Philosophy, Politics and Economics at Worcester College, Oxford University. During his time at Oxford, he joined the Oxford University Air Squadron and learned to fly. Upon graduating in 1934, he joined Unilever as a management trainee and in 1936 was appointed assistant commercial secretary in Unilever's home margarine executive. This proved to be useful in his wartime escape as the post required him to travel extensively in Germany and to learn to speak German. Service in the University Air Squadron automatically made Philpot a member of the RAFVR on its formation in 1936.

With the approach of the war, Philpot was recalled for service in August 1939 and posted as a pilot officer on probation to 42 Squadron, an 18 Group Coastal Command unit then operating Vickers Vildebeest torpedo bombers. The squadron re-equipped with the Bristol Beaufort in 1940 and took part in the Norwegian Campaign. Philpot was confirmed in his rank on 15 January 1941 and later in the same year was awarded the DFC. Promotion soon followed and it was Flying Officer Philpot who took off in Beaufort 'O-Orange' for an attack on a German convoy off Norway on 11 December 1941. The aircraft was shot down by German anti-aircraft fire and was ditched in the North Sea. Philpot and the three other crew evacuated the aircraft and took to the dinghy. After two days they were picked up by a German naval vessel. Philpot was suffering from exposure and was sent to a German military hospital in Oslo. After several weeks, he was moved to Dulag Luft, arriving in January 1942. Only a month later he was transferred to Oflag IX-A/H at Spangenberg castle in north-eastern Hesse. In April 1942 all the RAF prisoners at Spangenberg were sent to Stalag Luft III. Escape was always a thought, having first been considered while in the hospital immediately after capture, and at Sagan Philpot was involved in more than one attempt. In August he was promoted to flight lieutenant. In September 1942 he was among a number of prisoners transferred to Oflag XXI-B in Poland, the winter of 1942–43 being spent there before the camp closed and all prisoners returned to Stalag Luft III.

On his return to Sagan, Philpot was returned to the East Compound, where he had previously been held; in the interim period, most of his friends had been moved to the North Compound. Despite saying that he didn't think Codner and Williams had a hope in hell of getting out of getting out, Philpot agreed to become the third man in the wooden horse escape attempt. He had hit upon the idea of inventing an escape character and papers etc. before involvement with any escape, rather than the opposite way round. After some thought, he decided that his character would be a Norwegian margarine salesman called 'Jon Jörgensen'. The profession was based on Philpot's own civilian career and the nationality was common enough to be encountered in Germany, but with a reduced likelihood of meeting someone who spoke Norwegian, as Philpot did not speak the language. With the assistance of a Norwegian PoW, the character was fleshed out even to the extent of making him a Quisling.[3] The scheme using the wooden horse was then approved, with Group Captain Richard Kellett DFC AFC the Senior British Officer (SBO) at the time.[4]

On the evening of 29 October 1943, 114 days after the first digging commenced, Codner, Williams and Philpot made their escape. Williams and Codner were able to reach the port of

---

3. Quisling, which is used in Scandinavian languages and in English for a person who collaborates with an enemy occupying force, is named after Vidkun Quisling, who in the 1930s founded a pro-Nazi party. When Germany invaded Norway in 1940, Quisling attempted a pro-German coup against the government. From 1942 to 1945 he headed a pro-German administration. After the war Quisling was tried and convicted on charges of treason, and he was executed by firing squad on 24 October 1945.

4. In November 1938, as squadron leader, he had been one of the airmen who had established a new long-distance record-breaking flight in one of two Wellesleys from Ismailia to Darwin, Australia. On the night of 13–14 September 1942, while serving as SASO of 205 Group, he joined a 70 Squadron crew as second pilot on a Wellington IC for a raid on Tobruk. On the return journey the aircraft force-landed and the crew began to walk back towards the Allied lines, managing to evade capture until 20 September. He was the Senior British Officer at Luckenwalde at the time the camp was liberated by the Soviets on 22 April 1945.

Stettin, where they stowed away on a Danish ship and eventually returned to Britain. Philpot was able to board a train to Danzig (now Gdańsk) and from there stowed away on a Swedish merchant vessel called the *Aralizz* headed for Stockholm, from where he was repatriated to Britain, returning on a BOAC flight just before Christmas to be reunited with his family. He did not return to operational flying and after debriefing by MI9 he was posted to the Air Ministry as a senior scientific officer. He was subsequently awarded the Military Cross on 16 May 1944. Philpot resumed his career in management in the food industry. and in 1950 he wrote the book *Stolen Journey*, in which he recounts daily life as a prisoner in various PoW camps, ending with his escape via the wooden horse and his return to England. The book was illustrated by Ronald Searle.[5]

Accounts of the Wooden Horse escape were recorded in the short book *Goon in the Block* by Williams, which he wrote on the long sea voyage home on the RMS *Queen Mary*. In 1949 Williams rewrote his first book as a much longer third-person narrative under the title *The Wooden Horse*, an extended study of the mentalities of prisoners of war. Williams included many details omitted in his previous book, but because military censorship was still in force he changed his name to 'Peter Howard', Michael Codner to 'John Clinton' and Oliver Philpot to 'Philip Rowe' (and Leslie Sidwell to 'Nigel Wilde'). In 1950, when story was made into a film, *The Wooden Horse*, the three

---

5. Ronald William Fordham Searle CBE, RDI, born in Cambridge in 1920, was an English artist and satirical cartoonist, comics artist, sculptor, medal designer and illustrator who today is thought of as one of the world's foremost illustrators. During the Second World War he became a Japanese prisoner of war in Singapore. While in captivity he kept a sketchbook, providing a unique insight into PoW life. He is perhaps best remembered as the creator of St Trinian's School and for his collaboration with Geoffrey Willans on the Molesworth series. He died aged 91 in 2012.

main characters retained their pseudonyms.[6] In 1951 Williams wrote *The Tunnel*, a prequel to *The Wooden Horse*, that described his and Codner's escape from Oflag XXIB. Williams spent much of the time after 1962 living on his boat *Escaper* in the Eastern Mediterranean with his second wife, Sibyl Grain MBE.

Michael Codner said that he enjoyed himself when they were escaping. 'There was something about it. We were really living then. People don't live half the time … I think it's only when you're being hunted that you really live … I liked being hunted … the feeling that every minute was important, that everything you did would sway the balance …' After his successful escape he returned to combat in the Royal Artillery in Italy and was subsequently posted to India, where he served with his brother, Christopher John Codner, on the North West Frontier. After the war Michael Codner completed his degree at Oxford. In 1948 he married Florence Isobel Rosemary Moseley-Leigh. He joined the Colonial Service and became an Assistant District Officer in Malaya at the time of the Malayan Emergency. On 25 March 1952 Codner and eleven other men were killed in an ambush by communist guerrillas at Tanjung Malim, where they were repairing a sabotaged water pipeline. Codner, who had been wounded by machine gun fire, tried to crawl to cover and was shot dead beneath a bush. He was 31 years of age.

---

6. Lieutenant Peter William Shorrocks Butterworth of the Fleet Air Arm, who played his part in helping prisoners escape, was shot down during an attack on the Dutch coast in June 1940. He achieved three days of freedom before being spotted and captured by a member of the Hitler Youth. At Luft III Butterworth became close friends with Talbot Rothwell (later a writer on the Carry On series) and the two began writing and performing sketches for camp shows to entertain the prisoners (and to cover up the noise of other prisoners digging escape tunnels). Never having performed in public, Butterworth was petrified but gamely sang a duet with Talbot. This sparked his enthusiasm to enter show business after the war. Talbot helped and encouraged him and he soon became a familiar character actor in both films and television but, reputedly, when he auditioned for a part in the 1950 film *The Wooden Horse*, the film-makers considered him 'unconvincingly heroic or athletic enough'.

Chapter 4

O'Leary Line to Freedom

In Bronxville, New York, at 1018 hours on 16 February 1943 the English parents of Flying Officer Carter DFC* RCAF, a Halifax navigator on 35 Squadron at Graveley, in Huntingdonshire – the first Pathfinder squadron when the Pathfinder Force was formed in 1942 – received a telegram informing them that their son was missing in action. On 22 March the New York Daily News *noted briefly that he had been reported missing on 13–14 February; the night RAF Bomber Command bombed the German U-boat pens at the port of Lorient on the west Brittany coast. That same day another newspaper telephoned Mr Carter telling him that they had learned that his son had been killed. But, contrary to reports, he was very much alive and safely in the hands of the Resistance.*

Gordon Henry Francis Carter had been born in Paris on 1 June 1923 and the family had lived in the suburbs there until he was 13 when the family moved to the United States and set up home in Bronxville, New York. Gordon graduated from Roosevelt High School in Yonkers, New York, where he was on the board of the yearbook and played soccer. At Dartmouth Gordon majored in sociology, was a member of the French Club and played hockey and soccer. Gordon dropped out of Dartmouth before graduation because he 'found it cut off from the real world'. He went to Canada and enlisted in the Royal Canadian Air Force as soon as he became 18 in June 1941. His first commanding officer considered him 'calm and confident, very mature for his age, intelligent, deep thinker, dependable, responsible, serious, very good background' and a commission followed. Then it was across the ocean to England. In a tea shop in Bournemouth he listened intently to two Free French pilots at the next table discussing how to escape if they were shot down in France. He wondered if he would one day find himself in the same situation. Late in 1942 he was posted to 35 Pathfinder Squadron, one of the elite squadrons that led the waves of bombers to their targets and marked them for the main force.

Having completed thirteen sorties, the operation on 13–14 February to mark and bomb the U-boat base at Lorient (carrying escape kit No. 13) was Carter's fourteenth trip. His pilot, Flying Officer James Copeland Thomas, was an American in the RCAF. The crew had survived a crash-landing on W7923 ten days earlier on 3 February when approaching to land at base. The undercarriage could not be lowered and a belly landing was made without casualties. Now, on 13–14 February 'Tommy', as he was more familiarly known to his crew, had taken Halifax W7885 'B-Baker' off with its cargo of four green target indicators and three 1,000 pounders at 1820 hours. They crossed the north coast of Brittany on their way south and dropped their bomb load on the aiming point before being hit by heavy flak that destroyed the Halifax's port inner engine. Thomas ordered the crew to bail out, one of seven crews on the squadron that were lost that night on the Lorient raid.

Flight Sergeant John Napoleon 'Nap' Barry RCAF, the 24-year-old mid-upper gunner from Montreal; and Sergeants Richard Martin, 28, from St Anne's on the Sea in Lancashire, the 28-year-old air bomber; Daniel Christie Young, flight engineer, and Edward 'Eddie' Roland Turenne RCAF from Saint Boniface in Manitoba, the 27-year-old wireless operator/air gunner, jumped into the dark void 'in the nick of time'. The five men landed within a few hundred metres of each other near Spézet in central Brittany. Sergeant William Joseph Freeman RCAF, the tail gunner, was killed. Turenne, Martin and Young were taken under the wing of Operation Oaktree and soon found themselves together in a house in Châteauneuf-du-Faou. On 15 February Georges Jouanjean ('Geo', or 'Joe' to the English speakers) split them up, but they met up again on the evening of 17 February at Carhaix railway station when Geo and Jean Bach, a passeur of the Pat O'Leary aka 'Pat Line', took them to Paris on the overnight train, being joined by their American skipper, who had been staying with the Jouanjean family. Young, who had been suffering from a badly sprained ankle since his landing, went to stay with a French family in a PAO safe house in Paris but the home was raided by the Gestapo on 3 March and although Young made an escape via a back window, he was captured. Thomas was also staying at a safe house when it too was raided. He also made a run for it and, helped by railwaymen from time to time, he succeeded in reaching Switzerland on the night of 12–13 March 1943. He remained in Switzerland for eighteen months when, with France all but free of Germans, he returned to Allied lines, leaving behind his wife, who he had married on 2 November 1943 and a young son, Peter, born on 28 August 1944.

Flying Officer Gordon Carter, who admitted that his 'guts cramped with fear', had landed virtually into the arms of a young boy by the name of Lapous ('Bird') in a ploughed field about 15 yards from a house, beside a group of about thirty people. The boy's immediate words to Carter were '*Tu es mon frére*' ('you are my brother'). He took Carter's 'chute and hid it in a haystack near Loudéac, a few kilometres to the north-west of Kerlescoat. The canal de Nantes at Brest flows between these two localities and all the other members of the crew had fallen in a stick on the far side of the waterway.

Lapous led Carter to a stone farmhouse in Kerlescoat, 12km south-west of Carhaix, known as the 'Hamlet by the wood' in Breton, which soon became quite crowded. In addition to the young Lapous' parents and a wizened old grandmother by the hearth (as always in old Breton houses), many neighbours looked in to shake hands, to bring a bottle of cider or of wine or to bolster their spirits at the sight of les Anglais, for by then 'Nap' Barry had also been recovered from a field a little further away and was now among the throng. That night the two airmen slept together in the *lit clos*, a traditional Breton cupboard-like bed with sliding doors. Carter and Barry were awoken before dawn, given some civilian clothes, a shopping bag and some bread, and seen on their way before the German garrison in Carhaix showed up. They were scouring the countryside for the crew of the Halifax.

'Nap' and Carter, having planned to make for Spain using a Michelin map Carter had brought with him, decided that they should pass themselves off as French and Barry was given civilian clothing. However, Carter had previously made a study of escaping and was carrying with him when he was shot down several special aids, as well as simple civilian clothes that he wore underneath his uniform. He could also speak fluent French. Carter buried his escape kit to avoid having anything incriminating on him if searched. They set out in the half light, heading generally south-east towards remote Spain. As night was about to fall, they picked out an isolated farmhouse near a bridge over a stream at Pont Rouge between Priziac and Le Croisty and tried their luck. More by chance than anything, they introduced themselves as Canadian airmen. The reaction (in French) was: 'You're welcome. You wouldn't have been had you been English!' (Shades of the British shelling of the French fleet at Mers-el-Kébir on 3 July 1940.) His family fed them and put them up for the night. The daughter even washed their feet in a basin by the hearth.

Very early the next morning, Carter and 'Nap' walked to Guéméné-sur-Scorff with the man of the house pushing his bike, who then left them at a bus stop to take a bus to Pontivy. The bus was already packed with people and crowds were pushing and shoving to get in, mostly country women in their coiffes, Breton headwear. 'Nap' and Carter managed to squeeze their way to the rear door and Carter dared all, shouting to the conductor who was trying to close it that they were *des aviateurs Anglais*. That was good enough for him. He got them on board somehow. The bus was heading for Pontivy, due east, where a man on the bus who had overheard Carter told them that they should look up Pierre Valy at the Grand Café.

Valy showed them an RAF button compass and told them that their pilot was in the hands of a Resistance organisation and that he and one or two others were on their way. Valy introduced Carter and 'Nap' to a man who called himself Guy Dubreuil, who was in charge of an organisation receiving arms and ammunition by aircraft. As an agent working for London, organising the reception of arms drops, his (accurate) theory was that the thicker you laid it on, the less chance you had of being caught. He wore an Austin Reed shirt, called his dog 'RAF', carried a ferret called 'Hitler' around in a cage that sat on a million francs worth of banknotes (dropped by the RAF), slapped 'V-1918' licence plates on his motorbike, and had reversible Pétain/de Gaulle framed photographs at home, which then was a rented country house on the outskirts of St-Méen-le-Grand. He bluffed his way through thick and thin, even helping the Gestapo hunt the parachutist who had been seen coming down the night before. He passed himself off as a big-time black marketeer, who was known to be up to all sorts of tricks. Dubreuil was really BCRA[1] agent Guy Lenfant, who had been parachuted, along with his radio operator André Rapin, from a 138 Special Duties Halifax in December 1942. Both returned to the UK by Lysander in July. Dubreuil took Carter and Barry back to his house, where they stayed from 16 February until 8 March posing as refugees from Lorient. Dubreuil sent their details to London, and on about 4 March they received the news that they were to be taken off by boat when the BBC broadcast a certain message on the evening *Les Français parlent aux Français* (*The French talk to the French*) programme.

'Nap' and Carter went along with Dubreuil on his outings, lugging suitcases of Sten guns and ammo on their bicycles, always but always at the time of day when there were the most Germans about. He had

---

1. The *Bureau Central de Renseignements et d'Action,* forerunner of the SDECE, the French intelligence service.

the two evaders with him when his wireless operator transmitted to London from the bedroom of a couple of elderly ladies in Ploërmel, to which he travelled by train when the RAF had not shot up the engine. In Ploërmel 'Nap' and Carter went to the mairie (the town hall) and reported that they were bombed-out victims of the raids on Lorient and claimed ration cards and clothing coupons. They also had ID cards issued to them. Carter chose 'Georges Charleroi' as his *nom de guerre*, to keep his initials.

Guy Dubreuil arranged for his two companions to be picked up by a Royal Navy submarine off the north-west coast of Brittany. He sent his 'pathfinder cyclist' to check the spot and to report conditions in the Verboten Coastal Zone. 'Nap' and Carter, meanwhile, had been asked by the Pontiery police chief, a Monsieur Loch, who was an active member of the Resistance, to authenticate a tall USAAF airman the French nicknamed 'Petit Pierre'. Carter was told that if he – and no one else – considered him to be a plant the fugitive would be shot there and then. 'Petit Pierre' was in fact 25-year-old Staff Sergeant Clairborne Waddell Wilson, from Holly Springs in North Carolina, a B-17 tail gunner on *Chenault's Pappy* in the 306th Bomb Group at Thurleigh not far from Graveley in Hertfordshire, where Carter had recently lunched on spaghetti and meat balls. Carter was able to pin Wilson down on local details. Shot down on his thirteenth mission on 16 February 1943 over France, Wilson landed by parachute near Guillac and was picked up by a farmer near Josselin. His evasion was completed with the help of French citizens and members of the Resistance.

On Monday, 8 March, Dubreuil, 'Petit Pierre', 'Nap' and Carter set off in a taxi for a cove due north of Sibiril, 7–8km due west of St-Pol-de-Léon, north-west of Morlaix – to Plouégat-Moysan – which was as far as the driver would take them without authorisation to enter the boundary of the coastal zone in the Finistère department. From there they walked the 35 odd kilometres to Morlaix and then they took a train to St-Pol-de-Léon to meet a BOA (Bureau des Opérations

Aériennes) agent by the name of Julien Le Port. As they left this train and headed for the station exit, French and German police, checking passengers' Ausweise (passes), which travellers were expected to carry in the forbidden coastal zone, turned to 'Petit Pierre' for his. His companions were just in time to intercede in French – which Wilson did not speak – and explain that they were on their way to the Ausweis issuing office before the American panicked and gave the whole show away! As it was, they were issued Ausweise without any difficulty. The fugitives lunched on bigornots (winkles) in a country inn near the Ploujean Luftwaffe base; the only 'civilians' in a crowd of Luftwaffe officers. Carter and 'Nap' hoped to God that no one would notice their bulging breast pockets in which they had tucked their revolvers, which it would have been smarter to do without. As it was, the taxi owner had a fit when he later found bullets that one of them had spilled onto the back seat of his cab! They stayed overnight at the local Hotel des Voyageurs.

The pre-agreed message, *'Laplume de ma tante est rouge'* ('my aunt's red quill') on the BBC came over the clandestine airwaves and the fugitives set out at dusk for a beach 13km away on borrowed bicycles for their rendezvous at the cove. This had been described in the wireless exchange between Ploërmel and London as having a low cliff on which grew alder trees and a large rock in the middle. Night soon fell and the airmen's troubles began. Nearing Sibiril, they were stopped by a German sentry posted outside a house in which German officers were having a boisterous shindig. This was touch and go, for a shout by the guard and they would have had it. But Dubreuil was at his extravagant best and in a stream of French, English (!) and German, had the sentry bemoaning the fate of the German armies at Stalingrad. The airmen made off and, skirting some German positions in the countryside, finally reached the beach. They huddled by the rock and waited. In due course they saw a single flash at sea, the submarine's signal. But to their despair nothing happened and a couple of hours later they grudgingly made their way back, unhindered, to

St-Pol-de-Léon. (Carter found out later at MI9 that there were twin coves 200 yards apart and deduced that the submarine's dinghy had put in at the other one!) After three days of waiting, and not hearing anything on the radio, Carter, Barry and Wilson returned by train to Pontivy, where they stayed overnight on 14–15 March at the Pontivy Hôtel des Voyagers with owner André Weinzaepflen.

The fugitives were by now more than Dubreuil could cope with and after contacting the 'Pen Called' organisation that had helped their pilot, James Thomas, he turned the men over to monks at the Trappist monastery at Thymadeuc-en-Rohan, in central Brittany. The tradition whereby the monastery acted as a refuge for men for fourteen days with no questions asked was then still observed by the Germans. (They later raided the monastery and deported the fathers. Father Gwenael, 'White Angel' in Breton, died in one of the detention camps.) Carter, 'Nap' and Wilson spent an extraordinary week in the monastery where the vow of absolute silence prevailed. Only Father Hostelier could speak to them. By day the three men strolled in his gardens; at night, in their austere cells, they listened to the droning prayers of the monks. Meals were good, though, including the home-made liqueur of Mirabelle plums. They were joined at the abbaye by 1st Lieutenant Robert E. Biggs, a B-17 co-pilot in the 306th Bomb Group who had been shot down on 6 March.

On 8 March, Georges Jouanjean, a good-looking young tailor with chestnut brown hair and blue eyes, his face always lit up by a half smile, arrived to collect Carter, Barry, Wilson and Biggs. 'Geo', also known as 'Joe', was born in Carhaix in 1917. He had been taken prisoner in May 1940 while serving with the French artillery. He was interned in Stalag IIB, from where he escaped in 1942 by having himself sealed in a goods train loaded with seed potatoes bound for France. Thirteen days later he slipped out and away when the train reached Creil, just north of Paris. He eventually arrived home in Brittany. He soon joined the 'Mithridate' Resistance organisation and then the 'Pat O'Leary Line', aka 'Pat Line', the oldest and one of the most important escape lines, with which Louis Nouveau had established contact before his arrest in that same February. The line rescued Allied aircrew shot down over Western France, helped them to evade capture and organised and assisted their return to freedom. 'Geo', assisted by his family and friends, personally sought out, sheltered and guided sixty to seventy Allied airmen, either escorting them to Paris and turning them over to his network contact, or arranging for their escape by fishing boat from the west coast of Brittany. When his escape route was suddenly cut off, he found a refuge for them in northern Brittany.

'Geo' took his four fugitives to La Pie, where they met another American, 2nd Lieutenant Robert E. Kylius.[2] Next morning, 'Geo' took them to Carhaix, where they stayed overnight with 'Geo's aunt. Then it was on to Morlaix where they spent the afternoon with Geo's mother Marcelle before taking the 8.30 evening train to Paris, arriving in the French capital on the morning of Friday, 19 March. They made for Jouanjean's contact address, to which he had earlier delivered 'Tommy' Thomas. They all sat in a café in the Denfert-Rochereau district while 'Geo' went to an apartment at 19 rue d' Orléans, the Paris headquarters of Geo's organisation, to check that the way was clear. He reappeared in great haste for he had found the door to the flat sealed by the Gestapo and learned that three members of the organisation had been arrested. Had the fugitives shown up two days earlier they would have walked into the trap. 'Geo' told his fugitives that the French capital was not safe and the route south was now all but impassable, with Pat O'Leary under arrest and many other 'Pat Line' helpers also in German hands. There was no way out of their predicament so that evening the party returned to La Pie, where the five airmen were sheltered with Job Le Bec at the Moulin

---

2. Kylius was the bombardier on the same B-17 as Clairborne Wilson. See *First Over Germany: A History of the 306th Bombardment Group* by Russell A. Strong (1982).

de la Pie while Jouanjean returned to his home in Carhaix. About four days later, with Jouanjean and Le Bec unable to arrange their onward journeys, the airmen were split up. On about 24 March 'Nap' Barry was taken to Carhaix, where he was sheltered for more than six weeks by Madame Madeleine Marchais, a nurse who lived at 14 rue de l'Eglise, and Biggs with Madame Correc, a dentist, of Place d'Auguillon, both in Carhaix, while Wilson[3] and Kylius were taken just outside Carhaix to stay with brothers Louis and Jean Manach, flour dealers at the Minoterie de Kerniguez en Plouguer.

At first Carter stayed with 'Geo's aunt, Madame Rouillard, and grandfather, Edouard Rouillard, in Spézet. Shortly thereafter, 'Geo' decided to shelter him with his brother-in-law, Raymond Cougard, a grain merchant at rue de Quimper in Gourin who was married to 'Geo's elder sister Lucette Cougard, who lived in Gourin.[4] In order to make their bicycle ride from Carhaix to Gourin less conspicuous, 'Geo' asked his younger sister, 22-year-old Janine, an 'attractive blonde', to accompany them. Carter was younger than Janine, just 19; quite handsome even in his shabby clothes, 'tall, sleepy-looking, very dark and very reserved'. He cycled at her speed and repaired her chain while her brother was racing on ahead. Janine and Carter spent a happy fortnight or so in Gourin, where their neighbour was the Austrian Commanding Officer (whom Carter greeted every morning when they opened their shutters, their respective bedrooms being across the street from one another). Carter often visited Carhaix, passing himself off as a university friend of Raymond Cougard. He

---

3. Fed, clothed, sheltered, transported all the way to southern France, Wilson crossed the Pyrenees and arrived in Spain on 5 June. He was briefly interned there before being guided to Gibraltar, which he reached on 26 June 1943. Flown back from there to Bristol on 29 June 1943, returned to active duty in August 1943. He was promoted to master sergeant by General Ira Eaker upon his return to England.
4. Raymond was awarded the King's Medal for Courage for the numerous airmen he and his wife had sheltered before and after Carter.

also went back to Spézet to visit his first helpers, where he was told that James Thomas, Edward Turenne and Richard Martin from his crew were in the hands of Operation Oaktree and on their way to Toulouse.

Carter and Janine went for walks, visited the local cinema, attended football matches and so on ... and fell in love. The smitten RAF navigator wanted to take Janine with him to England but it was far too dangerous and it was obvious that she would have to remain behind when he took his leave of his brave hosts. 'Geo' and Raymond asked Carter one day whether he would go along with a scheme to hijack a new German MTB going out on trials in the next day or two from the western harbour of Douarnenez on the west Breton coast. Preposterous though it sounded, he said yes, as he had to grab any opportunity to relieve his helpers of his presence and get back home.[5]

Carter and 'Nap' Barry had left the next day for Douarnenez, having as a rendezvous point the railway station, located in the twin town of Tréboul. They were to contact someone there who would answer to the password 'Napoleon'. For the first couple of hours no one showed up. In desperation, Carter put to a man who had been lingering some distance away: '*Êtes-vous Napoleon?*' He was! The reason why it had taken so long to make contact was that the three evaders had been expected to arrive in a car belonging to a Resistance associate, Job le Bee, but this had proved to be unavailable.

They were led to a flat in Douarnenez at the head of a deep bay, where Claude Hernandez hid them, as well as a number of evading Frenchmen, until nightfall. After dark they single-filed at long intervals down to a shed on the quayside at Tréboul harbour, where they met yet other escapees and were briefed. Each one of them – nineteen in all – chipped in 10,000 francs to cover costs, principally diesel fuel, for by then they had learned that they were to escape in

---

5. Biggs arrived in Spain on 6 June and was back in England on 28 June.

a derelict fishing boat, a far cry from the MTB! As Carter had no money a local priest, the Abbe Cariou, put up the money for him. (He reimbursed him after the war.)

On 6 April Carter was taken to Tréboul, a small port near the tip of Brittany, where he joined a party of a dozen Frenchmen trying to get to England to join the war. They left in the *Dalc'h-Mad* ('Hang-on' or 'Persevere' in Breton), an old 40ft sardine boat captained by a 23-year-old local fisherman called Louis 'Lili' Marec and his two-man crew. As the German sentries on the quay moved away, they dropped down onto the harbour floor (the tide was out), ran for the *Dalc'h-Mad* and disappeared below deck. Absolute silence was impressed. After a long and somewhat anxious night 'Lili' Marec came openly on board, started the engine up and they headed out on the tide for the spot where all boats were checked out by the German military Customs, the Gast. Since the first day of the German occupation every vessel leaving Tréboul or Douarnenez had been boarded by the Gast during its check. The travellers had to be cleared without being boarded. 'Lili' Marec therefore idled the boat to within a few feet of the Gast dock, but too far for a jump on board. He explained that he was off to collect some fuel across the bay and would be right back. The Germans yelled back for him to heave to alongside. At that crucial moment, Hernandez and an accomplice breezed into the Gast office and started a rumpus of their own. One pretended to be an electrician who had repairs to carry out. The other bitched about having had something of his stolen. It was enough of a commotion for the Customs men to drop their guard and to shout them off with a '*Raus*!' (get going). They did, rounding Mistan Island and making for the still distant open sea. (The Customs men were later shot for letting the evaders through.)

They had a long chug out to the sea, sails straining to help the engine along, and headed due west to get as far from the German MTBs and destroyers in Brest as possible. They were probably saved from interception (their failure to return had by now been reported) by the worst storm at sea that Marec and the many sailors (Xavier Trellu was a famous yachtsman) and fishermen on board had ever experienced. Carter somehow struggled out of the mixture of vomit, diesel fuel and sea water sloshing all over them in the hold and joined Marec at the tiller, hanging on for dear life.

The next day they headed north, Carter navigating by 'astro', i.e. educated guesses as to their position in relation to the sun, at night, the stars. They ran up a French flag with a Cross of Lorraine tarred on it (their names were later embroidered on it and it is now in the National Resistance Museum in Bordeaux). After losing direction in fog, they spotted a small lumpy island in the distant haze that Carter guessed might be St Michael's Mount. They chanced it and soon saw cliffs on the horizon. Then appeared a fishing boat, heading for them. English? Irish? French? They stood by to either welcome it or do it in. It turned out to be a Cornish crabber from Cadgwith Cove! After a gruelling fifty-four-hour voyage dodging German shipping and braving fog and a Force 9 gale in the Channel they had made it!

They finally reached Coverack in Cornwall on 9 April after a Cornish crabber guided them through a minefield to the lifeboat slipway on Lizard Point. The BBC message announcing the safe arrival was *'Sainte Art les choses'* (*'Saint Anne took care of things nicely'*), for they sailed in sight of 'her' chapel at Sainte-Anne La Palud, a couple of miles up the coast from Douarnenez. 'Nap' Barry, Richard Martin and 'Eddie' Turenne were passed along the escape lines to Spain and reached Gibraltar safely. They were flown back to England on 13–14 July 1943.

For the thoroughness with which he prepared for the contingency, and the tenacity he showed in avoiding capture and returning, Flying Officer Carter was recommended for the immediate award of the Distinguished Flying Cross on 4 June 1943. A Bar to his DFC was awarded effective 10 January 1944 as per the *London Gazette* dated 18 January 1944. When MI9 learned of his successful escape to England they tried to persuade Carter to return to France for a role in the 'Shelburn' escape line[6] but he declined. If he went, he would not be able to stay away from Janine, the girl he had fallen in love with, and that would put her in great danger. His thoughts were always with her. Once back on 35 Squadron at Graveley Carter talked at length about his new girlfriend, who he described as his fiancée. On operations, he had *'Pour* [for] *Janine'* painted on a 1,000lb bomb loaded on his Halifax for a raid. Off duty he would compose love letters in immaculate French and send them in a sealed envelope to his Aunt Dot in Haslemere, Surrey, with instructions to send them to Janine once France was liberated if anything happened to him on operations.

Gordon Carter was promoted to flight lieutenant and he joined the crew skippered by 29-year-old Penetanguishene, Ontario-born and Toronto-educated Squadron Leader Douglas Julian Sale DSO, who had returned to operations after he was shot down on the Duisburg-Ruhrort raid on 12–13 May 1943 when he was a flight lieutenant. Sale's Halifax came down near the small Dutch town of Haaksbergen in Gelderland province near the German border by Oberleutnant August 'Gustel' Geiger of III./NJG1 flying a Bf 110. Julian Sale was blown out of the aircraft when it exploded and he landed in a pine tree. Four of his crew were taken into captivity and the other two were killed.

Sale had some knowledge of French and his general plan was to head for Spain, keeping to the east of Paris. He hoped to make contact with 'an organisation', but apart from being given some bread coupons he had to press on alone. He cycled through the day, approaching lonely farms each evening, almost always gaining access

---

6. The Shelburn Line was mainly in use between December 1943 and August 1944. It was different from many of the other mainland escape lines because it often took groups of evaders to safety, rather than just one or two men at a time. The escape line's route was primarily by sea. Evaders were taken to the Brittany coast, then from there they went by motor gun boats [MGBs] across the English Channel back to England.

to a barn. Few farmers accepted any payment for his food and he was regularly provided with enough for his journeys. For two days, he had only one pedal on his bicycle and punctures became a regular feature as he progressed south through Laon, Château-Thierry, Sens and on to Bourges, where he arrived at the demarcation line. As he had no repair outfit, he pushed his bicycle until he arrived at a small town, where he was able to get repairs. Throughout his journey, he used coloured card and tin to improvise a local licence plaque and he was very alert for police patrols whenever he entered a small town. The demarcation line between the Occupied and Unoccupied Zones of France was patrolled regularly and presented a major obstacle to the evader. Sale approached a landowner a few miles south of Bourges, who helped him cross at an unguarded bridge. Safely over, he continued south, aiming to cycle up to 100 miles each day, which he achieved to reach Castres on 1 June. A day later, he reached the small town of Revel, where he stayed on local farms for almost three weeks. Since leaving the Belgian border eight days earlier, he had covered just over 500 miles.

Shortly after arriving in Revel, Sale met a young Frenchman who had tried to escape to Switzerland, but had been forced to return to Revel because of the tight security near the border. They agreed to join forces to make an attempt to cross the Pyrenees. On 21 June Sale abandoned the Dutch bicycle that had served him so well. He and his companion left for Toulouse, where they caught a fast train to Carcassonne before transferring to a local train that took them to Quillan. After a 15-mile bus ride to Belcaire in the foothills of the Pyrenees, they stayed at a small hotel where they were able to contact a mountain guide who had gathered a party of six others who wished to cross the mountains. The party set off early on the morning of 24 June, but the guide became lost, which resulted in an overnight stop in the open. They started climbing early the next morning and had reached a point two miles from the frontier with Andorra by mid-afternoon when the guide refused to go any further. Sale and his

French companion continued alone, crossing a 7,000ft mountain and snow drifts to reach the frontier, which they crossed late on the night of 25–26 June. They stayed overnight in a shepherd's hut before walking into the small Andorran town of Canillo the next morning.

In Canillo they met a man who put them in touch with a Spanish smuggler who agreed to take them to Barcelona. A short car journey took them to the closely guarded Spanish frontier and that night they crossed the mountains on foot into Spain with the smuggler and some of his associates. Over the next ten days they descended from the mountains, reaching the town of Manresa after a 90-mile walk. Sale said that this was the most arduous phase of his journey. The guide left them to go ahead to Barcelona to make contact with the British Consul, who arrived on 7 July to take the two men to the Consulate. They remained there until their onward journey to Gibraltar could be arranged. Julian Sale left Gibraltar on 5 August, arriving in Liverpool five days later and three months after he had bailed out of his stricken Halifax. With the exception of three short train and bus journeys, he had walked and cycled over 800 miles without once being supported by any of the escape lines. Local Dutch, Belgian and French people had been his helpers along the route. It was one of the longest single evasions during the war. In October it was announced that Sale had been awarded the DSO for his epic journey, an extremely rare award for such an action. The citation concluded: 'His unconquerable spirit of determination, great gallantry and fortitude have set an example beyond praise.'

Back at Graveley, Julian Sale and Gordon Carter would get up at 0400 hours and go for long runs around the airfield. They also practised penetrating the perimeter fence and attacking parked aircraft. They had organised two exercises where they were taken out in a lorry at night and dumped in the middle of nowhere to get themselves back to Graveley without being picked up by MPs. Sale and Carter took these exercises so seriously that they even set fire to the odd haystack to divert attention from where they were actually headed. Both men also took to carrying civilian clothes with them on operations.

On the night of 20–21 December 1943 Julian Sale was returning from Frankfurt with a fire in the bomb bay of his Halifax. Hung-up TIs (target indicators) had exploded as the aircraft came below their barometric fuse altitude of 1,500ft. Sale ordered the crew to bail out but Flight Lieutenant Roger 'Sheep' Lamb, the mid-upper gunner, appeared beside him with a charred parachute so Sale dropped back into his seat, stuck his head out of the port window of the cockpit, which was filled with smoke, and calmly brought the blazing Halifax in for a normal circuit landing at Graveley before roaring off the runway and crashing in a ball of fire. Sale and Lamb reached safety before the bomber exploded. The four other men who bailed out were safe and only the rear gunner suffered any injury. Sale was awarded a bar to his DSO for his action.

On the night of 19–20 February 1944 four of the missing Halifaxes on a raid to Leipzig were from 35 Squadron, one of which exploded over Gohre and another was abandoned near Brandenburg. 'J-Johnny' piloted by Squadron Leader Julian Sale DSO* DFC was hit at 23,000ft near Beedenbostel in central Germany near Celle by a Ju 88 armed with Schräge Musik ('Oblique Music'). This device, invented by an armourer, Paul Mahle of II./NJG5, comprised two 20mm MG FF cannon mounted behind the rear cockpit bulkhead of the Bf 110 and Ju 88 night fighters and was arranged to fire forwards and upwards at an angle of between 70 and 80 degrees. 'J-Johnny's' port inner engine caught fire and Sale called, 'Bail out; bail out, bail out!' His highly decorated crew included the navigation leader, now Squadron Leader, Gordon Carter DFC*. Because he had been through it all before, Carter removed his helmet because 'a lot of chaps were hanged by their intercom leads going out' and bailed out. He had on his back under the parachute harness a pack of escape items such as wire cutters and some civilian clothes bought in France during his evasion.

ESCAPE FROM HITLER'S REICH

On landing in a lane in a forest in snow, Carter buried his parachute and then went into the trees and put the clothes on. He remembered that he was carrying a revolver that he had bought in Huntingdon in case he ever fell into a city where he thought that civilians might mob him. Carter decided that he had better get rid of it. Later he ditched his distinctive RAF Omega watch. He followed a track to a road. A sign pointed to Celle, a town between Hamburg and Hanover. The navigation leader was free for forty-eight hours and had travelled 40 miles when he met some children, who, trained to report any strangers, ran off to tell a sailor shooting crows in a field. He did not believe Carter's story that he was a French factory worker and he pointed his shotgun at him. Bitterly disappointed that he had not got any further, Carter was taken to a Luftwaffe airfield, where he was visited by Hauptmann Ludwig 'Luk' Meister, who told him that he was the pilot who had shot him down. Carter, who was still wearing his French clothes, was asked, 'Were you trying to do what your Skipper succeeded in doing last year?' Apparently, the Hauptmann had read about it in the Toronto ski club magazine. Carter opened his shirt and showed his interrogator his RCAF identity disc. Four others on the crew were also taken prisoner. Flight Sergeant Kenneth Knight, the 19-year-old rear gunner, had not answered the call to abandon the aircraft and he was found dead. Sale's parachute failed to open properly and his pelvis was broken in six places on landing and was taken prisoner. He died of internal injuries caused by his broken pelvis at the Air Force Hospital, Giessener Strasse near Frankfurt-am-Main, on 20 March. Prisoners who had been in hospital with him say that he died with the same old smile on his face.

Carter would spend the next fourteen months as a prisoner in Stalag Luft III. In Northern France on 6 June there was jubilation after the Allied landings in Normandy and soon most of the country was in Allied hands. That August the postman brought Jouanjean a huge bundle of love letters from Carter. She read them avidly while at the same time hoping that there might be news of her brother 'Geo' and her brother-in-law. In spring 1943 the Germans had succeeded in infiltrating the 'Pat O'Leary' network and they arrested 'Geo's mother and 80-year-old grandfather, holding them as hostages. 'Geo' was picked up in Paris by the Gestapo on 18 June. He was interrogated and imprisoned, first in Fresnes, south of Paris, then Rennes, Angoulême and Compiègne, whereupon his family were released. In April 1944 'Geo's interrogators were satisfied that he would reveal nothing, so he was thrown on the back of a cattle truck and taken to Auschwitz concentration camp. He was later incarcerated in concentration camps at Birkenau, Buchenwald, briefly, and Flossenbürg. In May 1945 when the camp was abandoned, the inmates were marched 400 miles along forest roads in southern Germany under the watchful eyes of SS guards. Thousands of the Flossenbürg inmates died on that notorious march, most of whom were shot as they fell behind, others committing suicide by dropping to their knees, stuffing dirt from the ground into their throats and choking to death. American troops and tanks arrived and saved 'Geo' and many of his fellow prisoners.

When 'Geo' returned to Carhaix, his arrival coincided with a visit by Gordon Carter, who after his release had returned to the UK on 9 May and then returned to France to find Janine on the 19th having received permission to make his way from England to Paris. He set off with a fourteen-day pass, taking the ferry from Newhaven across the Channel and travelled on to Paris, where he had been told that Janine had worked behind the counter in a pastry shop in rue Blanche. But she had long since gone back to Brittany and was working in her grandfather's tailor's shop in Carhaix. Carter took the next train the 300 miles to Morlaix on the north Brittany coast in a first-class carriage reserved for Allied officers. In Morlaix he learned that there was no connecting service to Carhaix, 25 miles away, until the next day but he was offered a lift in a car. An hour later he arrived outside Janine's grandfather's tailor's shop in Carhaix, unannounced and unexpected. The door opened. An aunt stood there. She looked at him and turned her head back inside. 'Janine,' she called out, 'c'est Gordon!' Gordon and Janine had not seen each other for about two-and-a-half years. The last time he had been in a shabby French suit but now he was in full RAF uniform, medals and all. Her heart jumped when she saw him. She was overwhelmed. Unable to take it in, she burst into tears.

Carter rekindled his romance with Janine and his proposal of marriage was accepted but her parents were not so sure and they were slow to give their blessing. His leave was running out and so he and his fiancée travelled to Paris, where Carter persuaded an RAF air marshal to extend his leave by another fourteen days. Gordon Carter and Janine married on 9 June 1945. She was given away by her brother 'Geo' Jouanjean. Just over a fortnight later she went with her husband to Buckingham Palace, where Carter received a bar to his DFC from King George VI. Before he left for Canada on the *Ile de France* to be demobbed in Montreal in August 1945 he took Janine to Graveley and showed her where he had written her name above his bunk.

After his military discharge Gordon Carter lived all around the world in various responsible positions with UNICEF, including director for South and Central Asia and later director for Europe. In retirement, from his home in Brittany he was involved with many historical, cultural and environmental organisations. He looked after two ancient houses, gardens and woods, attended RAF reunions and, with Janine, visited their children and grandchildren. Gordon Carter died on 22 March 2013. He was survived by Janine and their children Eric, Bridgette, France and Nathalie and seven grandchildren.

Chapter 5

Heydekrug

I remember 'Dixie' Deans, our camp leader, saying at a parade in December 1944, 'I've been here for six Christmases and it looks as if I'm going to be here for another bugger.' ... The RAF were kept in the special 'escape-proof' camp at Heydekrug in East Prussia. This was Stalag Luft VI, and also at Luft I, Barth. Heydekrug was the camp especially built for NCO prisoners. If promotion came through during internment you were promoted from a Stalag to an Oflag. The Germans were very punctilious about this sort of thing; they gave me a receipt for my fountain pen! Heydekrug was supposed to be more escape-proof and nasty than Colditz but 16 NCOs made 'home runs' as against 14 officers in the whole of the war. I built a mental bridge that made no sense whatever. I told myself that the war would be over in nine months. There was no logical reason for thinking this in September 1943. The invasion was almost unheard of. No one spoke about it or thought about it. We saw ourselves bombing Germany into submission. We knew nothing of the paratroops or gliders being prepared in readiness, although there were books published in 1943 that actually mentioned these preparations!

Sergeant Geoff Parnell, Stirling mid-upper gunner on 214 Squadron, who was shot down on 11 August 1943 and was incarcerated in Stalag Luft VI at Heydekrug until the end of the war

Warrant Officer Kenneth Albert Goodchild, who arrived at Heydekrug in early May 1943, had joined the Royal Air Force in 1940 and volunteered for aircrew. He was accepted and he qualified as a wireless operator. Most of his crew training involved flying on Wellington IAs, ICs and IIIs. By 1942, the Wellington, after sterling service, had been demoted to training duties and on completion of their OCU training the crew was detached to the HCU (Heavy Conversion Unit) at RAF Rufforth in February 1943 to convert to the Halifax. On completion they joined 51 Squadron at Snaith, Yorkshire, equipped with the Halifax II. 'We reported to the Flight Office, only to be told to report next morning to the Ground Training Centre for even more training! 51 Squadron comprised between 200 and 300 aircrew and about 28 aircraft. If a night raid was planned, the Flights would be informed and they would detail the crews. The crews were then given a time to attend a pre-operation briefing. We preferred night operations. They were safer from the German guns but carried their own dangers. Operations often consisted of 200 aircraft; all flying without lights and the danger of collision was always present. Navigation was also a problem. There were no modern aids, no radar. We would tune into a ground radio station and fly along its beam, using the directional aerial, providing it was working!

'Another method was to use marine navigation. This involved the use of a sextant to take sightings of the stars and co-ordinate the readings with positions on the map. This is fine if you're a ship moving at 10 mph! In an aeroplane, at four miles a minute, by the time the navigator has worked out the position, we've overflown it and need the next heading! We relied heavily on DR – Deduced Reckoning. This required the navigator to plot on his map where he thought our position was, check the compass for direction and take the wind speed. So, if the wind direction was north-east at 20 knots and we were flying south-west, then the wind must be behind us and we would be flying 20 knots faster than the ASI (Air Speed Indicator) reading. At night you can't look out of the window to check if you're flying over land or sea, so, after five hours' flying you have to have faith in your navigator.

HEYDEKRUG

'The other night-flying problem, too many aircraft in the same piece of sky. Bomber Command had adopted 'saturation-bombing', operated on the principle that if a lot of bombers raided one target, in spite of anti-aircraft defences and enemy fighters, many of the bombers would get through to the target. The principle was good, but it required all the aircraft to keep to a schedule and be in a certain place by a certain time. If the wind direction or speed were different to the navigator's calculations, then collisions would become inevitable. Precise navigation was as important as proficient piloting.

'Briefings for each night operation would be timed for early evening. On 12 May 1943 we were timed for take-off at 2250 hours on Halifax JB806 for Duisburg. My pilot was Sergeant Beverley Brown RAAF. The rest of the crew were: Sergeants W. B. Henderson, navigator; John D. A. M. Rae, bombardier; Arthur Lloyd George Knight, flight engineer; William Esmonde North-Lewis, mid-upper gunner; Phillipe Louis Marie Charles de Bourbon RCAF, rear gunner; and myself as wireless operator. We carried two 1,000lb bombs, 48 × 30lb general purpose high explosives and 63 × 4lb incendiaries. With a fuel load of 1,636 Imperial gallons, we were at maximum weight. Sergeant Brown revved up to full power and we took off at 2254 hours, our course to Stirling in Scotland and then back south to Scarborough, this strange route enabling us to gain our operational height of 20,000ft, then across the North Sea to Egmond and on to the target. All went according to plan but as we passed Egmond we began to experience heavy flak. I was on the flight deck with the skipper, keeping an eye out for enemy fighters. Flying alongside us was a Lancaster. I witnessed it receive a direct hit in the bomb bay and watched in horror as the aircraft disintegrated into a cloud of red and black flames.

'I moved back to my WOp position, directly beneath the pilot, and began receiving routine group broadcasts. Suddenly I felt a blast of cold air at my right elbow. I checked and found a large hole in the three-step staircase that led from my deck to the flight deck. I reported the damage to the pilot, who replied that there was also a hole in the cockpit roof. This confirmed that a shell had entered the fuselage next to me, missed the pilot by about a foot and passed out through the roof without exploding. That shell obviously didn't have our names on it! As we approached the Dutch route point another shell exploded right in front of us, completely wrecking the front turret and allowing a blast of cold air to enter the fuselage. With a great deal of effort, the navigator and I managed to close the forward bulkhead door and we pressed on.

'I noticed that we were losing fuel from the port wing tank but as the leak didn't seem to be endangering the aircraft, we flew on. The flak continued and a few minutes later Henderson the navigator slumped forward onto his table. He had been hit by shrapnel which had penetrated the fuselage by his seat. I called for assistance and with the engineer and bombardier's help, managed to move his limp body to the rest position, aft of the main spar. I gave him a shot of morphine. A brown, sticky fluid oozed from his mouth, causing us to assume that he had an injured lung. (Later we found out that the navigator had been eating chocolate when he had been hit, thus the brown, sticky liquid!) We flew on to the target and bombed the oil refinery. The pilot banked away and we set a course for home.

'On the Belgian–Dutch border we faced a barrage of searchlights and we knew they were guiding the anti-aircraft guns. Our fuel state was beginning to alarm us. I went up to the pilot's flight deck to check for enemy aircraft when the rear gunner called the pilot to weave as fighters (a Focke Wulf Fw 190 and a Ju 88) were on our tail. I moved to the astrodome on top of the fuselage, which gave me a good all-round view of the night scene. The enemy tracer seemed to approach us in slow motion. To my left I could see the port wing on fire. The pilot called for urgent assistance, the control column had jammed and even with Arthur Knight the engineer and me helping, the column remained stuck. Finally, the port engine fell away and the pilot yelled for us all to bail out. We got the injured navigator to the escape hatch first and, attaching his parachute ripcord to the static line, pushed him into the darkness. John Rae, the air bomber, was next followed by Arthur Knight. I nodded to the pilot and jumped. For ages I seemed to fall in an upside-down position until my parachute opened and jarred me right way up. An enemy fighter circled me and I reached for my revolver. Fortunately, the fighter pilot was keen to get back to the bombers and he ignored me. Or maybe I had scared him off by going for my revolver! That didn't really matter as I must have lost the weapon as I bailed out – but he didn't know that! I landed in a haystack. Looking around I spotted Arthur Knight. We had all survived. (Sergeant de Bourbon had been badly injured when his parachute had become entangled in the aircraft's tail. Henderson was in a German hospital.) Our Halifax landed on a bakery (at Weelde Station, Antwerp, near the border with Holland), killing the baker's wife and daughter. His visiting niece was badly burned and spent two years in hospital recovering.

'The Germans had seen us all float down on our parachutes and had arranged a welcoming reception. We were transported to Dulag Luft at Oberursel near Frankfurt. This was an interrogation centre for RAF prisoners. I was kept in solitary confinement for nine days and questioned regularly. Finally, the Germans accepted the "shot-down" story and I was moved on to Heydekrug on the border with Lithuania. This camp already housed 2,000 RAF prisoners in two lagers (compounds). I was sent to "A" Lager, the other one "K" Lager. Later, I was moved to a new compound, "J" Lager, and American prisoners took over "A" Lager.

'Life wasn't too bad. We had reasonable food, an easy time and the weather was decent. To pass the time, study sessions in almost every subject you could think of was arranged. Our compound became known as "Barbed Wire University"! Our PoW "management" also had an escape committee and a "canary", an aerial to listen in to British broadcasts. Ours was the volleyball net. The Germans never bothered us as long as we never bothered them. We also received a regular supply of Red Cross parcels. I reached my 21st birthday in November and the lads made me a cake and we had a party! We accepted life for what it was but we never noticed the subtle changes that were occurring. To celebrate Christmas our custodians allowed us half a tin of corned beef each and two boiled potatoes. I wolfed mine down – and spent the next twenty-four hours in bed suffering from acute indigestion! The weather turned very cold and we were locked up from dusk to dawn, about 4 pm to 8 am. Life then became a little more difficult. We seemed to be on each other's backs; nowhere to go, nothing much to do. From the radio we knew the Russians were advancing. Stalingrad had been retaken and there was a concentrated push on Berlin.

'In June 1944 we heard of the invasion, but we managed to keep quiet. If the Germans had heard us chatting about such things, then they would have discovered the radio. We didn't have to worry. Within a couple of days, the Germans announced over the camp Tannoy system news of the invasion. Their version was different. The announcer admitted there had been a minor invasion at Normandy but it had been repelled by the "gallant German army". The Russians were making massive steps along the Baltic coast and had entered Estonia, Latvia and Lithuania. Some of the prisoners saw the occasion as a chance to escape. They had been building a tunnel and it was planned for fifty prisoners to use it and escape. The Germans foiled the attempt by laying sensors along the perimeter fences which gave away the sounds of digging. The discovery shook the Germans. They set about organising a count of heads and a search of the camp. The prisoners reduced both to a fiasco.'

During the early part of 1944 six PoWs made successful escapes from Heydekrug but only two men made home runs. Warrant Officer Cyril Bruce 'Paddy' Flockhart, whose 76 Squadron Halifax piloted by Sergeant Thomas Augustine Byrne was shot down over Belgium on 5–6 August 1941 on the raid on Karlsruhe, escaped on 18 February. 'Paddy' had been one of the six crew members who were taken prisoner following the loss of the Halifax (one crew member was KIA). After capture he had been taken to Dulag Luft at

HEYDEKRUG

Oberursel, before being sent to a Stalag at Kirchhain. In May 1942 he was transferred to Stalag Luft III. Following an escape from the camp in May 1943, Flockhart was moved to Stalag Luft VI (Heydekrug) on 30 June 1943. The new camp was still under construction and the by-then experienced inmates decided that perfect papers and careful preparation would be needed to make any successful escape. The key to Flockhart's success was the escape of Sergeant George Grimson, the wireless operator on a 37 Squadron Wellington that was shot down by the anti-aircraft defences over Hamburg on 15 July 1940. He was one of only two survivors who bailed out before the bomber exploded. Born in Putney, south-west London, in October 1915, the son of a plumber, he had abandoned his architectural studies to join the RAF in early 1938 in order to help support his mother and siblings after their father died in 1937. Grimson was sent to Stalag Luft I at Barth, Stalag VIIIb, Lamsdorf, and back to Barth before finally being sent to Stalag Luft III. He had walked out of Heydekrug on 18 January 1944 disguised as a German guard, complete with a dummy rifle. Grimson contacted the local Polish Resistance and made arrangements for subsequent escapers, sending coded letters back to the camp with the details. It was the receipt of one of these letters that prompted 'Paddy' Flockhart, having shaved off his moustache and dressed in genuine German civilian clothing, to bluff his way into an unfinished section of the camp on 18 February 1944 and then use a forged pass to leave through the main gate. Flockhart walked to Heydekrug station and took a series of trains to Rybno before walking to the home of a local Resistance chief where Grimson was staying. On 21 February, Flockhart and Grimson took separate trains to Danzig and, after several false starts, Flockhart finally boarded the Swedish ship SS *Flora*, which left Weichselmünde on 25 February, arriving in Stockholm two days later. Flockhart left Stockholm for Leuchars on 10 March 1944 in the bomb bay of a BOAC Mosquito.[1]

---

1. *WWII escape and evasion Information Exchange.*

ESCAPE FROM HITLER'S REICH

Sergeant Jacob Gewelber, a Palestinian Jew, born in Poland, where his parents had been murdered, used the nom de guerre 'Jack Gilbert' to escape from Heydekrug on 3 April. On the 15th, he too caught a Swedish ship at Danzig, and arrived back in England in May. AC1 Gewelber was serving as ground staff for 33 Squadron RAF at Maleme when Crete was invaded and he was captured 23 May 1941. Gewelber worked as translator at Canea (Chania) hospital for two months before joining an RAF party working on a new aerodrome on the south of the island. In September he was sent to Athens (where he gave his name as Gilbert and claimed to be Welsh) and on via Dulag Luft at Oberursel to Stalag VIIIB. He escaped twice from Lamsdorf, the second time only being recaptured after living in Kraków for four months. After six weeks in a civilian prison there, he was returned to Lamsdorf in February 1943 for a day before transfer to Stalag Luft III at Sagan. Following a failed escape from Sagan in May 1943, Gewelber was transferred to Stalag Luft VI, Heydekrug, the most northerly of all the German PoW camps. He and Roland Brainerd Herbert Townsend-Coles, a lowly LAC (leading aircraftsman) shot down on an 18 Squadron Blenheim on 11 May 1940 and who was promoted to warrant officer in captivity, escaped from Heydekrug on 4 April 1944 when they bluffed their way out of the main gate; Gewelber disguised as a German 'ferret' and Coles as a civilian engineer. They had planned to walk to the Lithuanian border to try and contact Russian partisans but the bad weather persuaded them to take a train from Tilset, through Königsberg to Danzig. Gewelber stayed in Danzig until 19 April, when he was able to board a Swedish ship at Weichselmünde. He arrived in Sweden on 25 April and left Stockholm by air for Leuchars the night of 6–7 May.[2]

Now that the Gestapo had taken command, subsequent escapees who were recaptured, such as Sergeant George Grimson, Warrant

---

2. *See, WWII Escape and Evasion Information Exchange* website, part of the *Conscript Heroes* website.

HEYDEKRUG

Officer Townsend-Coles, Warrant Officer Edward 'Ned' Callander DFM RAFVR and Warrant Officer Ernest Phillip Lewis, were shot in cold blood. Warrant Officer Basil Sidney Craske, a Whitley pilot on 10 Squadron at Leeming who was shot down on 16 August 1941, was one of fifty-two men who made a mass escape on 11 May 1942 from Stalag Luft IIIE, Kirchhain. 'The manner and extent of the escape, and to get 52 prisoners out in a single night, was a miraculous achievement. I completed about 25km of the 1,500km required. Failure? Yes, if success is judged only as being my return to 10 Squadron to fight again, but not if the great cost to the German war effort, both materially and mortally, in dealing with such a large exodus is taken into consideration. The Germans thought so too, and a stir in high places brought a general from Berlin HQ to Stalag IIIE to investigate and produce a report. It was later ascertained that the tunnel was 227 feet in length and was shored with timber throughout – we used about a thousand bed boards in so doing. It is estimated that we shifted about 60 tons of sand. The Germans were impressed and took many photographs of our work. We never did find out who and how many of our keepers spent the winter on the Russian Front.

It was at Stalag Luft III that Basil Craske first observed Grimson – 'a dedicated and daring escaper' – at work. 'Unlike the majority of us he took the long-term view of the end of the war. He learnt colloquial German by taming a "goon" in the early stages of his captivity, and thus was very fluent. From an appropriate distance on one occasion, I observed Grimson, disguised as a German electrician complete with ladder, walk towards and over the tripwire and approach a guard tower to explain that there was a fault in the telephone lines which he had to find – they ran along the top of the perimeter fence. By means of accidentally dropping his dummy test meter among the wire between the inner and outer fences, he managed, with the help of a plank of wood, to get outside to retrieve it. In fact, at this stage, he was confronted by a guard patrolling the outside of the wire, and by his fluency and his forged pass had the guard resuming his patrol.

'Grimson played a major part in the organisation of escape routes during his many months on the outside of the wire. To achieve this situation there had to be collaboration of a few anti-Nazi Germans and some Germanised Poles, some willingly co-operative and some blackmailed by damaging photographic evidence. If ever there was an unsung hero it was Grimson.'

Grimson was last seen on 14 April 1944 in the Danzig area and was probably seized by the Gestapo before being shot. He was Mentioned in Despatches posthumously in December 1947 for bravery during his escaping attempts and for his work to assist fellow escapers. Townsend-Coles escaped on 3 April 1944 when he walked out of the camp dressed as a civilian drainage inspector. He was court-martialled on a charge of espionage and collaboration with the Polish underground and was shot dead at Tilsit for allegedly 'showing resistance'. His date of death is given as 15 July 1944. He was 30 years old and left a widow, Vera Hazel Townsend-Coles, of Streatham, London.

'Ned' Callander, who was born in Dumfries in 1917, had left home at 19 due to lack of work and joined the French Foreign Legion. In spring 1940 he earned the Croix de Guerre in the Battle of Narvik in northern Norway. When France fell Ned returned to England and became a rear gunner on Wellington bombers on 75 Squadron RNZAF. He completed a tour and was awarded the DFM in September 1941. After a spell as a gunnery instructor Ned, now a warrant officer, volunteered for a second tour and served at Marham, Norfolk, on 115 Squadron, again as a rear gunner. On the evening of 6–7 May 1942 his Wellington was shot down on a raid on the Bosch factory in Stuttgart. He bailed out and was captured and sent to Stalag Luft III. Transferred to Heydekrug, he tried to escape for a third time in early March 1944 and this time he succeeded by hiding in a water tank for fifty-six hours before getting free. He got as far as the docks at Danzig, where he hid among French working PoWs and hoped to board a Swedish ship. It is believed a French worker at the docks tipped off the authorities; the Gestapo captured him and then took him to Mauthausen concentration camp, where he was subjected to intense interrogation by the Gestapo and then shot. Ned was mentioned in despatches on 13 June 1946.[3]

On about 25 March 1944 Warrant Officer Ernest Philip Lewis got out of Stalag Luft VI by crawling through a trench into the wash house, which had been wired off for repairs. He then walked through a gate dressed as a civilian worker. Lewis was the pilot of a 10 Squadron Whitley V at Leeming that was shot down on Bremen on 27–28 June 1941 by Unteroffizier Arnim Behrend of 5./NJG1 flying a Bf 110E[4] and he was the only survivor of the five-man crew. He had planned to try to get into France but was recaptured in July and he too was shot in cold blood, on 1 August 1944. He is buried at Malbork.[5]

Anyone on the German side of the wire who had aided the PoWs were never seen again. Unteroffizier Adolph 'Little Munkert', the liaison officer who had done so much for the Escape Committee by smuggling supplies and documents into the camp, was 'horribly' tortured before being executed. The Polish–German camp photographer was also under suspicion and had been locked up. Rather than face torture, he hanged himself. The Gestapo were ruthless. All future escape plans were shelved.

---

3. See *Fighter! Fighter! The story of Edward Callander DFM, Croix de Guerre hero of two nations* by John Brenan and Richard Frost. (RedBek, 2008).
4. Return fire from the Whitley hit the Bf 110 and the German crew were killed while attempting to land at Stade airfield.
5. See *Footprints on the Sands of Time* by Oliver Clutton-Brock (Grub Street, 2003).

Chapter 6

Comet Line Escape
Flight Sergeant Stanley Munns

The Le Réseau Comète (Comet Line), which went from Brussels to the Pyrenees through France to the British consulate in Madrid and on to Gibraltar, involved 2,000 Resistance members and was able to escort 700 Allied servicemen to Spain. Altogether, 2,803 Allied airmen were helped to escape or evade capture via the help of Resistance groups, including the Comet Line. The first crossing of the Pyrenees by the Comet line was on 17 October 1941, when the first three men, Privates Jim Cromar, Bob Conville and Alan Cogan, were taken over by Andrée de Jongh. The first man in the RAF to successfully use the line was Jack Newton. Eight hundred members of the Comet Line were arrested by the Gestapo, of whom 140 were executed, including Frédéric de Jongh (in June 1943). Andrée de Jongh was captured in January 1944. After her arrest, the line continued under Baron Jean Greindl and then Baron Jean-Françoise Nothomb. Unwilling to believe Andrée could have organised the network herself, the Gestapo let her live. She was sent first to Fresnes prison in Paris and eventually to Ravensbrück and Mauthausen concentration camps. Andrée was liberated by the advancing Allied troops in April 1945 and was awarded the George Medal by Great Britain after the war. Her government made her a countess. She died on 13 October 2007 aged 90.

'Our group of young sergeant air gunners stood on the edge of the aircraft runway. It was the end of the Operational Training course in mid-summer 1943 and the group were being addressed by an experienced operational air gunner. We had all gained our sergeant's stripes and air gunner badges and I had not passed my nineteenth birthday. We had been flying outdated Whitley aircraft with a crew of five. I was the rear gunner. Now that Operational Training was finished, we were moved to another station to gain experience in flying Halifax bombers and to pick up two more crew.

'After three weeks we were sent to 428 ['Ghost'] Squadron at Middleton St George near Darlington, Yorkshire. This squadron was part of the Royal Canadian Air Force and was carrying out bomber raids on Germany. It was the custom that the pilot had to complete two operational raids with an experienced crew before being allowed to operate as a crew on our own. Each crew had to complete thirty operational trips, known as a "tour", before being stood down for non-operational raids. We discovered the score for the two squadrons on the station was six crews having completed a "tour" and sixty crews were missing. With the prospect of only one crew in ten completing the thirty required operational flights I was not feeling confident. But there was no going back and we duly took off early evening for our first raid on Germany. Early evening was chosen because our Halifax aircraft from Yorkshire had further to go than the faster Lancaster bombers based more southerly. Other than avoiding searchlights and the mass anti-aircraft fire (flak) over the target, the trip was very successful. I was now an experienced operational air-gunner on the crew skippered by Flight Sergeant H. C. Shepherd RCAF. The losses on Bomber Command were appalling during this period known as the Battle of Berlin (November 1943–March 1944).'

On the night of 18–19 November 1943 the Halifax squadrons of the Canadian Group were on a diversion raid to Mannheim. It was planned that Lancaster bombers only would raid Berlin, the inference being that the slower and lower-flying Halifaxes were too vulnerable to take part in the Berlin operation. Twenty-three aircraft – a dozen Halifaxes, nine Stirlings and two Lancasters – were lost.

The following night, 19–20 November, the target for 266 Halifaxes and Stirlings was Leverkusen [when bad weather on the Continent prevented many night fighters from operating]. Only four Halifaxes and a Stirling were lost. Halifax V 'S-Sugar' (LK956) took off from Middleton St George at 1606 hours piloted by Flight Sergeant Harold Calvin Shepherd RCAF and successfully bombed the target.

'Somehow, as we turned away from the target,' wrote Stan Munns, 'we were off course and leaving the main stream of bombers. We were out on our own and probably flew over the well-fortified town Aachen. An aircraft on its own is an easy target for the German anti-aircraft guns and numerous flashes and puffs of smoke appeared alongside the aircraft, together with clanging noises as shrapnel tore its way through the fuselage. ['Sugar' was damaged severely by flak near Bonn and finished off in an attack by Hauptmann Paul Förster of 2./NJG1, flying a Bf 110G-4 from Venlo airfield.] The pilot's voice came over the intercom asking me if the rudders were still in place as he had no control over them. As I was sitting in between the rudders in the rear gun turret I was happy to say they were and we came to the conclusion the control wires through the fuselage must have been damaged. A bomber aircraft cannot be landed without rudder control so we knew we would have to bail out sooner or later. It turned out to be sooner as the engines became damaged and the propellers turned in the wind like windmills dragging us down.

'When the navigator [Flying Officer David Roy Knight RCAF] estimated we had crossed the border into Holland the pilot gave the order to bail out while we still had some height. To do this, I had to get into the fuselage of the plane from the gun turret as my parachute was stowed there in a rack. Having obtained my 'chute, I clipped it on in almost complete darkness as the bulkhead door was closed to the dimly lit centre of the fuselage; fumbling in the darkness for the bulkhead door latch, panic seized me as I made no contact. I wondered if I had time to get back into the turret and turn it round, so that the turret doors could be opened and I could drop out backwards. I decided against it and tried using my forearm to locate the door latch, all the time thinking how much longer I had before the plane plunged downwards with only me in it. At last, the latch struck my arm. I quickly opened the door. I saw the fuselage escape hatch was open where some of the crew had bailed out, but there was no sign of any other members of the crew. I glanced at my parachute; the wires around the chute were clipped into the harness clips as well as the parachute holding lugs. I had a quick thought that the trapped wires of the parachute would cause the chute to malfunction, but the necessity to jump overcame my fears as I slid through the escape hatch. I felt myself falling through space. I pulled the ripcord. This was a stupid thing to do as the chute could have caught on the tailplane, however, it soon pulled me up with a jerk and I was floating down in pitch darkness. Within seconds of my chute opening a huge glow lit the sky as the aircraft hit the ground. I had escaped with only seconds to spare. A few more seconds and I landed flat on my back in a dry dyke, probably the only one in Holland. I had made a perfect landing.

'I unclipped my harness and parachute and left them in the dyke. I heard planes in the distance going home and I swore at them in the frustration of being stranded on a dark and cold evening in a German-occupied country. However, the optimism of youth prevailed and I thought the thing to do was to walk to the Spanish border, so I set off in a north-westerly direction away from the Dutch–German border but also heading for Belgium.

'The going was heavy; mud was building up on my flying boots and I was wet around the lower legs. As I approached a barb-wired fence my legs felt as though they had weights attached to them, so I just rolled over the fence. Fortunately, I was still wearing my flying suit and Mae West so although the wire tore my clothing I was not hurt. Upon finding a haystack I took a rest sitting on loose hay around the base and with my back to the stack, but the evening was cold and despite my flying attire I was soon shivering and found sleep impossible.

'My thoughts at this time were not to contact anybody but to just keep going. I guessed German soldiers were out looking for me and I felt I was leaving them a trail: my parachute harness with my name and number printed on it was discarded in a field and my life-jacket somewhere in a ditch. By late evening I had found an open barn, just a roof on four legs. I found my hideout fairly comfortable and protected from the cold wind and I slept the night, but I was awakened early morning by voices in the farmyard nearby. I decided to wait until darkness before making a move. I opened my escape kit that consisted of maps and a compass, various nourishing tablets and Dutch, Belgium and French monies and Horlicks tablets.

'I was hungry as I had now been a good many hours without eating. As soon as it was dark, I proceeded on my way. A signpost indicated a small village called Nuenen and as I passed a small isolated house, I thought I might try my luck for food and shelter. Knocking on the door, it was opened partially and a man's face appeared rather furtively, so I said to him "RAF". He looked blankly at me so I repeated "RAF". He started to close the door and then suddenly opened it again and said "RAF" with a guttural accent. He motioned me into a dimly lit room and disappeared into the kitchen, returning with some bread and butter. But as soon as I had eaten, he motioned me to go. Clearly, he was very frightened.

'I continued along the road and before I had gone very far, I heard a vehicle behind me. I jumped into the roadside ditch, but I was unlucky it was filled with water. There was nothing else I could do but to stand there with the water lapping around my knees until the car had passed, as it was almost certain to be a German transport. I realised my plan to walk to Spain was impossible in these wintry conditions, so I thought I had better find help and a nearby farmhouse seemed a good place to start.

'The door was opened by a woman, I said to her "RAF" in a similar accent as used by the man at the previous house. She understood right away and without showing any sign of fear said in Flemish, "You eat and drink." (The words were similar to English and easy for me to understand.) She took me into the living room where her husband was sitting and sat me at the table and offered me ham and a glass of milk. I tried to engage the man in conversation asking him if he was Dutch. He thought I was saying "Deutsche" and assured me he was not German, but he did not understand any English. I was feeling very tired and the woman indicated for me to sit on a couch. I took off my wet boots and lay down and fell asleep. I was awakened later by a man speaking English, who informed me he was an ex-Dutch army officer and asked me if I wanted to get back to England. He did not know himself how it could be done, but thought it may be by submarine.

'I told him I was willing to try to escape if he would help. Whilst I was in Holland, I heard that one of my crew had given himself up to the Germans, possibly thinking he was safe for the rest of the war and although I could not blame him for such thoughts, the prospect of a prisoner of war camp appalled me. The man told me there were small children in the house and the farmer and his wife were frightened they may talk about me if I stayed in hiding, so he took me on the back of his bicycle along a narrow lane to another farmhouse where I was to stay the night. I slept that night with the farmer in the main front bedroom. I awoke startled during the early morning to see the farmer crouching below the window with a wicked-looking knife in his hand. There were German soldiers about. I hoped he was not going to use the knife, however, they appeared to move on and all was well.

'In the afternoon two men (from the Dutch Resistance) arrived on bicycles to bring me civilian clothes, which included a light raincoat, a razor and bicycle for my use. We set out for the nearby town of Eindhoven. On arrival at the house, I was met by two men. A third man joined us who seemed to be a senior person. Plans were made, but no names were exchanged. Finally, he said if I was caught, please do not give anyone away. I replied with bravado they would have to shoot me before I would talk and he replied, "I believe the word of an Englishman." After a meal, I was left on my own and a man who

I had not seen before came into the room and started talking. He said, "Are you sure you are English because if we find out you are not, we will shoot you, do you understand?"

'He then pulled out an automatic gun from his overcoat pocket to emphasise the point. I assured him I was English and he then said, "When the clock on the wall says 8 o'clock I want you to walk out of the front door, turn left and walk down the road and take the first turning on the right and go to the church and then left." I followed the instructions and was sure I was being followed. I thought I might be leading a German agent to the Resistance organisation so I walked past the church. As I did so a priest came rushing out to me and said, "Did you not see the church?" I told him of my fears and he said I was only being followed to make sure I did not get lost. I was given a railway ticket and informed I was to be taken on a short journey. My guide said he would do all the talking necessary and I was only to show my ticket at the barrier. We entered a vacant compartment on the train and almost immediately two German soldiers came in and sat down opposite. Although it was a short journey, I was apprehensive all the way.

'Following this, a new guide, a young girl, took me in the town of Weert by train. She seemed to have no fear and she spoke to me in English throughout the journey irrespective of being overheard. She took me to a small house where I was introduced to a New Zealand airman and an American airman [Flight Officer Robert E. Sheehan, a P-47 Thunderbolt pilot in the 56th Fighter Group, who had bailed out on 7 November after his engine caught fire at 30,000ft while escorting B-17s to Wesel. Eight years later, on 23 January 1953, he would die as a fighter pilot in Korea]. As we waited in a small lounge the American suggested a plan: if we were approached by one lone German, we would make a fight of it; but if there was more than one, we would give ourselves up. Some minutes after agreeing to the plan the door opened and in walked a man with a long dark overcoat and a peaked cap. I looked at the other two, but the first man was quickly followed by another in the same guise so we were confined to our fate. Fortunately, the men turned out to be Dutch policemen who were to take us to the Belgian border nearby. One of the policemen said he played in a dance band and asked if we could tell him the words to the song 'Stardust'. This could have been a further test to prove our identity. After blurting out the words to 'Stardust' we three airmen and the two policemen set out on bicycles towards the Belgium frontier, supposedly under arrest, although had we been stopped, I felt this ploy would not have held up under questioning.

'We arrived at a small village [Hamont] close to the border and I stayed the night with a family in a gypsy-type caravan. When I joined the others the two policemen then took us on foot across the border, where we were met by two members of the Belgian police who took over the escort duty. They took us across the fields to a large detached house, the owner being a wine merchant. That evening we were plied with strong brandy until we were highly inebriated. We were then given pencil and paper and asked to answer a number of questions. These questions were mainly associated with the RAF and if the other two airmen did not know the answers it did not matter because I was so high on the brandy, I was shouting out the answers like a wireless quiz.

'Our next move was to the town of Neerpelt, where the New Zealander and myself stayed with the local shoe repairer. After a two-day stay, I was taken (we were only moved one person at a time in this instance) to the nearby railway station, where I met a short, dark-haired man who was to be my guide to Antwerp. This I found out after the war was a new escape route as Allied airmen and their guides had been caught on the existing route to Brussels.

'On arrival at Antwerp, I was taken to a cafe called The Swan, where the wife of the proprietor was British. I only stayed overnight at the cafe and the next morning boarded a train for Brussels with the new guide. On arrival at Brussels railway station, I was met by a young girl who was to act as my guide. After she had made a telephone call, we made our way to a flat in the city. Unbeknown to me, some American airmen were already in the flat and had been teaching another young girl some basic English. As I came through the door of the flat the girl shook my hand and said "Hello you fucking bastard," to which the Americans roared with laughter.

'I was later taken to a house to stay for a few days. The house was occupied by an elderly lady and her two adult sons, one of whom had been in the hands of the Gestapo and seemed to be in a mental state and very rarely spoke. The other son was a civil servant and apparently very helpful in his position to the underground movement in Brussels. The movement, I later discovered, was known as the Comet Line that was organised for the escape of Allied airmen and I was the 243rd airman helped by the organisation to evade capture by the occupying forces.

'Whilst I was staying in this house, I managed to get my first bath since bailing out, although I had only a few inches of lukewarm water. After a few days a man came to see me and said he would be taking me to the railway station the next day and in the meantime I was to get my identity tags which were tied around my neck sewn inside my trousers. As I did not see any point to this I did not bother, but the next day on public transport with this man he asked me if I had done as he said, and as I replied "no" he then took a penknife from his pocket and cut the string holding the tags around my neck. He put the tags in his coat pocket. I thought he would give them back to me at later date, but after seeing me to the station and meeting another guide I never saw him again and therefore lost my only means of identity. We were given tickets and boarded the train and were told to get out when the guide did. We travelled to a small country town near the French border. It was dark on arrival and we were taken to a farmhouse and given a meal. Later, with our guide, we crossed the French border in a local train.

'When we reached our destination, we were handed over to three guides who were to take us individually on a fast train to Paris. I was

Above: Sergeant Cyril Rofé, observer on the crew of a Wellington bomber on 40 Squadron.

Right: Flight Sergeant George Henry Steinhauer RCAF, KIA 30–31 March.

Above left: Joe Pack and Margaret Dillon on their wedding day.

Above right: Gertrude Moors, one of the heroines of the Comet Line, who returned twenty-five airmen to England.

Andrée Dumon, code-named 'Nadine' or Dédée.

Above: Stalag Luft III.

Right: Second Lieutenant Richard Michael Clinton Codner MC.

Above: A dramatic scene in the film *The Wooden Horse*.

Below left: Pilot Officer Thomas William Spencer Wilson, one of many at Sagan who assisted in the 'Wooden Horse' escape.

Below right: Georges 'Geo' Jouanjean of the 'Pat O'Leary Line'.

Above: Mademoiselle Janine Jouanjean, 'an attractive blonde' who Gordon Carter met while evading in France. They fell in love and married on 11 June 1945.

Right: Sergeant Kenneth Albert Goodchild, who was shot down on 12 May 1943 and sent to Stalag Luft VI, Heydekrug.

Sergeant Stanley Munns. (Munns Family Archive)

Pilot Officer Leonard Alfred Len 'Barney' Barnes.

Above left: American-born Virginia d'Albert-Lake, who was arrested on 12 June 1944 and imprisoned by the Germans in Ravensbrück concentration camp and other camps for the remainder of the war. She helped sixty-seven British and American airmen evade German capture.

Above right: Squadron Leader Francis John Hartnell-Beavis DFC (right) with his brother David, a Parachute Regiment pilot.

Right: Souse Lieutenant Bernard W. M. Scheidhauer. (Franciose Magne)

Squadron Leader Roger Bushell (left). Bushell was posthumously mentioned in Despatches on 8 June 1944 for his services as a PoW.

Flight Lieutenant Cy Grant, Lancaster navigator on Lancasters on 103 Squadron, who was shot down on 25 June 1943 and sent to Stalag Luft III to spend the rest of the war behind the wire.

Group Captain Herbert Martin Massey (SBO) with German officers and Swiss representatives who were visiting Stalag Luft III.

Photograph taken at the Foyle's Book of the Month luncheon at the Dorchester Hotel, London, 18 March 1949, for publication of the book *The Wooden Horse*. Seated L–R: Leslie Sidwell; Eric Williams (author); Michael Codner and Oliver Philpot. Standing: Sir John Slessor (then Marshal of the RAF). Because military censorship was still in force, when *The Wooden Horse* was published Eric Williams had changed his name to 'Peter Howard', Michael Codner to 'John Clinton', Oliver Philpot to 'Philip Rowe' and Leslie Sidwell to 'Nigel Wilde'. (Daily Express)

The 'Long March'.

Colditz Castle in 1945.

Right: Alain Le Ray, who earned the distinction of being the first prisoner to get clean away from Colditz, on 12 April 1941.

Below: Lieutenant Leo de Hartog holding 'Moritz', one of the two dummy heads of PoWs made to mislead German guards during daily roll calls at Oflag IVC, Colditz, in 1941. 'Moritz' and 'Max' (the second dummy) were made of plaster by a fellow Polish PoW and painted by another Dutch PoW, Lieutenant Diederick van Lynden. Then they were used during the successful escape attempt by Lieutenants Hans Larive and Franz Steinmetz (both of the Royal Netherlands Navy) on 15 August 1941.

Lieutenant Airey Neave, who made the first British 'home run' from Colditz on 5 January 1942.

On 5 June 1941 prisoners on their supervised daily walk to the park near the castle paused by a gate leading out to let a German woman through. The German guards said nothing, but as the woman walked away from the castle, one of the prisoners noticed she had dropped her watch. 'Hey, Fräulein, your watch!' he said. She did not respond, so a guard went after her – and found 'her' to be Lieutenant Chasseurs Alpins Bouley, a Frenchman. Untimely chivalry cost Bouley his freedom.

Lieutenant Hans Larive MWO, DSC*, who with Lieutenant Franz Steinmetz (both of the Royal Netherlands Navy) escaped from Colditz on 15 August 1941.

Flying Officer Dominic Bruce, who was described as 'the most ingenious escaper' of the Second World War. Shot down on 9 June 1941, in all he made seventeen attempts at escaping from PoW camps and was awarded the Military Cross. He died age 84 on 12 February 2000.

Lieutenant Pierre Marie Jean-Baptiste Mairesse-Lebrun, who made his first escape attempt from Colditz on 9 June 1941. He got clean away on 2 July and reached Switzerland in eight days on a stolen bicycle.

Around Christmas 1942, Willi, the castle's electrician, entered the French quarters to replace a blown fuse. About 1730 hours Willi (in reality Lieutenant A. Perodeau disguised as Willi) tried to walk out through the park gate but when asked for his pass he had the wrong one. Although his disguise was near perfect, Perodeau's scarf was not the same colour as that worn by the real Willi and this may have tipped off the guard.

Parade of nations at Colditz.

The only known photo of the original 'Colditz Cock' glider inside Colditz, by US War Correspondent Lee Carson shortly after the castle was liberated in April 1945.

accompanied by a woman guide. As we disembarked, I noticed the large Paris station was packed with German troops and was amazed to see two high-ranking officers give the Nazi salute as a greeting. The woman guide took me on the Metro to a Paris suburb where I was placed with an old couple in a small flat. There were already two Americans [Thelma B. 'Jockey' Wiggins and Elton F. Kevil] staying so we had to bed down in one room on the floor.[1]

'The following day was 25 December and this must have been the strangest Christmas of my life, although not an unpleasant one. The old couple's granddaughter and other members of the family came to visit in the evening. Our Christmas meal had oysters as starters, and as I thoroughly dislike such things I forced them down, and when asked if I had enjoyed them, being polite I said "yes" and I was promptly given some more. However, the rest of the evening was enjoyable enough. After a few drinks the two Americans and myself sang songs in English at the top of our voices which must have been heard from yards around, but we were not asked to stop.

'Shortly after Christmas we were taken to a photographic studio to have our photographs taken for fake identity cards, but because men in France up to the age 25 years had special youth identity cards, and these were unavailable to the Resistance people, my blank card was made up showing my age as 26 years.

'As I was a young-looking 19-year-old and taking into account the loss of my identity tags, I was not feeling very happy about my present situation. However, I set off the following day with another woman

---

[1]. Tech Sergeant Thelma Berto Wiggins Jr, a radio operator/gunner was a Southerner, with his home in Lithonia, Georgia, who was shot down on the infamous raid on Schweinfurt on 14 October 1943 in B-17 42-29952 *Sizzle* of the 305th Bomb Group at Chelveston, flown by 2nd Lieutenant Douglas Murdoch (KIA). Staff Sergeant Elton F. Kevil, another Southerner, who was from Ballinger, Texas, was left waist gunner on B-17G 42-37751 in the 305th Bomb Group flown by 2nd Lieutenant W. E. Emmert that was shot down on the Bremen raid on 8 October 1943.

guide on to the Metro heading for another of the large Paris railway stations to catch the night train to Bordeaux. As we changed trains on the Metro at one point, I was striding out along the interchange platforms, my guide suddenly stopped me and said, "You must stop walking like an Englishman and take small steps like a Frenchman." This made me realise how vulnerable I was and how easily I could give myself away. [Slipped aboard a train before other passengers arrived, he was told to pretend to be asleep.] My guide accompanied me on the journey to Bordeaux. Also on the train were the two Americans I stayed with in Paris and also another American [Tom Applewhite, a stocky 22-year-old born on 1 July 1921 in Oskaloosa, Barton County, Missouri] I later came to know. Each of us had our own guide and we were in separate carriages throughout the train.[2]

'On arrival at Bordeaux, we boarded an early morning train to Bayonne with the same guides. This was an uneventful journey except at the end of it my guide insisted I gave her my raincoat, because she said it was needed in Paris for another escapee. I was now dressed in a light sports jacket, and light trousers in the middle of winter and with a dodgy identity card in my pocket.' [The overnight journey, with a change of trains in Bordeaux, put them in Bayonne on 27 December. But instead of being picked up at the station by their next guides, the four escaping airmen were promptly placed on another train and sent back north to the town of Dax. This apparent change of plans may have been caused by the disastrous crossing of the Bidassoa River into Spain by the previous group the night of 23–24 December when two men drowned.] At Bayonne a new guide, a man, who issued us with tickets for a railway journey to the small town of Dax, took over the four of us. As we were nearing the

---

2. 1st Lieutenant Thomas Beasley Applewhite Jr, bombardier, was the only member of the crew of B-17F *The Wild Hare* in the 548th Bomb Squadron, 385th Bomb Group, that was shot down on 11 November 1943 on the Münster mission, to successfully evade capture.

Spanish border, we were given to understand that the train would be searched by German soldiers. The guide only showed us to our seats on the train, two to a compartment, and then left us on our own to get out of the train at Dax station. It was obvious the guide thought the journey too dangerous to accompany us, but I sat in a seat with a full view of the corridor.

'The sight of German soldiers entering the corridor, then the first compartment, sent my heart thumping and as they came closer I began to wish I had not been able to see them because I was sure that by the time they reached us they would be able to hear my heart jumping up and down.

'Eventually a soldier entered the compartment and speaking in French asked for identity cards. The French passengers were the first to hand over their cards for inspection and the soldier seemed to just scan them and hand them back. He then took my card and to my horror he spoke to me in French. I did not understand what he said, but I thought he may be referring to my age, so I just sat there tight-lipped.

'He repeated what he had said before, more aggressively, I just looked blank at him. He realised he was not going to get an answer from me and with a look that said, "I give up" handed back the card.

'The train duly arrived at Dax. We stepped out onto the platform and were joined by the other two Americans. We seemed to be the only people leaving the train, so we promptly handed in our tickets and left the station as we had been instructed. In the station yard were two men [25-year-old Jean-François Nothomb ('Franco'), a member of an aristocratic Belgian family, who succeeded Andrée de Jongh as leader in France and who was arrested in an apartment in Paris on 18 January 1944)[3] and Marcel 'Max' Roger], one of whom greeted us in

---

3. He survived several Nazi concentration camps. Awarded the Distinguished Service Order.

English telling us to take a bicycle each from the six cycles propped up against the wall.

'This was the beginning of a long [70km] cycle ride to the foot of the Pyrenees and I was glad the weather was mild as I had no coat or gloves for the journey. I found out later our two guides were of Basque nationality and were going to take us through the mountains to Spain. This would not be easy as the French–Spanish border was guarded on both sides and I knew the Spanish jails were worse than the German prison camps, so it was no consolation to be caught in Spain.

'However, we started out on the long ride, the two guides in front and the four escapees following. I soon lagged behind and struggled on for what seemed hours, just following the road. I was slow on my own and hoping that the guides did not make a detour. Exhausted, I eventually caught up with them outside a bungalow-type building [38-year-old Jeanne Marthe Villenave-Mendiara's restaurant, 'Larré', in Sutar, 5km from Bayonne] where we were to have a meal and to stay the night.'[4]

Before entering Sutar a guide would check to see if the party were safe to enter the village and arrive at the restaurant, as the latter was frequented regularly by German officers of the Wehrmacht. A red scarf on the washing line from Marthe Mendiara (as she became known), signified they should wait. Marthe, whose husband Felix Antonio Mendiara was a PoW in Germany, provided them with a good meal and they met Pierre Elhorga, a retired Customs officer, and his wife, Marie; close associates of 'Franco', who were involved in the transfer of airmen to Spain via the alternate Larressore route. Tom Applewhite signed the evader registry, deliberately misspelling his name as 'Appelwhite' so that one day he could determine where he was. He also wrote a thank you message in Pierre Elhorga's

---

4. The restaurant was also used to plan the escape of Comet head Andrée de Jongh from the Villa Chagrin prison in Bayonne.

notebook. Marie Elhorga, a motherly type, tucked the four men in for the night, insisting that they get their rest. Late on the 28th they set off on bikes with 'Franco' for the village of Villefranque on the east side of the river Nive, where a rowboat was waiting to carry them across. From the west side of the river, they cycled to the town of Ustaritz, where they stopped at a home with children and picked up three Basque guides, (Pierre Etchégoyen, Pierre Aguerre and his brother Baptiste, Jean Elizondo – all friends of Pierre Elhorga. With 'Franco' accompanying them, they made their way on foot to a sheep herder's barn outside of Larressore, where they were directed to replace their shoes with the traditional Basque zapatos and provided with hiking staffs.

If they now proceeded directly south to enter Spain, they risked coming too close to a German border patrol post at border marker 76. Instead, their group gave the patrol post a wide berth by swinging west toward the official border crossing at Dancharia before turning south again and crossing into Spain near marker 74. The Pyrenees crossing was a tremendous ordeal for the four airmen. It had been snowing and raining. Their zapatos and their clothes were soaked up to their waists from crossing streams and sliding in the snow. Their feet were freezing and their toes bleeding.

'The next day, early morning, we started out on foot to make our way through the mountains and to cross the Spanish border, climbing ever higher and stopping only to rest for a little food and some wine from a goatskin bag. By nightfall we were following narrow tracks, sufficiently high in the mountains to be walking through snow.' [At this point 'Jockey' Wiggins' heel wound from flak, which had been on the mend in Brussels, opened up and at one point he collapsed.] 'I had been walking quite well during the day and was leading the group at the time and as I came back to see what was happening one of the Basque guides had been able to get the American into a sitting position and urging him to get up, but without much success. When the guide saw me standing nearby, he said to the American

"Look how well your English [sic] friend is walking", to which the American replied "Fuck him", but the guide's remark was sufficient to galvanise the American to get to his feet and with his arms around the guide's shoulders he carried on.

'We eventually arrived on the bank of the mountain river where ['Franco'] left us to see if it was possible to cross by a bridge downstream, but he returned to say the bridge was guarded by Spanish police as the river was the dividing line between France and Spain. So, there was nothing else for it but for us to wade through the freezing river and as we climbed out onto the bank on the other side, we had to stamp around in the snow to try and dry our wet clothing.

'At last, I was in Spain, the Comet Line had done its job and four more airmen had escaped from the occupied territories. However, Spain at this time was no friendly haven, so our journey continued in secrecy and we were hidden in a stable in the hayloft above the horses. There was no glass in the windows of the loft and the bitter wind blew straight in as we settled down in the hay for the night.

'There was a stone fireplace in the corner of the loft, but other than burning the hay we could not think of any way of having a satisfactory fire until Tom Applewhite suggested we took out every other step of the wooden ladder leading to the loft. This we did and sat around the fire drying out before trying to get more sleep. Applewhite kindly came to my rescue with regards to the bitter cold by using his heavy overcoat as a blanket for the pair of us.[5]

'We did not see our guides the next morning but about midday a young man and a girl brought us some food on tin plates. The food consisted of red beans, potatoes and mutton with the sheep's wool still attached. As we had not eaten for some time the meal was most

---

5. On the third day of the crossing, as a result of a fall in the rocks, Stan Munns injured his leg so badly that he could no longer walk by himself. He made it the rest of the way across the Pyrenees with his right arm around Tom Applewhite's shoulders.

welcome. For the rest of the day, we sat around the loft debating whether to try to make our way to the nearest town on our own and perhaps obtain help to contact the British or American authorities in Spain.

'It was agreed that we would only wait all day and if the guides did not show by midday, we would go it alone. We waited anxiously for several hours next morning, but fortunately for us the two guides turned up and we were able to continue on our journey. The sun was shining as we made our way along the lower slopes of the mountains on the Spanish side and it was quite pleasant. As it became dark, we were taken into a farm house where we were fed a type of corn cake baked on the hearth and later slept the night in a chicken run, sleeping on animal furs.

'On the following day we walked through the rocky foothills [to the Baztan Valley] and to a small road where a car was waiting for us. We were bundled into the car and the driver gave us a cigarette apiece, but I never finished mine as I fell asleep exhausted with the lighted cigarette still in my hand. When I awoke, we were in the town of San Sebastian on the Atlantic coast and we were driven to a hotel with British proprietors.

'We were made most welcome at the hotel and for the first time in weeks I was able to bath in loads of hot water and to sit down to good meals. Eventually a car arrived from the Bilbao consulate, complete with Union Jack flying from the mudguard, to take us to the embassy in Madrid. With a Spanish chauffeur at the wheel, we set off on the long ride to the capital.

'As we drove through the town of San Sebastian the front wheels of our car became entangled with the tramlines, which jammed the wheels tightly against the car bodywork. We could not leave the car to help the chauffeur straighten out the wheels in case we were arrested for illegal entry (the car being considered as British territory). So, as we sat in the car, crowds gathered around us. Someone produced a plank of wood as a lever and with the help of several onlookers the wheels were levered into the correct position. Thankfully the police did not arrive on the scene, much to our relief.

'The journey through Spain was a fascinating one: at one time in the mountainous regions of the north it was snowing hard, contrasting with the warm lowlands as we neared Madrid where people were sitting outside their houses in the sun. It was dark as we arrived at the British Embassy and strange to see light streaming from windows after years of blacked-out Britain. I was informed I was the youngest escapee to reach there. [For six days they rested in the temporary barracks built in the embassy gardens as more men spilled across the Pyrenees. With eighteen evaders having arrived, the men learned it was time to continue on to Gibraltar.]

'We were taken by a British ambulance to the port of Seville on the Guadalquivir River, capable of handling seagoing merchant ships, on 28 December, and on 7 January 1944 under the cover of a drunken party of British expatriates we slipped aboard the *Lisbeth*, a free Norwegian ship, in the harbour. The party was to confuse the Spanish harbour guard. So many people were going on and off the ship that the guard did not realise we had stayed on board when all the other guests had departed. Even so, the ship was searched before it sailed and we four sat on a small platform in the bilge until sailing time. We soon arrived in Gibraltar, where the three Americans[6] were sent to an hotel but I was told to report to the local RAF camp. There I met our Canadian bomb aimer, "Mac" MacGillivray, who had arrived in Gibraltar a few days earlier. "Mac" and I were given fresh uniforms and flown home. After interrogation at the Air Ministry in London, "Mac" was told he could return to Canada as his flying duties were

---

6. In actuality, there were four, with the addition of Lieutenant John Kennard Hurst, a 25-year-old Texan navigator on B-17F *Shatzi* in the 390th Bomb Group that was shot down on the mission to Düren on 20 October 1943. Hit by German fighters, the aircraft broke in two and crashed. Two crew members were killed, seven taken prisoner, with Hurst as the only escapee.

completed. Being British was another matter: I had to report to an RAF station to make up a new crew for further operational flights.'

All seven men on Flight Sergeant Shepherd's crew had survived. Shepherd evaded for a time and he and Sergeant N. H. Michie, the mid-upper gunner, with the help of the Resistance ended up in Brussels. Michie went off into the countryside where he remained until liberation but Shepherd was trapped by the Gestapo in Brussels on 26 January 1944 and apprehended. He ended the war in a PoW camp at Stalag XI-B Fallingbostel, located just to the east of the town in Lower Saxony. Flying Officer David Roy Knight, Sergeant John Montague Carlton Walker, the RAF flight engineer, and Sergeant Sidney James Stevens, the RAF wireless operator, were captured and sent to languish in prisoner of war camps in the Reich.

Chapter 7

The Ides of March

The Ides of March had not been a lucky day for Julius Caesar and they were to prove equally unlucky for Pilot Officer Leonard Alfred 'Barney' Barnes' crew of 'P-Peter' (ND530), one of twenty Lancasters on 630 Squadron at East Kirkby on the Battle Order for Stuttgart on the night of 15–16 March 1944. Barnes had recently celebrated his 24th birthday but tonight he had got off to a bad start. As usual he had put his lucky little teddy bear, which his fiancée Merville had given him, on the compass. But as soon as he started the engines the little bear fell to the floor because of the vibration. 'Barney' felt that this was a bad omen. Up until now his lucky mascot had brought nothing but good fortune.

Shortly after 1800 hours on Wednesday, 15 March 1944 'Barney' Barnes took Lancaster 'P-Peter' off from East Kirkby. At Stuttgart bombing took place between 2315 and 2329 hours from 20,000 to 23,000ft. Everyone on board 'P-Peter' was relieved to be making the homeward journey after Sergeant Malcolm Elliot (aka 'Ginger') Gregg, the 21-year-old bomb aimer and former Nottingham clerk, born in West Bridgford, Nottingham, on 7 January 1923 had dropped the bomb load on Stuttgart. 'Barney' Barnes had pulled sharply away from the city and all seemed to be going well but 24-year-old Oberleutnant Dietrich Schmidt of 8./NJG1, flying a Bf 110G-4 from St-Dizier airfield, who had claimed a Halifax at Bonneuil-les-Eaux, south of Amiens, at 0118 hours, was determined to get a second kill this night. At about 0056 hours, at 6,300m altitude to the west of Reims, he carried out a typical Schräge Musik attack with his upward-firing guns on the unsuspecting crew of 'P-Peter'; about 100ft below and 50ft behind the bomber. Inside the homeward-bound Lancaster there was a state of absolute carnage. The hydraulics had been destroyed and they were now a 'sitting duck'. Schmidt attacked for a second time from behind. In the rear turret, Sergeant Thomas Austin Fox, the 21-year-old rear gunner, better known as 'Freddie', a nickname he acquired after the famous jockey of the 1920s and '30s, could have known little of what happened next and he died in a hail of shrapnel. A keen amateur boxer, who had reached the finals of the fly-weight division of an inter-squadron boxing tournament in March 1943, he had trained as a butcher under his father, who was a master butcher. His son had wanted to be a pilot but at only 5ft 1½in, 'Freddie' was considered too short. When he had joined the RAF in May 1941 he became a motorcyclist and despatch rider before training as a gunner.

Sergeant James Henry Overholt, the 20-year-old Canadian mid-upper gunner from Eastwood, Ontario, was by now lying on the rest bed, his oxygen supply to the mid-upper turret having been cut off. As 'P-Peter' was attacked, again from underneath, Overholt was killed. Barnes, unaware that his bomber was on fire, put the Lancaster into a 360mph dive from 12,000ft to try to shake off the fighter. Finally, the starboard engines were hit and set ablaze and the rudder controls were badly damaged, so the order to bail out was given. Sergeant Ken Walker, the 20-year-old flight engineer; Sergeant George Plowman, the 21-year-old wireless operator and former leather worker from London; and Flying Officer Malcolm Geisler, the 26-year-old navigator and former Manchester salesman, jumped one after the other. 'Ginger' Gregg, who had sustained shrapnel wounds to his hand, managed to bail out with the rest of the crew. Upon landing (in a tree), he made his way across country and came upon a convent. When he asked for aid, he was given some food, but was subsequently captured and spent the rest of the war in Stalag Luft I. The bodies of

Overholt and Tom Fox were discovered in the remains of the aircraft, which lay scattered in fields at Mont-sur-Courville close to St-Gilles (Marne) on the west bank of the Ardre river, 24km west of Reims.

'Barney' Barnes, having realised that both starboard engines had been badly hit and were ablaze and the rudder controls badly damaged, had repeated the order to his crew to bail out. Ensuring they had left the aircraft, he prepared to make his own escape. However, the Lancaster lurched to one side and he missed the escape hatch. After hitting the bombsight and knocking himself out in the process, he regained his senses. The next thing 'Barney' remembered was falling through the air with an unopened parachute, his scarf slapping him gently on his cheek. One of his eyes was very swollen. Tumbling through the night sky, he pulled his ripcord and floated to the ground, landing in a farmer's field obscured by a small wood about 4 miles north-east of Dravegny in the department of Aisne. 'Barney' lit a cigarette and buried his parachute, Mae West and the tops of his flying boots and set off in a south-westerly direction using his compass. After about a mile he saw a parachute hanging in a tree. 'Barney' dragged it clear and buried it but forgot to look for the name on the 'chute. (He discovered much later that it belonged to Ken Walker.)

Meanwhile in London on the morning of 17 March, Merville, 'Barney's fiancée, had pinned on her lapel the RAF wings brooch that he had given her. As she bent forward the brooch fell to the ground. The clasp was still fastened! Merville wondered if this was a bad omen. But 'Barney's luck was in.

He reached Dravegny and walked through the town. A short while later he arrived in the village of Arcis-le-Ponsart, where he bathed his swollen eye in the drinking trough but made a hasty getaway as a dog started barking. 'Barney' continued across the fields to Cohan, which he reached about 0530 hours on 16 March. In the distance he saw a farmer leading his horses towards a farm. He watched the farmer cross the yard and go into the house and then slipped into

THE IDES OF MARCH

the barn and hid under the hay. It was about 0530 hours. At 1030 hours, when he thought there was no one around, he came out of his hiding place and took out his maps. He was looking at them when a man appeared and, as he had seen him, 'Barney' declared himself to him and asked for help. The man brought him food and drink and 'Barney' allowed him to bathe his swollen eye. Two more men appeared and showed him his position on the map. Barney returned to the barn and at 1500 hours a young girl, who could speak English, came to see him. She questioned 'Barney' closely and examined his kit. She left shortly afterwards but not before telling him to wait for signals and that under no circumstances was he to leave his hiding place, adding that she would send a friend to see him. That evening a man came for him and from this point 'Barney's journey to Ferme-le-Reraye was arranged. The man turned out to be a middle-aged ex-French Army captain. He kitted Barnes out with the de rigueur beret and an overcoat and fortified by sips from his companion's bottle of whisky, 'Barney' accompanied the captain to what was to become his home for the next ten days. The farm belonged to Pierre Martin and 'Barney' was marooned here with what seemed an endless diet of red wine and French bread. During his stay he was taken to see the burnt-out wreck of 'P-Peter'. Pierre told him that the villagers had stolen the bodies of the two gunners from the Germans under cover of darkness at midnight in order to give the airmen a decent burial in the local cemetery. The reason 'Barney' was being kept so close to the site of the crash was that it was hoped that the Germans would by now be spreading their search area further afield. Unfortunately, they began to retrace their steps, and Barney's position became precarious. It was time to move.

Late in the evening of 25 March, 'Barney' was escorted to the village cemetery at Seringes-et-Nesles, where he was left to hide among the gravestones in the dark for hours until further contact was made. Around midnight he heard a noise, followed by a voice whispering 'Tommy, Tommy'. 'Here,' he answered. From out of the darkness a few maquisards of BOA (Bureau des Opérations Aériennes), a small Resistance group led by Grand Léon Coigne, armed with Sten guns appeared. The youngest was probably about 15 years old. Léon indicated to 'Barney' to follow them. At the outbreak of war Léon Coigné, a tall, quiet man, was an aircraft mechanic in the French Navy. He was taken prisoner and escaped twice and then returned home to his old job as a plumber at the factory next to his house in the Rue de la Goutte d'Or on the bank of the Orque, which flows through Fère-en-Tardenois.

Suddenly, while walking in silence along a small country lane, the men in front dived into a ditch. The rest, including 'Barney', followed suit and waited silently until a small German patrol had passed by. To attack would have been too risky and if a German had been shot they would not have hesitated to shoot a few villagers in revenge. Once the danger had passed, they continued walking to 'La Cabane' (the 'Shack'), Léon Coigne's white-painted house with its large garden in Fère-en-Tardenois that he shared with his wife Madeleine ('Mimi'), their 14-year-old daughter Christiane and their 11-year-old son Jean.[1]

'Barney' remained with the Coigne family for nearly six weeks. His presence inadvertently became known to the neighbours, but no harm was done. Only a trusted few knew of Léon Coigne's nocturnal existence leading his group through the fields to wait for RAF aircraft to drop weapons and explosives that were then used in sabotage actions, blowing up railways, bridges and telephone poles, or that he was in communication with London with a secret radio hidden in the next village of Arcy-Sainte-Restitue. On the night of 8–9 May, during an outing to recover supplies dropped by the RAF, Léon's group fell into an ambush set by the Germans and ten men were killed. However, Léon managed to escape and he had to hide

---

1. See *Journey to the Horizon: Escape and Evasion during World War II* by Hans Onderwater and Brian Lissette.

THE IDES OF MARCH

for ten days in the chimney of a disused factory in Fère-en-Tardenois. Christiane, who often carried messages hidden in her socks, carefully took him food until he could leave his hiding place and continue his action with another group.

Because of the tense situation, 'Barney' was taken by Madame Pinard, a member of the BOA, to Madame Lesguillier's property, the Chalet des Bruyères, in the same village. There, another evader, Flying Officer William Angus Jacks, a 23-year-old 77 Squadron Halifax rear gunner, shot down on the night of 22–23 April attacking railyards at Laon, was already hiding.[2] 'Barney' remained there a week, after one night sleeping in the woods with only wild pigs for company. Then on 13 May, disguised as a butcher, 'Barney' and Jacks were moved on to Paris by 'Jeanne' (Odile de Vasselot de Régné), a young woman of 22, to be handled by the Comet Line. The only incident of the trip by train occurred when Jacks, having unintentionally bumped into a German guard, apologised in English. Fortunately, the German simply snarled 'Mensch, sei vorsicht' (Man, be more careful).

Arriving in Paris, 'Barney' and Jacks went to a house near the Elysée, the home of an unidentified couple, and stayed there until 22 May, when they were visited by Rosine Witton (also known as 'Rolande') a 38-year-old French woman who spoke very good English (and whose British husband had been interned by the Germans in 1940) and by other members of the Comet network. Rosine told the two airmen that the network had received the order from London not to send the airmen to Spain, but rather to direct them to a camp in the Forêt de Fréteval, south-west of Châteaudun, south-west of Paris.

---

2. Jacks was a last-minute replacement on Squadron Leader Kenneth Frank Pennington Bond's crew, as the usual crew rear gunner, Sergeant Jack Waddilove, was taken ill at the last minute. After dropping its bombs, the Halifax was attacked by Oberleutnant Johannes Hager of 6./NJG1. The two left engines were set on fire, which spread to the entire aircraft. Bond was the only fatality.

She said she would still contact her network to try to smuggle them to Spain.[3] Bertrand Lesguillier took Jacks and Barnes to his mother's apartment at 11 Avenue Emile Deschanel. On the 23rd, 'Jeanne' gave the two airmen their French papers and guided them to a garage to see a man, who said he could take only one in the next 'delivery'. They went to Rue Vaneau in the 7th arrondissement with Philippe d'Albert-Lake, who spoke English with an American accent, acquired from his American wife Virginia, whom he fell in love with during a visit to France in 1936 and had married on 1 May 1937.

Virginia Roush was born in Dayton, Ohio, on 4 June 1910. After her marriage she retained her American citizenship although the couple resided in France. Philippe was in the French Army when the war began in 1939. After France surrendered to Germany in 1940, Virginia chose to remain in France with Philippe. The couple could not live in the family château near Dinard in Brittany because the Germans occupied it, so they moved to Paris. In December 1943, Philippe had met with Jean de Blommaert, a Belgian working for the British intelligence agency MI9, and became his second-in-command of the Paris sector of the Comet Line. He soon became chief of the Paris Sector, which had at the time twenty-nine members (usually called helpers[4]), of whom twenty-one were women. Virginia became a guide and keeper of safe houses for escaping airmen until such time as arrangements could be made for them to travel southward toward Spain. Altogether, she helped sixty-seven British and American airmen evade German capture in apartments in Paris

---

3. Rosine Witton was arrested by the Gestapo and sent to Ravensbrück concentration camp. She survived for two years in the camp and was awarded the George Medal, Legion of Honor, Croix de Guerre and the Medal of Freedom from the USA.
4. An estimated 3,000 civilians, mostly Belgians and French, assisted the Comet Line. They are usually called 'helpers'. Seven hundred helpers were arrested by the Germans and 290 were executed or died in prison or concentration camps.

THE IDES OF MARCH

or in the d'Albert-Lakes' country house at Nesles-la-Vallée, 25 miles north of Paris.[5]

One of Virginia's tasks was to quiz Allied airmen to determine they were who they said they were. To make sure that 'Barney' was genuine there followed the usual rigorous interrogation. Then he was introduced to a further twenty or so Allied airmen who were in hiding. They included three USAAF evaders – P-47 Thunderbolt pilots Lieutenant Colonel Thomas 'Speedy' Hubbard and 2nd Lieutenant Jack 'Jacko' Donald Cornett, and Major Donald 'Willy' Willis, a P-38J Lightning pilot – and RAF Sergeant Ron 'Curly' Emeny, a 20-year-old Lancaster mid-upper gunner on 207 Squadron who had been shot down on the Mailly-le-Camp raid on 3–4 May.[6] They would accompany 'Barney' on the remainder of his journey to Spain the next day. 'Curly' lived but two minutes from 'Barney's' home in the East End! Their journey, though not without its dangers, was successful but when they neared the Spanish–French border they were still not safe. 'Barney' was not happy that they had been following a river upstream instead of towards the coast. They were lodged in a farmhouse but discovered that they were uncomfortably close to the Spanish border. 'Jacko' Cornett, who in his past had smuggled contraband across the Mexican border, was able to understand the Spanish being spoken. The children were being ordered by their mother not to tell the airmen where they were or to let them leave, which 'Barney' found puzzling. He was determined they should move

---

5. Virginia was at special risk of being arrested as she spoke French with an American accent and her identity papers showed her birthplace as the United States. She was arrested on 12 June 1944 and imprisoned by the Germans in Ravensbrück concentration camp and other camps for the remainder of the war. Philippe managed to flee France after her arrest and did not know if his wife was dead or alive until they were reunited after the war. See *An American Heroine in the French Résistance: The Diary and Memoir of Virginia D'Albert-Lake*, Judy Barrett Litoff, editor (New York: Fordham University Press, 2006).
6. See *Last of the Lancasters* by Martin W. Bowman (Pen & Sword, 2014).

on and the five airmen left without their guides, ignoring their frantic shouts to return. They discovered later that they had been intending to hand the airmen over to the Germans in return for a sack of corn for each betrayed pilot! Later 'Willy' Willis wrote in his diary: 'We had been saved by the "impetuous Englishman" who wanted to keep on the move.'

'Barney' remembered waking up after a rest in the sun to the sight of a gun barrel as they were 'arrested' by Spanish police. They were transferred to the care of the British Consul. Then 'Barney' and Ken Walker, his flight engineer, were flown back to England from Gibraltar. Walker had managed to evade capture by travelling overland to a French town/village called La Ferté-Gaucher. Here he sought refuge in a farmhouse just outside the village where the farmer allowed him to hide and supplied him with food and aid for his wounded leg hit by shrapnel. He had travelled approximately 70 miles and walked for a week. Finally, in September, the Americans liberated the area where Ken Walker was in hiding. Upon 'Barney's return to England he completed the remaining twenty-six ops on the squadron. In October 1945 he and Merville were married and, having disbanded 630 Squadron as adjutant, 'Barney' returned to his job as a printer for Glyn Mills & Co.[7]

---

7. See also, *Free To Fight Again: RAF Escapes and Evasions 1940–1945* by Alan W. Cooper (Airlife, 1988).

Chapter 8

The Great Escape

If you can quit the compound undetected
  And clear your tracks nor leave the smallest trace
  And follow out the programme you've selected
  Nor lose your grasp at distance, time and place.

If you can walk at night by compass bearing
  Or ride upon the rails by night and day
  And tempter your illusiveness with daring
  Trusting that sometimes bluff will find a way.

If you can swallow sudden sour frustration
  And gaze unmoved at failure's ugly shape
  Remembering as further inspiration
  It was and is your duty to escape.

If you can keep the great Gestapo guessing
  With explanations only partly true
  And leave them in their heart of hearts confessing.

If you can use your 'Cooler' fortnight clearly
  For planning methods wiser than before
  And treat your miscalculations merely
  As hints let fail by fate to teach you more.

If you scheme on patience and precision
  It was not in a day they build-ed Rome
  And make escape your sole ambition
  The next time you attempt it – YOU'LL GET HOME.

ESCAPE FROM HITLER'S REICH

Written by Flight Lieutenant Edward Gordon Brettell DFC after an early bid to escape had failed. In the summer of 1942, he had been posted to 133 (Eagle) Squadron RAF at Lympne as a flight commander, the only British officer within the volunteer US unit. To Terence Brettell, his adoring younger brother, he seemed to be 'not merely a brilliant pilot, but quite indestructible. He had survived a crash at Brooklands before the war when his car went over the top of the banking. He had also survived when, separated from his squadron in a dogfight, he was pounced on by upwards of 12 Messerschmitts. He shot one of these down and fought his way back to England, though wounded in the head and in a state of collapse from loss of blood. As to his last mission, [on 26 September 1942] it went tragically wrong and not only for him. He was shot down by anti-aircraft fire and, since the cockpit canopy had jammed, went into the ground at over 200 mph. How he was not killed instantly I will never know, although he was severely injured. He recovered from his injuries remarkably quickly and was sent to Stalag Luft III at Sagan. He escaped two or three times. Even then the Germans were thinking of making an example. He and a friend were travelling to Munich by train, as French workers. Unfortunately, the RAF began a raid and the train was stopped and then searched. The two of them were arrested as suspected French agents. They had to admit who they were and they were taken before a Luftwaffe officer. He asked them why they wanted to escape. They replied that they considered it their duty to do so. He banged the table and said: "Yes, it is your duty to do so!" After a time and some phoning, he told them: "Gentlemen, you are lucky. I am to return you to your camp." It sounds like the Luftwaffe officer had orders to hand them over to the SS or Gestapo and it also sounds as though, perhaps, he managed to talk someone out of it.'

Stammlager Luft (or main camp for aircrew) III was a Luftwaffe-run prisoner-of-war camp in the German province of Lower Silesia near the town of Sagan (now Żagań in Poland), 100 miles south-east of Berlin. The site of the camp was selected because it would be difficult to escape by tunnelling. Despite being an officers-only camp, it was referred to as a Stalag camp rather than Oflag (Offizier Lager) as the Luftwaffe had their nomenclature. The camp's 800 Luftwaffe guards were primarily either too old for combat duty or young men convalescing after long tours of duty or from wounds. Because the guards were Luftwaffe personnel, the prisoners or 'Kriegies', as they called themselves, were accorded far better treatment than that granted to other PoWs in Germany. Luft III was commanded by Oberst Friedrich Wilhelm Gustav von Lindeiner genannt von Wildau. Born on 12 December 1880, he had entered the Prussian Army on 15 March 1898. By 10 August 1914 he was the Commander of the Infantry Staff Guard at the Kaiser's General Field Headquarters. He was wounded during the First Battle of Ypres on 17 November 1914 and again the following year, and then severely wounded on 5 December 1915 in fighting around Roye-Noyon. Von Lindeiner retired on 20 September 1919, working in several civilian posts and he married a Dutch baroness. In 1937 von Lindeiner joined the Luftwaffe as one of Hermann Göring's personal staff, after being refused retirement. Deputy Kommandant Major Gustav Simoleit, a professor of history, geography and ethnology before the war, spoke several languages, including English, Russian, Polish and Czech. Transferred to Sagan in early 1943, he proved sympathetic to Allied airmen. Ignoring the ban against extending military courtesies to PoWs, he provided full military honours for Luft III PoW funerals, including one for a Jewish airman.

The East Compound was completed and opened on 21 March 1942. The first prisoners to be housed at Stalag Luft III were British and Commonwealth airmen as well as Fleet Air Arm officers, arriving that April. The Centre Compound was opened on 11 April, originally for British sergeants, but by the end of 1942 replaced by Americans. The North Compound for British airmen opened on 29 March 1943. Later camp expansions added compounds for non-commissioned officers.

Captured Fleet Air Arm (Royal Navy) crew were considered to be Air Force by the Luftwaffe and no differentiation was made. At times non-airmen were interned. A South Compound for Americans was opened in September 1943 and US Army Air Forces prisoners began arriving at the camp in significant numbers the following month, with the West Compound opened in July 1944 for US officers. Each compound consisted of fifteen single-storey huts. Each 10 × 12ft bunkroom slept fifteen men in five triple-deck bunks. Eventually the camp grew to approximately 60 acres in size and eventually housed about 2,500 RAF officers, about 7,500 USAAF and about nine hundred officers from other Allied air forces, for a total of 10,949 inmates, including some support officers.

The camp had a number of design features that made escape extremely difficult. The digging of escape tunnels, in particular, was discouraged by several factors. The barracks housing the prisoners were raised approximately 60cm off the ground to make it easier for guards to detect any tunnelling activity. The camp itself had been constructed on land that had very sandy subsoil. The sand was bright yellow, so it could easily be detected if anyone dumped it on the surface (which consisted of grey dust), or even just had some of it on their clothing. In addition, the loose, collapsible sand meant the structural integrity of any tunnel would be very poor. A third defence against tunnelling was the placement of seismograph microphones around the perimeter of the camp, which were expected to detect any sounds of digging just below the surface.

The recommended dietary intake for a normal healthy inactive man is 2,150 calories. Luft III issued 'non-working' German civilian rations, which allowed 1,928 calories per day, with the balance made up from American, Canadian and British Red Cross parcels and items sent to the PoWs by their families. As was customary at most camps, both Red Cross and individual parcels were pooled and distributed to the men equally. The camp also had an official internal bartering system called a 'Foodacco' – PoWs marketed surplus goods for 'points' that could be 'spent' on other items. The Germans paid captured officers the equivalent of their pay in internal camp currency (lagergeld), which was used to buy what goods were made available by the German administration. Every three months a weak beer was made available in the canteen for sale. As NCOs did not receive any 'pay' it was the usual practice in camps for the officers to provide one third for their use but at Luft III all lagergeld was pooled for communal purchases. As British government policy was to deduct camp pay from the prisoners' military pay, the communal pool avoided the practice in other camps whereby American officers contributed to British canteen purchases.

Luft III had the best-organised recreational programme of any PoW camp in Germany. Each compound had athletic fields and volleyball courts. The prisoners participated in basketball, softball, boxing, touch football, volleyball, table tennis and fencing, with leagues organised for most. A pool, 20ft by 22ft by 5ft deep, used to store water for fire-fighting, was occasionally available for swimming. A substantial library with schooling facilities was available where many PoWs earned degrees such as languages, engineering or law. The exams were supplied by the Red Cross and supervised by academics such as a Master of King's College who was a PoW in Luft III. The prisoners also built a theatre and put on high-quality, bi-weekly performances featuring all the current West End shows. The prisoners used the camp amplifier to broadcast a news and music radio station they named 'Station KRGY', short for 'Kriegsgefangenen', a term meaning 'PoWs', and also published two newspapers, *The Circuit* and the *Kriegie Times*, which were issued four times a week.

To prevent Germans from infiltrating the prisoner population, newcomers to the camp had to be personally vouched for by two existing PoWs who knew the prisoner by sight. Anyone who failed this requirement was severely interrogated and assigned a rota of PoWs who had to escort him at all times until he was deemed to be genuine. Several infiltrators were discovered by this method and none are known to have escaped detection in Luft III. The German guards were referred to as 'Goons' and unaware of the western connotation, willingly accepted the nickname after being told it stood for 'German Officer or Non-Com'. German guards were followed everywhere they went by prisoners, who used an elaborate system of signals to warn others of their location. The guards' movements were then carefully recorded in a logbook kept by an assigned rota of officers. Unable to effectively stop what the prisoners called the 'Duty Pilot' system, the Germans allowed it to continue and on one occasion the book was used by von Lindeiner to bring charges against two guards who had slunk away from duty several hours early.

Notable military personnel held at Stalag Luft III included Squadron Leader Philip John Lamason DFC* RNZAF, born in Napier, New Zealand, on 15 September 1918 and educated locally. He worked as a livestock inspector before joining the RNZAF to train as a pilot. In April 1941 he sailed for England, where he joined 218 Squadron flying the Stirling. On 8 June 1944 Lamason was serving as a flight commander on a Lancaster on 15 Squadron, on his forty-fifth operation, when he was shot down during a raid on railway marshalling yards at Massy-Palaiseau near Paris. Two of his crew were killed, three eventually made it back to England. For seven weeks Lamason and his 25-year-old navigator, Flying Officer Kenneth Walter Chapman, were hidden by the French Resistance before they were betrayed to the Gestapo, who interrogated them at the infamous Fresnes prison near Paris. Lamason was wearing civilian clothes when he was captured and was therefore treated as a spy rather than as a prisoner of war. On 15 August, five days before Paris was liberated, Lamason and Chapman were taken in cattle trucks with a group of 168 other airmen to Buchenwald, a journey that took five days. As the most senior officer, Lamason insisted on military discipline and bearing. He did not do this just to improve morale but also because he saw it as his responsibility to carry on his war duties despite the circumstances. On 19 October Luftwaffe officers arrived at Buchenwald and demanded the airmen's release and they were transferred to Stalag Luft III.

The Americans in the South Compound organised their 'S' Committee in much the same way as the RAF at Sagan did. 'Big S', 28-year-old Lieutenant Colonel Albert Patton Clark Jr, was a gangling, red-headed West Pointer, who answered to the nickname 'Bub' and also either 'Junior' or 'Red' and sometimes 'Flamingo' because his lanky legs did seem to bend a little backwards at the knees.[1] He was in charge of all escape activity including approval of escape plans. On Sunday, 26 July 1942 Clark was serving as the Exec in the 31st Fighter Group when he was shot down on the US Army Air Force's first fighter action in the ETO flying a Spitfire Vb during a sweep to Abbeville in France. He had crashed in a field in the Pas de Calais after being attacked by a Focke Wulf Fw 190 flown by Oberfeldwebel Walter Meyer of 6./JG 26 and was taken prisoner by German soldiers manning the coastal gun batteries just south of Cap Gris-Nez near Ambleteuse.[2]

Clark's assistant was Major David Mudgett 'Tokyo' Jones, who was known as 'Little S'. After earning his wings in June 1938, Jones served as a Northrop A-17 pilot with the 95th Attack Squadron of the 17th Attack Group, at March Field, California. In 1939 the 17th was redesignated a medium bombardment group and transferred to McChord Field, Washington. By September 1941 it became the first unit of the Army Air Forces to be fully equipped with the new B-25 Mitchell medium bomber. In early 1942 Jones volunteered for the Doolittle Project, a secret bombing raid to be launched on Japan in retaliation for the December 1941 attack on Pearl Harbor, and acted as the squadron navigation and intelligence officer.

---

1. *Behind the Wire: Allied Prisoners of War in Hitler's Germany* by Philip Kaplan and Jack Currie (Pen & Sword Aviation, 2012).

2. Lieutenant Colonel Clark's experiences are described in his memoir *33 Months as a PoW in Stalag Luft III: A World War II Airman Tells his Story.*

ESCAPE FROM HITLER'S REICH

On 18 April 1942, the Doolittle Raid led by Lieutenant Colonel 'Jimmy' Doolittle launched from the carrier USS *Hornet* dropped bombs on Tokyo and four other Japanese cities. Lacking the fuel to make a safe landing after the raid, Jones bailed out over China, where he was assisted by the Chinese people in evading capture. He received the DFC for his participation as a flight commander in the planning, training and completion of the mission. After escaping capture, 'Tokyo' Jones was flown to India, where he spent three months flying further B-25 missions against the Japanese. In September 1942, Jones was assigned to the new 319th Bombardment Group, preparing for combat in North Africa to develop low-level bombing tactics and techniques due to his experience with the Doolittle project and his belief in low-level bombing. He was shot down over Bizerte, Tunisia, on 4 December 1942 and would spend two and a half years as a prisoner of war in Stalag Luft III. As a result of his constant agitation and harassment of the enemy, he was selected for the 'escape committee' by fellow prisoners. The committee reviewed escape plans and directed escapes. Jones led the digging team on tunnel 'Harry'.

Colonel Delmar Taft Spivey, a 38-year-old expert on aerial gunnery and the highest-ranking USAAF officer shot down and captured in the European Theatre of Operations, on 12 August 1943, was serving as an observer on a B-17 Flying Fortress of the 92nd Bomb Group on the mission to evaluate how to improve gun turrets. Two weeks after entering Stalag Luft III, Spivey assumed command as Senior American Officer (SAO) of Centre Compound. Amazed by the prisoners' ingenuity, he had a carefully coded history of the camp created so that future PoWs would not have to 're-invent the wheel'. This carefully hidden record was retrieved and carried at no little risk when the camp was hastily evacuated in late January 1945 as the Germans marched the prisoners away from the rapidly advancing Russian armies.

Another key man at Sagan was Major Jerry M. Sage, a larger-than-life Army paratrooper and a member of OSS and later Special Forces who conducted judo classes. His first assignment was to organise behind-the-lines operations against Erwin Rommel in North Africa. As an OSS (Office of Strategic Services) officer, Sage would have been executed had his identity been known. But at the time he was captured, Sage jettisoned his OSS hardware and claimed he was a shot-down flier. His true identity was never discovered by his Nazi captors and he went behind the wire at Luft III in April 1943, where Sage conducted classes in silent killing with a hand-picked group of Americans. He was part of the 'X' committee, so secret that nine tenths of the men in the compound were never aware of the project, although in almost every hut there were prisoners who were involved in the escape activities, such as producing maps and identification and escape clothing for escapees. Sage earned the nickname 'Cooler King' because he was placed in solitary confinement fifteen times in Stalag Luft III. After escaping from South Camp twice, the Germans got tired of his trouble-making and sent him to the US Army officers' camp, Oflag 64. He again escaped when this camp was evacuated in January 1945 and got home early through the Russian lines.

American, Flying Officer George Rutherford Harsh RCAF, described as 'grey as a badger' and looking like a 'Kentucky colonel; a wild, wild man with a great spreading nose and a rambunctious soul', was a member of the Great Escape's executive committee and the camp's 'security officer'. Harsh was the 102 (Ceylon) Squadron Gunnery Officer, who had been shot down in a Halifax on 5 September 1942. Born in 1910 to a wealthy and prominent Georgia family, life had started out with great expectations. Educated in North Carolina and at Oglethorpe University in Atlanta, he lost his father when he was 12 but at his death $500,000 was put in trust in his name. Then at age 17 Harsh shot a man in a grocery store hold-up. Harsh was sentenced to die in the electric chair but at age 18 his sentence was commuted to life in prison and he spent the next twelve years on a Georgia chain gang. Harsh wielded a shovel for fourteen hours a day; slept in a stinking cage; fought off the sexual attacks of other prisoners and learned how to survive a hell that would have killed most men. In January 1941 Georgia Governor Eugene Talmadge released him on parole and finally granted him a full pardon. Less than a year later Harsh had volunteered for the RCAF and by 1942 he was a rear gunner on a Halifax of 102 Squadron at Pocklington.

At 1600 hours on the afternoon of 5 October, all air crew members were ordered over the Tannoy system to report to the briefing room. The target for more than 250 aircraft was Aachen. Although George Harsh was not scheduled to fly that night, he ended up as rear gunner on W7824, the third-from-last Halifax II, skippered by 20-year-old Warrant Officer Frederick Arthur Schaw RNZAF when he replaced the gunner, a huge farm boy from Yorkshire. En route the crew became lost. Harsh looked down at the ground 8,000ft below and spotted the majestic twin spires of Cologne Cathedral. Schaw must have instinctively sensed that something was wrong for his voice crackled in the earphones. 'Hullo navigator! Where are we?' For what seemed like interminable seconds there was dead silence. Then the well-bred, English public school accent of the navigator came over the intercom: 'I'm fucked if I know old boy.'[3] They were then shot down and Schaw was killed but the seven crew all bailed out safely and were captured. Harsh spent two weeks in a hospital in Cologne before being incarcerated in Stalag Luft III. He had charge of tunnel security in the 'X Organisation'. 'Home for Christmas' was the standard joke in prisoner of war camps but tunnelling went so smoothly at Luft III that Harsh said thoughtfully one morning, 'You know, this time it might really be home for Christmas for some of us' and for once nobody laughed.

At the beginning of March 1944, Harsh and eighteen other PoWs were ordered to pack and they were marched out of the gate at Sagan to Stalag VIIIC at Belaria, 5 miles away. The move probably saved

---

3. *Lonesome Road* by George Harsh (Sphere Books London, 1972).

THE GREAT ESCAPE

Harsh's life and that of some of the others, including two of the tunnellers and Robert Stanford Tuck, who all worked in the escape organisation and would have been among those at the head of the queue when the Great Escape took place.

Some held at Stalag Luft III went on to notable careers in the entertainment industry. British actor Rupert Davies had many roles in productions at the theatre in the camp. Singer Cy Grant, born in British Guiana, who served as a flight lieutenant navigator on Lancasters on 103 Squadron, was shot down on Friday, 25 June 1943 on only his third operation.

'My arrival at Stalag Luft III created a bit of a stir amongst the Germans,' he recalled. 'A black officer! The Kommandant sent for me. I was ushered into the presence of a very handsome middle-aged man, not the type of man one would have expected to see in charge of a prisoner of war camp. He had an intelligent, dignified manner and was extremely polite to me. He asked me where I came from and thrust a page of the *Volkischer Beobachter*, the newspaper of the National Socialist German Workers' Party, in front of me. It featured the picture of me, taken after five days of solitary confinement. There was no point now in not telling him where I came from. I told him I was from British Guiana. His face lit up. Unbelievably he had been there!

'I recalled that as a very small boy a German Moravian minister had stayed with my family. My father had himself been a Moravian minister. Our guest had been a charming, soft-spoken man who had served in the trenches during the First World War. He had told me the story of how his Bible had saved his life. He always kept it on his person, in his breast pocket and it had stopped a piece of shrapnel entering his chest!

'We talked about Guiana in very general terms. I cannot remember what he had done there, but thereafter the Kommandant always saluted me whenever we chanced to meet on his rounds around the camp.

'The camp was divided into six compounds, each holding approximately 1,000 prisoners. The centre compound, where I was to spend my first six months of captivity, was about 200 yards long and 75 yards wide. There were about ten barrack blocks, each holding one hundred prisoners. Each block was again subdivided into ten 'messes', with ten prisoners to each mess. A mess was equivalent to a family, of sorts, within our PoW community. Each week a new consignment of PoWs arrived. We would all flock to the perimeter fence to welcome them. We each hoped that other members of our respective crews would show up. Some of them joined our mess, staying together when we were eventually moved to Belaria, a smaller camp for British officers 5km south. We were to remain there until the end of January 1945.

'The first few months of captivity were the hardest, for until a camp is properly organised it can be quite a daunting environment. There was no access to reliable news about the progress of the war, only the occasional letter from home (heavily censored). There was also a shortage of decent food and the uncomfortable two-tiered wooden beds. Uncertainty about the outcome of the war did not help the situation. Incarceration was a period for deep reflection upon the fact that if one had not been shot down one would be still be on operations. We were all well aware that only a small minority of aircrews finished their first tour. I passed the time by keeping a log, reading, playing the guitar in the band and playing games – hockey and volleyball. I had played hockey for my county in British Guiana. I also was in great demand to make portraits of girlfriends of prisoners – enlargements of photographs.'

Henry Wallace 'Wally' Kinnan, one of the first well-known US television broadcast meteorologists, was a B-17 Flying Fortress pilot with the 429th Bombardment Squadron, 2nd Bomb Group, based at Massicault Airfield, Tunisia, as part of the Twelfth Air Force. Kinnan's aircraft was shot down over Eygalières, Vichy France, on 17 August 1943. He sustained shrapnel injuries that were compounded when he bailed out too close to the ground and made hard impact. His injuries prevented him from attempting evasion and he was captured. He was first taken to a hospital in Arles. Kinnan strongly credited his German captors in France with great humanity and care of his injuries. However, after just only over a week in France, he was transferred to another hospital that was part of Dulag Luft near Frankfurt, where his treatment was much sterner. Once processed he was transferred to Stalag Luft III in mid-September 1943.

American novelist and screenwriter Len Giovannitti was held in Stalag Luft III's Centre Compound. A navigator in the 742nd Bomb Squadron, 455th Bomb Group, in the Fifteenth Air Force, he was on his fiftieth mission when his B-24 Liberator was shot down over Austria on 26 June 1944. Writer and broadcaster Hugh Falkus, who was shot down over France in June 1940 flying a Spitfire, was an inmate at Stalag Luft III from around 1943. Falkus reportedly worked on thirteen escape tunnels during his time as a PoW, although was never officially listed as an escapee.

Another notable prisoner was Paramasiva Prabhakar Kumaramangalam DSO MBE of the then British Indian Army and the future Chief of the Indian Army. He was taken prisoner by the Italians late in 1942 and held in a PoW camp in Italy. With the Italian Armistice in September 1943, he escaped on 19 November but he was captured again in January 1944 and transferred to Stalag Luft III. Fighter pilot Roland Beamont, later to fly the English Electric Canberra and Lightning as a test pilot, arrived at Stalag Luft III just after the Great Escape, having been shot down in his Hawker Tempest on 12 October 1944 by ground fire while attacking a troop train near Bocholt on his 492nd operational sortie. Confined firstly to Stalag Luft III, then to Stalag III-A at Luckenwalde, Brandenburg, he remained a PoW until the end of the war in Europe.

Stalag Luft III inmates also developed an interest in politics. Justin O'Byrne, who later represented Tasmania in the Australian Senate for thirty-four years and served as President of the Senate, was born in

Launceston, Tasmania, and was educated at St Patrick's College. At the age of 18, during the Great Depression, he travelled to Queensland where he spent ten years working a variety of jobs including drover, fencer, bullock driver, tank sinker and station overseer. In 1940 he enlisted in the Royal Australian Air Force, becoming a pilot on 452 Squadron RAAF, which operated in 11 Group RAF during the Battle of Britain. He was shot down over France in 1941 and was a prisoner of war at Stalag Luft III for three years and nine months.

Professor Frederick Basil Chubb, author and political science lecturer, who was shot down and captured during a bombing raid on Leipzig on 19 February 1944, spent fifteen months in Luft III. Peter John Mitchell Thomas, later Baron Thomas of Gwydir, PC, QC, who enjoyed a political career as a Welsh Conservative politician and Cabinet minister under Edward Heath, was shot down in 1941 while serving as a bomber pilot in 1941 and spent four years as a prisoner of war, including at Stalag Luft III.

Flight Lieutenant Paul Chester Jerome Brickhill an Australian-born Spitfire pilot on 92 Squadron who was shot down on 17 March 1943 over Tunisia, was a prisoner at Stalag Luft III from 1943 until release. He was originally scheduled to be an early escapee but when it was discovered that he suffered from claustrophobia he was dropped down to the bottom of the list. He later said he figured this probably saved his life. Put in charge of security for the forgers, he was responsible for placed 'stooges', the relay teams who would alert prisoners that German search teams had entered the camp.

One of the forgers, Squadron Leader Francis John Hartnell-Beavis DFC, who on 26 July 1943 was shot down piloting a Halifax on the raid on Essen, learned of the 'X-Organisation' shortly after his arrival at Sagan. Born in Hong Kong in 1913, educated at Uppingham School and later spending nine months at Grenoble University and nine months at Freiburg University in the Black Forest, living with a German family, Hartnell-Beavis had qualified as an architect after training. Very soon after his arrival at Sagan an RAF prisoner came around swiping three bed boards from each bunk in Hartnell-Beavis' hut. The bunks were wooden double-deckers, with palliasses containing wood shavings as mattresses, each laid on eight bed boards. After spacing five boards across the bed, he laid the palliasse on top and laid on top of that, Hartnell-Beavis felt as if he was lying on a rather large section of corrugated iron roofing!

'Here, you can't do that,' the new arrivals chorused.

'Wanted for "X",' was the cryptic reply.

'What's "X"?' Hartnell-Beavis asked.

'You'll find out,' was the reply.

Hartnell Beavis soon discovered that 'X' was the escape committee and the boards were required for shoring up the escape tunnels![4]

The 'X' organisation at Stalag Luft III had been modelled on that created at Dulag Luft and Stalag Luft I by the SBO, Wing Commander Harry Melville Arbuthnot Day. 'Wings' as he was universally known, was over 40 years of age when the war began. He commanded 57 Squadron, which moved to Metz as part of the air component of the British Expeditionary Force, equipped with the Bristol Blenheim light bomber. On 13 October 1939 he volunteered to carry out the squadron's first operation, a flight to reconnoitre Hamm–Hannover–Soest. His Blenheim was shot down by a Me 109 flown by Unteroffizier Stephan Lütjens, of 11/JG 53 near Birkenfeld. Day bailed out, suffering burns to his face and hands, but otherwise landed safely by parachute. His two crew were killed. He was immediately captured and placed in the custody of Luftwaffe doctor Hermann Gauch. 'Wings' Day appointed Lieutenant Commander James Brian Buckley DSC as his adjutant and in October 1940 he put him in charge of escape operations by which all escape attempts, intelligence gathering and escape preparations were controlled. Buckley was a Royal Navy Fleet Air

---

4. *Final Flight* by Squadron Leader John Hartnell-Beavis DFC (Merlin Books Ltd, Braunton, 1985).

Arm pilot attached to the RAF, who was shot down on a bombing raid during the defence of Calais on 29 May 1940 and was captured by the Germans on the same day.

Squadron Leader Roger Joyce Bushell became Buckley's deputy. Bushell was born in Springs, Transvaal, South Africa, on 30 August 1910 to English parents Benjamin Daniel and Dorothy Wingate Bushell. His father, a mining engineer, had emigrated to the country from Britain and he used his wealth to ensure that Roger received a first-class education. He was first schooled in Johannesburg. Then, aged 14, he went to Wellington College in Berkshire. In 1929, Bushell then went to Pembroke College, Cambridge, to study law. Keen on pursuing non-academic interests, from an early age, he excelled in athletics and skied for Cambridge in races between 1930 and 1932 – captaining the team in 1931. Paul Brickhill stated that 'at the age of six, he [Bushell] could swear fluently in English, Afrikaans and Xhosa and spit an incredible distance'.

One of Bushell's passions and talents was skiing: in the early 1930s he was declared the fastest Briton in the male downhill category. He even had a black run named after him in St Moritz, Switzerland, in recognition of the fact that he had set the fastest time for it. He also won the slalom event of the annual Oxford–Cambridge ski race in 1931. At an event in Canada, Bushell had an accident in which one of his skis narrowly missed his left eye, leaving him with a gash in the corner of it. Although he recovered from this accident, he still had a dark drooping in his left eye as a result of scarring from his stitches. Bushell became fluent in French and German, with a good accent, which became extremely useful during his time as a prisoner of war. Despite his sporting prospects, one of Bushell's primary wishes was to fly and in 1932 he joined 601 Squadron Auxiliary Air Force, often referred to as 'The Millionaires' Mob' because of the number of wealthy young men who paid their way solely to learn how to fly during training days at weekends. By now Roger Bushell had become a barrister-at-law of Lincoln's Inn.

Bushell was given command of 92 Squadron in October 1939 and his promotion to squadron leader was confirmed on 1 January 1940. During the squadron's first engagement with enemy aircraft on 23 May, while on a patrol near Calais, Bushell was credited with damaging two Bf 110s of ZG26 before being shot down himself (probably by future ace Oberleutnant Günther Specht). He crash-landed his Spitfire and was captured before he had a chance to hide. On arrival at Dulag Luft he was made part of the permanent British staff under 'Wings' Day.

Three escape tunnels, one of which was completed in May 1941, were started. In June 1941, 'Wings' Day, Buckley and sixteen other ranks tunnelled out of Dulag Luft in the first mass escape of the war. Day travelled on foot alone, aiming to walk down the Moselle Valley and into France, but was recaptured five days later, looking like a tramp. All the escapers were recaptured and after spending a few days in jail at Frankfurt am Main they were transferred to Stalag Luft I, Barth, on the Baltic coast. Day once more assumed the role of senior British officer, and again appointed Buckley as head of the escape committee. 'Wings' Day partly oversaw a mass escape attempt in August 1941 when twelve officers tried to escape using a tunnel; however, the attempt was discovered as the third person left the exit, and all three escapers were recaptured. On the day of the escape Roger Bushell had wanted an earlier getaway so that he could catch a particular train, so he cut through the wire surrounding a small park in the camp grounds. He was recaptured on the Swiss border, only a few hundred yards from freedom, by a German border guard. He was treated well and returned to Dulag Luft, before being transferred to Stalag Luft I with all the seventeen others who had escaped in the tunnel (including 'Wings' Day and 'Jimmy' Buckley).

After a short period, Bushell was transferred to Oflag XC at Lübeck, where he participated in the construction of another tunnel. This was abandoned unfinished on 8 October 1941 when all British and Commonwealth Officer PoWs were removed from the camp and entrained for transfer to Oflag VIB at Warburg. During the night of 8–9 October the train stopped briefly in Hannover, where Bushell and 24-year-old Pilot Officer Jaroslav 'Jack' Zafouk, a Czech navigator on a 311 Squadron Wellington who was shot down on 16–17 July 1941 on a raid on Hamburg, jumped from the train and escaped unnoticed by the German guards. They made their way to Prague in occupied Czechoslovakia and made contact with the Czech underground movement, staying in 'safe houses' while arrangements for their onward journey was being made. However, following the assassination of Reinhard Heydrich in May 1942 the Germans launched a massive manhunt for the assassins and during the round-up Bushell and Zafouk were arrested. Both were interrogated by the Gestapo and were very roughly treated. Bushell was eventually sent to Stalag Luft III at Sagan, arriving there in October 1942 after further questioning by the Gestapo. Zafouk was sent to Oflag IVC at Colditz Castle.[5]

By this time the compound at Stalag Luft III was becoming overcrowded and 'Wings' Day and Jimmy Buckley were among those transferred to Oflag XXI-B at Schubin, where, on 5 March 1943, both men and thirty-three others (including future MP and journalist Aidan Crawley, journalist/author Robert Kee, German–Jewish RAF pilot Peter Stevens and future Chancellor of the Exchequer Anthony Barber) crawled through a 150ft tunnel, which started from the camp Abort (toilet block). All were recaptured within a few days, except for Buckley and his travelling companion, a young Danish officer, Jorgen Thalbitzer (who was using the name 'Flying Officer Thompson' to hide his real identity from the Germans). The pair travelled to Copenhagen before attempting a crossing by canoe to

---

5. See, *The Great Escaper: The life and death of Roger Bushell, Love, Betrayal, Big X and the Great Escape* by Simon Pearson (Hodder & Stoughton, 2013). Nineteen Czechoslovakian airmen – thirteen from Bomber Command and six from Fighter Command – were prisoners at Colditz Castle.

neutral Sweden but they never arrived. Thalbitzer's body was washed ashore sometime later but Buckley's was never found.[6]

'Wings' Day had headed east to Poland, hoping to get on a ship to Sweden, but he was recaptured and sent back to Schubin, before being transferred back to Sagan. He was SBO there until the arrival of 44-year-old Group Captain Herbert Martin Massey, who was shot down in a Short Stirling of 7 Squadron during the second thousand bomber raid on the night of 1–2 June 1942. Massey had lost half of his leg in Palestine in the First World War but was among the small band of amputees who remained in the RAF and continued flying. A veteran escaper himself, he had been in trouble with the Gestapo. He let 'Wings' continue as SBO.

On his return to Stalag Luft III Roger Bushell had taken over control of the 'X' escape organisation, inheriting the code name 'Big X' from the late Jimmy Buckley. Bushell had developed an intense hatred for the Nazis and his plan was to strike back at them as best he could – by organising mass breakouts from the PoW camps he was in. In spring 1943 he masterminded a plot for a major escape from the North Compound from three tunnels: 'Tom', 'Dick' and 'Harry' dug simultaneously. 'Everyone here in this room is living on borrowed time,' he told his fellow prisoners. 'By rights we should all be dead! The only reason that God allowed us this extra ration of life is so we can make life hell for the Hun ... In North Compound we are concentrating our efforts on completing and escaping through one master tunnel. No private enterprise tunnels allowed. Three bloody deep, bloody long tunnels will be dug – "Tom", "Dick" and "Harry". One will succeed!'

Falling back on his legal background to represent his scheme, Bushell not only shocked those present with its scope, but injected into every man a passionate determination to put their every energy

---

6. His date of death is recorded as 21 March 1943. He was 38 years old when he died. He was posthumously Mentioned in Despatches for his services as a PoW.

into the escape. 'Tom' began in a darkened corner of a hall in one of the buildings. 'Dick's entrance was carefully hidden in a drain sump in one of the washrooms. The entrance to 'Harry' was hidden under a stove. More than 600 prisoners were involved in their construction. The tunnels were very deep, about 30ft below the surface. They were very small, only 2ft square, although larger chambers were dug to house the air pump, a workshop and staging posts along each tunnel. The sandy walls of the tunnels were shored up with pieces of wood scavenged from all over the camp. One main source of wood was the prisoners' beds. At the beginning, each had about twenty boards supporting the mattress. By the time of the escape, only about eight were left on each. A number of other pieces of wooden furniture were also scavenged. A variety of other materials was also scavenged. The metal in the 'Klim' ('milk' spelt backwards) tin cans could be fashioned into a variety of different tools and items such as scoops and candle holders. Candles were fashioned by skimming the fat off the top of soup served at the camp and putting it in tiny tin vessels. Wicks were made from old and worn clothing. The main use of the 'Klim' tins, however, was in the construction of the extensive ventilation ducting in all three tunnels. As the tunnels grew longer, a number of technical innovations made the job easier and safer.

One important issue was ensuring that the person digging had enough oxygen to breathe and keep his lamps lit. A pump was built to push fresh air along the ducting into the tunnels, invented by Squadron Leader 'Bob' Nelson on 37 Squadron. The pumps were built of odd items including major bed pieces, hockey sticks and knapsacks, as well as 'Klim' tins. With three tunnels, the prisoners needed places to dump sand. The usual method was to discreetly scatter it on the surface. Small pouches made of towels or long underpants were attached inside the prisoners' trousers. As the prisoners walked around, the sand would scatter. Sometimes, the prisoners would dump sand into small gardens that they were allowed to tend. As one prisoner turned the soil, another would release sand while the two appeared to carry on a normal conversation. The prisoners wore greatcoats to conceal the bulges made by the sand and were referred to as 'penguins' because of their supposed resemblance to the waddling flightless sea-bird. In the sunny months sand could be carried outside and scattered in blankets for sun bathing. More than 200 were recruited who were to make an estimated 25,000 trips. The Germans were aware that something major was going on, but all attempts to discover tunnels failed. In an attempt to break up any escape attempts, nineteen of their top suspects were transferred without warning to Stalag VIIIC. Of those, only six were heavily involved with tunnel construction.

Eventually, the prisoners felt they could no longer dump sand on the surface as the Germans became too efficient at catching prisoners using this method. After 'Dick's' planned exit surface became covered by a camp expansion, the decision was made to start filling up the tunnel. As the tunnel's entrance was very well hidden, 'Dick' was also used as a storage room for a variety of items such as maps, postage stamps, forged travel permits, compasses and clothing such as German uniforms and civilian suits. A number of guards co-operated in supplying railway timetables, maps and the large number of official papers required to allow them to be forged. Some genuine civilian clothes were also obtained by bribing German staff with cigarettes, coffee or chocolate. These were used by escaping prisoners to travel away from the prison camp more easily; by train, if possible.

The prisoners later ran out of places to hide the sand and snow cover now made it impractical to scatter it over the ground. Underneath the seats in the theatre was a huge enclosed area, but the theatre had been built using tools and materials supplied on parole – that is, the prisoners gave their word not to misuse them – and the parole system was regarded as inviolate. Internal 'legal advice' was taken and the SBOs decided that the completed theatre building itself did not fall under the parole system. A seat in the back row was hinged and the sand dispersal problem solved.

'Tom' was discovered in August 1943 when nearing completion. As the war progressed, the German prison camps began to be overwhelmed with American prisoners. The Germans decided that new camps would be built specifically for the US airmen. In an effort to allow as many people to escape as possible, including the Americans, efforts on the remaining two tunnels increased. However, the higher level of activity drew the attention of guards and in September 1943 the entrance to 'Tom' became the ninety-eighth tunnel to be discovered in the camp. Guards hiding in the woods watching the 'penguins' noticed sand was being removed from the hut where 'Tom' was located. Work on 'Harry' ceased and did not resume until January 1944. When 'Harry' was finally ready in March, the American prisoners, some of whom had worked on 'Tom', had been moved to another compound seven months earlier. No American prisoners of war actually participated in the Great Escape, which had been planned for the summer as good weather was a large factor of success. However, in early 1944 the Gestapo had visited the camp and ordered increased efforts in detecting possible escape attempts. Bushell ordered the attempt be made as soon as the tunnel was ready.

Having the necessary qualifications, in November 1943 Squadron Leader Hartnell-Beavis had been asked to join Flight Lieutenant Plunkett's staff of map makers. Desmond Lancelot Plunkett – 'a nuggety little man with a fierce moustache – was born in 1915 in India, where his father was a civil engineer. After the family returned to England, he was educated at King's College, Wimbledon, then joined the Hawker aircraft company at Kingston, Surrey. He learned to fly at Redhill flying club and graduated as a flying instructor with the RAF Volunteer Reserve. Days before his wedding in 1941, he qualified as a bomber pilot and was posted to 218 Squadron at RAF Marham in Norfolk. On only his eighth operation, on 20–21 June 1942, the Stirling Plunkett was co-piloting was shot down by a night fighter over occupied Holland on a raid on Emden. By bribing a guard Plunkett obtained a large and detailed map of Europe, which formed

THE GREAT ESCAPE

the basis of an eventual supply of 2,500 maps in five colours. He abandoned tracing as being too time-consuming; instead, he conjured up an ingenious mimeograph using gelatine created from the crystal jelly sent in Red Cross parcels.

'There were about a dozen of us in Plunkett's "firm" employed as draughtsmen,' recalled Hartnell-Beavis, 'and about a dozen stooges, whose job it was to keep tabs on the ferrets, usually four or five at a time, who were in the camp, wandering around and to give us the warning in time for us to pack up our work and carry on with a camouflage lecture or talk. The stooges had a complicated system of flashing danger signals around the camp – a red book in a certain window might mean immediate danger, a blue towel hanging on a line, all clear, etc.

'We worked for a long time in the chapel afternoons from 1 o'clock till four. If the padre had seen all the secret hiding places and panels in the floor and walls, he would have had a severe shock. Actually, I don't believe he ever knew that any illegal activities used to take place in his chapel every day. During the course of the year or so that I spent with "Plunk's" mapping firm, we produced many thousands of maps of different types. We would receive miniature flimsies from home, usually sent out in special gramophone records or cigarettes, mark out the escape routes on them and enlarge these strips up five or six times, using special inks, which we had manufactured or acquired by other means. The negatives so produced were then printed on specially treated jelly, obtained from medical comforts parcels. From a good jelly, and good negative we sometimes obtained as many as thirty-five prints.

'We experimented with coloured dyes got from boiling indelible coloured pencil leads and finally had perfected a five-colour printing process. Thus, with woods in green, railway lines black, roads red, rivers blue and autobahns yellow, the prints were fairly easy to follow and read even in bad light. All our work inks, pens, rulers, dividers, paper, etc., had to be used in such a manner that it was possible for everything to be concealed in a matter of a few seconds, when the alarm was given, especially when "Rubberneck" was in camp.

'Our rival firm, "Dean and Dawson" under the leadership of Flight Lieutenant Gilbert "Tim" Walenn,' recalled Hartnell-Beavis 'was employed in manufacturing passports, Ausweise (identity cards), papers, etc; and a marvellous job they made of it.[7] Special paper was brought into the camp through various means. They worked from a small selection of genuine papers, which had either been lifted from guards' pockets or obtained from them by bribery. Extreme care was needed in copying these documents, as all the printing had to be done by hand with fine mapping pens and one document would take a week or more to produce, but the pains and trouble were justified, as it was impossible for the ordinary person to tell the forgery from the original. One snag about the work was that it was extremely hard on the eyes and usually after a few months, or sometimes weeks, the workers had to retire. I believe that "Dean and Dawson" produced as many as 400 sets of papers complete for the big tunnel escape of March 1944.

'The departments of "X" were many and varied. There were the dressmakers and tailors, employed in making civilian clothes and German uniforms, out of greatcoat linings and old clothes, dyed with beetroot juice, boot polish, or boiled book covers. The photographic section, having by some means obtained a Leica camera, were producing passport photos. An Australian invented a neat little compass, which he turned out by the hundred, made from melted

---

7. Walenn was piloting a Wellington Ic on 'B' Flight of 25 OTU on the night of 10–11 September when his aircraft was hit by anti-aircraft fire and had to be abandoned. All five crew abandoned the bomber before it crashed in the Ijsselhaven at Rotterdam. Before joining the RAF, he had designed wallpapers and fabrics for his uncle's design studio. Shy with gentle manners, he became a well-known character in the prison camp system for his skilful drawing, as well as for his enormous handlebar moustache, which had to be shaved off for the escape due to its unmistakable RAF style.

gramophone records and razor blades. The needles were magnetized from the electric light supply. The "tin bashers", engineers and carpenters produced tools for tunnel digging and all sorts of escape aids, water flasks, etc.; also railway trolleys for the tunnel railways.

'Besides these specialised departments, there were the tunnel experts themselves – men who had previous mining experience, who took charge of digging operations, "Penguins", who were employed on sand dispersal and stooges, or look-out men. The total personnel belonging to the "X" organisation numbered, I believe, about 500.'[8]

Of the 600 prisoners who worked on the tunnels, only 200 officers, all of whom wore civilian clothes and possessed a complete range of forged papers and escape equipment, would be able to escape. In addition, twenty officers should be kept in reserve to follow on if time permitted. For the purpose of selection, the party of 200 was divided into two main groups, the first thirty in each main group being selected for 'services rendered' by the Senior British Officer and by Squadron Leader Bushell. The other seventy in each main group took their position by lot. The first twenty-five were to travel entirely by rail, the next twenty-five partly by rail and partly on foot and the remainder entirely on foot. The twenty-five who were to travel entirely by rail were given precedence in order to give them a chance to catch their trains. The first group of 100 prisoners called 'serial offenders' were guaranteed a place and included those who spoke German well or had a history of escapes, plus an additional seventy men considered to have put in the most work on the tunnels.

Squadron Leader Henry Cuthbert Marshall, a Spitfire PR.III pilot on 3 PRU between June 1941 and February 1942, had assisted in the construction of four escape tunnels, the last of which demanded considerable physical endurance. However, before he was able to escape by this tunnel, he was transferred to Stalag Luft III in April

---

8. *Final Flight* by Squadron Leader Francis J. Hartnell-Beavis DFC (Merlin Books Ltd, Braunton, Devon, 1985).

1942, where he became a member of the escape committee. 'Johnny' Marshall, as he was more familiarly known, had been forced to make a crash landing during a sortie over France. He sustained severe injuries to his knee and on landing was handed over to the German police. He attempted to escape but was handicapped by his injury and was recaptured after several shots had been fired. While being transferred from Oberursel to Barth by train, he and other officers attempted an escape. The train was in motion at about 30mph when Marshall jumped from it and he suffered further injury to his knee. Despite this, he and a companion continued the attempt but were finally recaptured in Berlin in a very exhausted condition.

The chief tunnelling engineer was Flight Lieutenant Clarke Wallace Chant 'Wally' Floody, who was born on 28 April 1918 at Chatham, Ontario; a 6ft 6in, pre-war Canadian mining engineer and latterly a 401 Squadron RCAF Spitfire pilot who was shot down on 28 October 1941. Under him were other specialists in tunnelling, including Flight Lieutenant Gerald 'Crump' Ker-Ramsay, who was shot down near Calais on 13 September 1940 while flying a Blenheim, and Squadron Leader Leslie G. 'Johnny' Bull DFC, a Wellington bomber pilot shot down on 5 November 1941. In March 1944, the German guards at Sagan, always suspicious of escapes, spotted the telltale sign of sand being dropped by one of the 'penguins' out of the bottom of his trouser legs and immediately rounded up Floody and nineteen others and transferred them to another camp in Belaria.[9]

By March 1944 escape from Sagan now depended on the state of the moon so that ideally the Kriegies could leave under the cover of complete darkness. But the Camp Security Police were getting suspicious. Obergefreiter Karl Griese, 'a dedicated but hateful ferret'

---

9. Floody agreed to be technical adviser on the 1963 feature film *The Great Escape*, which was filmed at locations in Germany during the summer of 1962. He is popularly considered the real-life counterpart to that film's fictional 'Tunnel King', Danny Velinski, played by Charles Bronson.

better known as 'Rubberneck', succeeded Hermann Glemnitz, the 'Chief Ferret', in the North Compound. Glemnitz has been described as 'a wise man who had seen much of the world and who spoke several languages'. Although he was responsible for unearthing more than a hundred tunnels, he possessed a sense of humour and was respected by the inmates. On a rainy day his favourite line was, 'It is bad weather to be above the ground, isn't it?' Glemnitz sometimes played tough and used to swagger into the reception block to greet a new group arriving at the Stalag, saying, 'Good morning gentlemen. Velcome to Stalag Luft III. Here you will find that the beer is piss poor but the gin is shit hot.' 'Rubberneck' was the prisoners' most dangerous adversary. 'An ardent Nazi, he was really keen on his job and always looking for trouble.'

The Escape Committee decided that the escape should take place on the moonless night of 24–25 March because they could not take the risk of waiting for another three weeks before the moon was again favourable. As night fell, those allocated a place in the tunnel moved to Hut 104. 'As regards the order of the escape,' recalled Henry Marshall, 'Johnny Bull was sent through first to keep watch at the exit for the first twenty escapers. I was the first on the list and went into the tunnel at 2000 hours. I was followed by my partner, Flight Lieutenant Arnošt Valenta,[10] who in view of his excellent knowledge of German was responsible to Squadron Leader Bushell for intelligence matters such as finding out what passes were required in the various circumstances. Bushell was number 3 and his partner, 22-year-old Souse Lieutenant Bernard W. M. Scheidhauer, a German-born Spitfire Vb pilot on 131 Squadron, was number 4[11] and

---

10. A Czechoslovak Army officer who became a RAFVR radio operator on 311 Squadron and who was shot down on 6 February 1941.
11. Nineteen-year-old Bernard Scheidhauer was studying in France as the Germans approached Paris. His father advised him to go to England and after a few attempts he obtained passage aboard a small trawler. On 5 November 1940, he had joined the Forces Aériennes Françaises Libres (FAFL), the air arm of the Free French Forces. He started training to be a pilot with the RAF in 1941.

Lieutenants Johannes Gouws, a P-40 Tomahawk pilot, and Rupert Stevens SAAF, shot down in a Martin Maryland on 14 November 1941, were numbers 5 and 6 respectively. Gouws and his British-born South African partner Rupert Stevens apparently planned to head for Switzerland via Breslau.'

The second group of 100, considered to have very little chance of success, had to draw lots to determine inclusion. Called 'hard-arsers', these would be required to travel by night as they spoke little or no German and were only equipped with the most basic fake papers and equipment. 'Johnny' Marshall told Bushell that they could not possibly make the break in such cold weather but when 'Big X' asserted that they certainly could 'Johnny' Marshall responded by saying that 'it did not give the cross-country boys much chance'. Bushell had replied, 'Johnny, they haven't much chance anyway. You know as well as I do, they'll nearly all be caught. We can't lose "Harry" just because conditions are tough. It isn't only to get people home. It's to muck the goons about too and get them to divert troops to look for us.'[12]

Marshall was dressed for the escape in a pair of RAAF blue serge trousers, an RAF airman's jacket modified to look like a civilian's, a skiing cap and an airman's overcoat dyed dark grey with civilian buttons. 'The first ten of us to escape assembled at a point about 200 yards from the mouth of the tunnel and then split up in pairs as pre-arranged. Valenta and I were to make our way immediately to the railway station at Sagan. In order to enable the first twenty-five escapers to catch their trains "Zero Hour" for the opening of the tunnel was fixed at 2045 hours but the exit trap door of "Harry" was found to be frozen solid and freeing the door delayed my escape until just after 2200 hours.'

---

12. *The Great Escaper: The Life and Death of Roger Bushell, Love, Betrayal, Big X and the Great Escape* by Simon Pearson (Hodder, 2013).

THE GREAT ESCAPE

An even larger setback was when it was discovered that the tunnel had come up short. It had been planned that it would reach into a nearby forest but at 2230 the first man out emerged just short of the tree line and close to a guard tower. As the temperature was below freezing and snow still lay on the ground, any escapee would leave a dark trail while crawling to cover. Because of the need to now avoid sentries, instead of the planned one man every minute, the escape was reduced to little more than ten per hour. Word was eventually sent back that no prisoner issued with a number higher than 100 would be able to escape before daylight. As they would be shot if caught trying to return to their barracks, these men changed into their own uniforms and got some sleep. At 2300 hours an air raid on Berlin took place and as a consequence the camp electricity supply was cut off and the tunnel was thrown into darkness, slowing the escape even more. At around 0001 hours the tunnel collapsed and had to be repaired.

Finally, at 0455 hours on 25 March, the seventy-seventh man was seen emerging from the tunnel by one of the guards. Henry Marshall knew that seventy-six men passed through successfully 'but four were caught in the immediate vicinity of the tunnel and were returned to the camp forthwith'.

Those already in the trees began running while New Zealand Squadron Leader Leonard Henry Trent, who had just reached the tree line, stood up and surrendered. (Trent had been a Ventura pilot on 487 Squadron RNZAF and he was awarded the Victoria Cross for his action on 3 May 1943 when he was the only survivor from the fateful raid on the Amsterdam power station.) The guards had no idea where the tunnel entrance was, so they began searching the huts, giving the men time to burn their fake papers. Hut 104 was one of the last huts searched and despite using dogs the guards were unable to find the entrance. Finally, Unteroffizier 'Charlie' Pilz crawled the length of the tunnel but found himself trapped at the other end. Pilz began calling for help and the prisoners opened the entrance to let him out, finally revealing the location.

When the escapees arrived at Sagan station most had difficulty in finding the entrance until daylight revealed it was in a recess in the side wall of an underground pedestrian tunnel. Consequently, many men missed their night-time trains and either decided to walk across country or wait on the platform in daylight. Marshall and Valenta planned to take the train from Sagan to Breslau, where they would change to catch a train at 0300 to head 80 miles south to Mittelwalde, just 2½ miles from the Czech border. Once there they hoped to contact an underground organisation and, if that failed, to make for Yugoslavia, where they would join Tito's partisans. Just before Marshall and Valenta found the tunnel entrance the air raid alert was sounded, which meant that they could not now get on to the platform. 'We decided,' recalled Henry Marshall, 'that in view of the great danger in remaining so close to the camp we should not wait for the train but try to reach Regensburg via Kohlfurt on foot, a distance of 90 miles. [March 1944 was the coldest recorded in thirty years and snow lay up to 5ft deep, so the escapees had no option but to leave the cover of woods and fields and use roads.]

'We started walking but were eventually arrested at Heillgersee near Kohlfurt at approximately 0400 hours on 26 March by two members of the Landwacht (the German Home Guard) near the Polish village of Tiefenfurt, about 15 miles from Sagan. Later in the morning we were taken to Sagan jail, where we were stripped, searched and put into a cell with approximately seventeen other recaptured prisoners. At 0100 hours on 27 March, we were taken under armed police guard to Görlitz jail, where we were again put into cells. We were taken to KRIPO [Kriminalpolizei] Headquarters on the 28th for interrogation, which was carried out by a civilian, a woman typist and an interpreter in army uniform. Throughout the interrogation threats and intimidation were used and many remarks were made with the obvious object of causing fear.

'I was marched back to my cell, in which were also Leigh, Cameron and Humphreys. After this I was moved around continuously from cell to cell and I saw or talked to over 30 of them. On the 29th or 30th a guard told us that further interrogations were to be carried out and from then on various parties were moved away under what I was told were Gestapo guards. The parties moved off as follows: 30 March: Casey, Wiley, Cross, Leigh, Pohe and Hake. 31 March: Humphreys, McGill, Swain, Valenta, Hall, Kolanowski, Stewart, Birkland, Langford, and Evans. 1 April: Ogilvie, McDonald, Thompson and Royle. Grisman, Street, McGarr, Gunn, J. F. Williams and Milford. The last party left on the afternoon of the 6th: Shand, Bethell, Cameron, Armstrong [sic], Churchill, Nelson, Broderick and myself. Flight Lieutenant J. L. Long was left behind in Görlitz jail.[13] The lists of names were compiled from memory after I had heard them called out in the corridor. It was absolutely necessary for me to remember these names as, to the best of my knowledge, I was the only member of the Escape Committee in the jail at Görlitz. As the parties left those of us remaining had no premonition about their fate because we had been told by a guard that they were being taken away for a second interrogation and would then be returned to Stalag Luft III.'

On 28 March the Reich Criminal Office, Berlin, reported that: 'By 2400 hours 27 March, 65 of the escapers had been recaptured. For the most part the arrests were made on trains and at railway stations. While some tried immediately to reach the northern, western and southern frontiers of the Reich, others tried to conceal themselves both in the nearby and outlying surroundings of the place of escape. In addition to a few localities in Silesia: Metz, Meulhausen, Reichenberg, Strassnitz and Stettin are of note as being places where arrests took place today. In one case two of the escapers found refuge in a camp for foreign workers, which fact was reported by a V-man (agent). One of the recaptured wore the uniform of an obergefreiter of the Luftwaffe and was in possession of a corresponding paybook.'

---

13. Flight Lieutenant James L. Long was shot in cold blood on 12 April at Breslau.

This was followed on 5 April: 'Of the 80 escapers, Sydney Henstings Dowse, Bedrich Dvorak, Stanislaw Krol, Jens Einar Müller, Desmond Plunkett, Peter Rockland and Bram Van Der Stok are still at large. The escapers may, as in the case of those hitherto arrested, be in possession of passes for foreign civilian workers, in some cases very well forged. Organisations engaged on the Kriegsfahndung [War Emergency Manhunt] should not let themselves be influenced by apparently confident appearance. The following are especially to be searched: hotels in ports, places with heavy railway traffic and foreign workers' hostels.'

On 6 April the Reich Criminal Office reported that: 'Stanislaw Krol and Sidney Henstings Dowse had been recaptured in a barn in the Oels district', and on 13 April, that 'two foreign workers without leave passes were discovered when a train check was carried out at Klattau station on 8 April ... It was found that they were Flight Lieutenants Plunkett and his escape partner, Czech airman Bedrich Dvorak.' At his own request (no one else would volunteer for the unlucky number) Desmond Plunkett was the thirteenth man to crawl to freedom. He had reached the safety of the tree line before the Germans discovered the existence of the tunnel. He and Flight Lieutenant 'Freddie' Dvorak, a Czech Spitfire Vb pilot on 312 Squadron, went to the local railway station and boarded a train for Breslau. The two men succeeded in getting into Czechoslovakia, where, after several days in the relative luxury of a hotel, they hid in a barn. They eventually got as far as the Austrian border before being apprehended. While Plunkett enjoyed the hospitality of the Gestapo (boiled blood was on the prisoners' menu every Tuesday and Thursday), Dvorak was sent to Colditz. Plunkett was finally released by the Gestapo into the custody of Hradin prison in Prague. Later, in January 1945, he was sent to Stalag Luft I.

Finally, on 17 April, the Reich Criminal Office announced that: 'Jens Einar Muller of Norway, Peter Rockland of London and Bram van der Stok of Pladjoe, Sumatra' were still at large and urged 'Arrest! Further Energetic Search!'

THE GREAT ESCAPE

Henry Marshall's party, meanwhile, had been taken straight back to the camp, where they were all placed in the arrest block. 'On arrival we found that all four members of the third party to leave Görlitz were also in the arrest block, Later, that same day, we were told by the camp adjutant that a Memorial Service had just been held for 40 escapers who had been shot. Nelson and I discussed this information and could not believe it to be true. We thought that it was an attempt on the part of the Gestapo to discourage any further attempts at mass escape. It was not until we were released three weeks later that we heard that the shooting had been confirmed by the Commandant and that a list had been produced to the Senior British Officer giving the names of 47 prisoners who had been killed. The names of three more were added later.'

The day after the mass escape Hitler gave personal orders that every recaptured officer as well as Commandant von Lindeiner, the architect who designed the camp, the camp's security officer and the guards on duty at the time, were to be shot. Reichsmarschall Hermann Göring, head of the Luftwaffe; Field Marshal Wilhelm Keitel, head of the German High Command, who had ultimate control over prisoners of war; Major General Westhoff and Major General von Graevenitz, who was head of the department in charge of prisoners of war; all argued against any executions as a violation of the Geneva Convention. Göring pointed out to Hitler that a massacre might bring about reprisals to German pilots in Allied hands. Hitler agreed, but insisted 'more than half' were to be shot. Reichsführer Heinrich Himmler, chief of state security, fixed the total at fifty and passed the selection on to SS-Gruppenführer Arthur Nebe. The general orders were that recaptured officers would be turned over to the Criminal Police and fifty would be handed to the Gestapo to be killed. Nebe was later executed for his involvement in the 20 July plot to kill Hitler.

As the prisoners were captured, they were interrogated for any useful information and taken out by motor car, usually in small parties of two at a time, on the pretext of returning them to their prison camp.

Their Gestapo escorts would stop them in the country and invite the officers to relieve themselves. The prisoners were then executed singly or in pairs at close range from behind by pistol or machine pistol fire. Roger Bushell and his partner, Bernard Scheidhauer, who were dressed as French workers and had been arrested at the Saarbrücken railway station, probably on 27 March, were driven to a remote spot just outside Saarbrücken, where they were shot in the back by Dr Leopold Spann, a local Gestapo official. Scheidhauer died instantly but Bushell was only injured and lay writhing on the ground. Spann ordered his driver, Emil Schulz, to 'finish him off'.[14] Johannes Gouws and Rupert Stevens were recaptured on 29 March near the Bodensee beside the border of neutral Switzerland, taken to Munich central Gestapo offices, and later that day they were shot and cremated.

Near Dirschau (Tozew) Bridge over the Weichel (Vistula), while attempting to reach Danzig, Flight Lieutenant Edward D. Brettell was caught together with Flight Lieutenants Romualdas Marcinus, the only Lithuanian pilot to serve in the RAF during the Second World War;[15] Henri A. Pickard, a Belgian Spitfire pilot on 350 (Belgian) Squadron at RAF Kenley who on 27 August 1942 was shot down by Focke Wulf Fw 190s over the English Channel off Abbeville; and 'Tim' Walenn. All four officers were executed by the Gestapo on 29 March.

Only three escapers made home runs: Per Bergsland, a Norwegian Spitfire pilot on 332 Squadron RAF who was shot down during the

---

14. Spann was killed in air raid at Linz on 25 April 1945. Schultz was one of eighteen members of the Gestapo put on trial for the murder of the fifty escapers and he was executed at Hameln (Hamelin) on 27 February 1948.
15. Marcinus, who participated in an early trans-European flight on 25 June 1934, had enlisted in the French Air Force a few months before the Soviet occupation of Lithuania, and after the Battle of France and the French capitulation, escaped to Britain, where he flew on 1 Squadron RAF. He was shot down on 12 February 1942 during Operation Cerberus.

raid on Dieppe on 19 August 1942; Jens Einar Müller, a Norwegian Spitfire V pilot on 331 Squadron RAF who on 19 June 1942 was shot down just off the Belgian coast after running out of ammunition; and Bram van der Stok, a Dutch Spitfire Vb pilot on 41 Squadron RAF who had been shot down on 12 April 1942. Bergsland and Müller made it to neutral Sweden first, by boat, while van der Stok travelled through France before finding safety at a British consulate in Spain.

'Wings' Day made his way to Stettin disguised as a renegade Irish colonel who had been held prisoner since 1940 and had been converted to Nazism under guard by another escapee Flying Officer Paweł 'Peter' N. Tobolski, who was dressed in the uniform of a Luftwaffe corporal and acting as the escort of 'Colonel Brown'. Tobolski was a Polish navigator on 301 Squadron who was shot down on the thousand-bomber raid on Bremen on 25–26 June 1942. Both escapers travelled by train, through Berlin, reaching Stettin on the evening of the next day. There they sought help from some French workers and were taken to a workers' camp. However, they were betrayed by an informer in the camp and arrested the following day. After a brief stay in the local jail, Day was taken to Berlin and was interviewed by Arthur Nebe, the man who selected the fifty escapers to be murdered, which included Tobolski. Day was spared execution. He said later that Hitler had ordered his execution personally, but that Hermann Göring had asked him to relent because Day and his family were so well known to the public.

The British government learned of the deaths of the fifty escapers from a routine visit to the camp by the Swiss authorities as the Protecting power in May; the Foreign Secretary Anthony Eden announced the news to the House of Commons on 19 May 1944. Shortly after the announcement the Senior British Officer of the camp, Group Captain Herbert Massey, was repatriated to England via Switzerland due to ill health. Upon his return, he informed the British Government about the circumstances of the escape and the reality of the murder of the recaptured escapees. Anthony Eden, the Foreign Secretary, updated

Parliament on 23 June, promising that, at the end of the war, those responsible would be 'brought to exemplary justice'.

Just before midnight on 27 January 1945, with Soviet troops only 16 miles away, the remaining 11,000 PoWs were marched out of camp with the eventual destination of Spremberg. In below-freezing temperatures and 6in of snow, 2,000 prisoners were assigned to clear the road ahead of the main group. After a 34-mile march the PoWs arrived in Bad Muskau, where they rested for thirty hours before marching the remaining 16 miles to Spremberg. On 31 January the South Compound prisoners plus 200 men from the West Compound were sent by train to Stalag VIIA at Moosburg, followed by the Centre Compound prisoners on 7 February. Thirty-two prisoners escaped during the march to Moosburg but all were recaptured. The North, East and remaining West Compound prisoners at Spremberg were sent to Stalag XIII-D at Nürnberg on 2 February. With the approach of US forces on 13 April, the American prisoners at XIII-D were marched to Stalag VIIA. While the majority reached VIIA on 20 April, many had dropped out on the way with the German guards making no attempt to stop them. Built to hold 14,000 PoWs, Stalag VIIA now held 130,000 from evacuated stalags with 500 living in barracks built for 200. Some chose to live in tents while others slept in air raid slit trenches. The US 14th Armoured Division liberated VIIA on 29 April.

After Nazi Germany's capitulation in May 1945, the RAF Police (RAFP) investigative branch launched a special investigation into the killings following the Great Escape from Stalag Luft III in March 1944, having branded the shootings a war crime despite official German reports that the airmen had been shot while attempting to escape from captivity following recapture. An extensive investigation into the events following the recapture of the seventy-three airmen was launched, which was unique for being the only major war crime to be investigated by a single branch of any nation's military. The investigation started seventeen months after the alleged crimes had been committed, making it a cold case. Worse, according to an account of the investigation, the perpetrators 'belonged to a body, the Secret State Police or Gestapo, which held and exercised every facility to provide its members with false identities and forged identification papers immediately they were ordered to go on the run at the moment of national surrender'. The small detachment of investigators, numbering five officers and fourteen NCOs, remained active for three years and identified seventy-two men, guilty of either murder or conspiracy to murder, sixty-nine of whom were accounted for.

Of these, twenty-one were eventually tried and executed (some of these were for other than the Stalag Luft III murders); seventeen were tried and imprisoned; eleven had committed suicide; seven were untraced, though of these four were presumed dead; six had been killed during the war; five were arrested but charges had not been laid; one was arrested but not charged so he could be used as a material witness; three were charged but either acquitted or had the sentence quashed on review and one remained in refuge in East Germany. Despite attempts to cover up the murders during the war, the investigators were aided by such things as Germany's meticulous book-keeping, such as at various crematoria, as well as willing eyewitness accounts and many confessions among the Gestapo members themselves, who cited that they were only following orders. Wing Commander Wilfred Bowes OBE headed the fifteen-man investigation team from the RAF that relentlessly tracked down, arrested and interrogated the alleged war criminals responsible for the murders.

American Colonel Telford Taylor was the US prosecutor in the High Command case at the Nuremberg Trials. The indictment in this case called for the General Staff of the Army and the High Command of the German Armed Forces to be considered criminal organisations; the witnesses were several of the surviving German field marshals and their staff officers. One of the crimes charged was of the murder of the fifty. The first trial specifically dealing with the Stalag Luft III murders began on 1 July 1947, against eighteen defendants. The trial was held before No. 1 War Crimes Court at the Curio Haus in Hamburg. The accused all pleaded 'not guilty' to the counts of the names of the victims that they were accused of murdering. The verdicts and sentences were handed down after a full fifty days on 3 September of that year. Three were sentenced to life imprisonment, two others received ten years' imprisonment each and the other thirteen condemned prisoners were hanged at Hamelin Jail in February 1948 by British executioner Albert Pierrepoint. A further four were hanged by the authorities in Czechoslovakia for a variety of war crimes against humanity. A second trial began in Hamburg on 11 October 1948, with verdicts and sentences being reached by 6 November. In the interim, however, Ernest Bevin, the British Foreign Secretary, announced a Cabinet decision not to prosecute any more war criminals after 31 August 1948.

Chapter 9

'Home by Christmas 1945?'[1]

From his own wartime experiences Leslie Sidwell writes about the hurried evacuation of Stalag Luft III in January 1945 when 10,000 RAF/Allied Air Force officers began their long journey to the west and eventual freedom. He gives a detailed account of how one typical little group fared on an unknown journey; how they lived and coped day to day, through the bad times that were mixed in with the bizarre and humorous when high spirits inevitably surfaced. The group were forced to march through deep snow and blizzards, then transported in overcrowded cattle trucks for two days through air raids, mainly locked in with little water and suffering sickness and diarrhoea. There was then a brief stay behind barbed wire and a 'spring march' northwards, living off the land, with a growing sense of freedom and official liberation close to the Baltic.

'Any "Home for Christmas" hopes had been upset by the autumn Arnhem setback and the surprise German Ardennes offensive had further lowered our spirits by the end of 1944. With no immediate hope from the West, our thoughts turned to the East and our optimism rose when the new Russian offensive opened up in mid-January: the breathtaking advances and the reported bridgehead attack on the River Oder at Steinau caught our imagination – it put them at under fifty miles from Luft III. It was surmised that our area could be on the

---

1. Adapted from *Wingless Journey* by Leslie Sidwell with the kind permission of James Sidwell, Leslie's grandson.

"tongue" of a Russian pincer movement. Rumours intensified – what might happen to us …? The Kommandant's private opinion (having had no orders from Berlin) was that they would just quit and leave us behind if the Russians threatened the area. But many could not accept this and went on converting kitbags into rucksacks – to carry our kit if it came to a march … Our Polish friends smiled at our naivety about the Russians, especially at one popular story that their advance units carried British liaison officers with them to handle liberated PoWs. But change was surely in the air, substantiated by the sight of large numbers of passing refugees seen through the wire. Even hard-bitten PoWs from 1940 days sat up. Instead of their usual response to wild optimism; ("We've seen it all before, dear chap, haven't we?"), they joined the rest of us in sorting out our things as speculation grew. If we had to march it became plain that two things would be crucial: food and the cruel weather.

The six compounds of Luft III held 10,000 RAF/Allied Air Force officers. Food supplies had dwindled throughout 1944, both the scant German rations and the vital Red Cross food parcels. As stocks of the latter fell – and with so many mouths to feed – we had been reduced to half parcels issue for over three months and exercise had been accordingly cut down. In a harsh winter a lean Christmas had been in prospect with talk centred on hopes of the coming Russian offensive. But incredibly and against all the odds in such severe weather, a big load of USA Christmas parcels had got through on 21 December as temperatures sank lower so we unexpectedly had the great treat of full food parcels issue for Christmas week. Then, reverting to half parcels, we grew hungrier and colder. But a second food surprise came: one day in mid-January, as we were excitedly studying the lines of pins and cotton which marked the latest Russian advances on our wall-map, great cheers greeted the news that a further load of Red Cross food had somehow got through the worsening blizzard conditions. An immediate issue put us back on full parcels for a further week or two and the searing cold that penetrated our bones seemed more bearable.

'HOME BY CHRISTMAS 1945?'

December had been a bitter month with heavy snows and frosts of minus 14C before Christmas. January 1945 had added to the snowfalls and frosts became harder by several degrees. But our spirits rose as temperatures dropped lower and it seemed odds on that we would march. Time was running out fast at the snowbound Luft III. 27th January was another day of blizzards. All our uncertainties were abruptly terminated that evening: guards entered East Compound at 2000 hours with terse orders – "Stand by to march in an hour!"

'The two Red Cross food arrivals were to prove vital to us. We not only had full issues to "stoke" us up before we marched, we were also enabled to carry a lot of food on the unknown journey ahead of us to help us through the very harsh weather and to offset the German inability to organise any rations for us. Possession of the Red Cross food (and cigarettes) was to prove a priceless asset in the coming hardships. Unquestionably the Red Cross supplies that had so miraculously arrived in time proved a major factor of survival in the first stage of our adventures. Food and weather – the two crucial things: possession of the one enabled us to withstand the severity of the other.

'With a blizzard raging and deep snow on the ground, final sortings of possessions have to be made and priorities worked out. Warm clothing, blankets and food are a "must", plus cigarettes for bartering. And we know that Nescafe and ordinary Red Cross soap are also good trading things. Those who haven't already converted their kitbags into rucksacks set to work on them. As all we know is that we are marching westwards and that we have to carry everything, only our short-term future governs our thoughts on what to take in this severe weather. Things like summer clothing join the accumulating piles of throw-outs in the corridors as "Not wanted on the voyage". The unfit are told to report to the Senior British Officer's office. Russian forces are reported to have crossed the Oder in three places.

'Our officials announce that the entire stock of Red Cross food parcels will be handed out as we leave the camp and, with the aim of devouring all the food we cannot carry with us, the biggest food "bash" in "Kriegie" history begins. Individual messes place their hoarded reserves on the tables to be freely eaten as wanted and feeds of long-forgotten quantities take place in an unreal atmosphere of plenty, so that nothing can be left. For the first time fuel shortages are non-existent – wood for the stoves is torn down from anywhere to cook as much as possible in anticipation of the riches we are to collect on our way out. The question of the hour's notice is disregarded.

'Wood from doors and beds is used for sledge-making and hammerings and bangings are heard everywhere; the wooden huts are literally torn apart and bonfires blaze outside. The normal lock-up in our own blocks after dark goes by the board tonight as "Kriegies" blithely trip from block to block to see friends or to swap things with each other. The "Goons" are too busy with their own problems to interfere with anything; as the hours pass it is plain that they are in a mess with such a quick evacuation of the six big compounds and that we won't be moving yet, especially when the news filters through to us that we shall be the last compound out of Luft III. The extra time is an incentive for more sledge-making work. Most just aim at a functional job to carry our belongings but the skilful types use the time to construct better models. There is a fantastic air of unreality in such a hive of activities after the static years. Spirits are high as tremendously exciting prospects open up, even though unknown challenges may appear … Thoughts of movement, of getting into the outside world, are a tonic although there are some misgivings because of unfitness in the snow. And, although we are to stock up with food parcels on the way out, there are still mixed feelings about devouring the reserves; mess food reserves have always been held to be sacred – but times are now changing. Those who are ill-shod for marching in snow seek better footwear in the piles of rejects. We are trying to contact our messmate, Tom Wilson, who had to go into sickbay after an ice accident a few days ago. Snow continues to fall.

'Plans become finalized. Messes of eight or so are usual in camp; most now arrange for smaller groups out on the road, down to "combines" of two or three, with odd "loners" opting to go solo. Six from our mess decide to stay together with pooled resources to see how we fare in the unknown circumstances outside: "Johnny" Hynd, "Don" Hockey, "Tony" Burcher (all Australians), Adam Chisholm, Frank Phillips and me.

'We make one big sledge to carry as much of our belongings as possible. The advice of our expert on dietetic matters (David Lubbock) is widely followed: to mix chocolate, condensed milk, rolled oats and Bemax into a concentrated "cake" form. This escapers' "Dogfood" is invaluable stuff because a little goes a long way nutritionally and it is easy to carry. Orders come from the SBO to keep together and not try to escape; and delaying tactics are to be used. Gunfire sounds are exciting; can the Russian advances overtake us …?

'Decisions aren't easy on what personal things to take, now that the moment has come. I'm loath to abandon a lot of stuff that I've been hanging on to but obviously much will have to be finally discarded. I opt for two blankets (including the lightweight one left by Mike Codner after the "Wooden Horse" escape), with one serviceable pair of slacks to wear with the SD tunic which I recently "bought" from "Danny" Bateman for chocolate. I pack my battledress tunic and my warmest shirts, socks, woollies and underwear. And another reminder of the "Wooden Horse": the blue/grey haversack left by Eric Williams will be useful for carrying things.

'I shall wear my long, voluminous Polish cavalry greatcoat that I acquired during my first PoW winter at Oflag XXIB. It is of thinnish khaki material but there is such a lot of it. I am luckier than most in having good Red Cross boots for the snow. I also have my old flying boots but they are useless now outdoors as the summer heats have perished the rubber; I hate to scrap them and they may have a use. I've built up a good stock of cigarettes, in cartons of 200, and will take as many as possible. I throw out some of my books and papers and bundle up the rest that I must keep with all my letters.'

After leaving the camp on 27 January, Sidwell's account continues.

'Exhilaration is in the air despite the conditions; there is a sense of freedom in being outside the wire and part of the open countryside – bleak though it is – plus the possibility of being overtaken by the Russian spearheads. The snow underfoot has been beaten down by the passage of preceding columns and the runners of the sledges move quite well at first. But, being unfit, we tired quickly and are glad to be replaced on the ropes. Welcome long stretches of fir woods line the route on both sides, giving some protection from the blizzard. Many loads have to be lightened as tiredness increases: flying boots, books and papers and countless cartons of cigarettes lie in the wayside snowdrifts – truly an amazing sight in a country that is short of everything! The snow-blanketed silence of the countryside contrasts with the sounds of the column around: the scraping noises of the sledge runners; the jingling of the mugs and pots hanging from waists; the rattling of the guards' heavy equipment; the periodic talk and speculation that goes on as we walk. Eating and drinking are a matter of improvisation during the halts. Invaluable little "Tommy's Cookers" (fed continuously with tiny chips of wood or minute twists of paper) are whipped out for a tea or coffee "brew", using melted snow to boil. Hot soups from powder or even tinned stews were prepared in the longer breaks. Cheese, chocolate, biscuits or cold Spam are all eaten when hunger comes on. There is no anxiety about the lack of any German rations thanks to the Red Cross! Chunks of the excellent "Dogfood" are nibbled to keep us going. There are kindnesses at cottage doors and sometimes hot soup is offered, when our mugs are quickly detached from our belted waists for such welcomed gestures.

'Most of the guards are veterans from the Great War or were wounded on the Russian Front and they find conditions tough. One who trudges alongside us was a frostbite casualty in the east. A few guards have bicycles, not for riding but to help carry their kit while they push them. The sense of the SBO's order prohibiting escapes is generally recognised. These dangers do not deter everybody; a few do disappear to try their luck, mostly struggling back to rejoin the scattered columns. It is easy just to slip away but those who return say it is a grim experience in the desolate white wastes. We become mixed up at times with vast crowds of civilian refugees from the east, who are fleeing from their farms and homesteads; they have the very fixed idea of keeping out of Russian hands. "Kriegies" mix with the refugees; they have travelled hundreds of miles from their homes and we pity them as most are old and sick. The abler ones walk and carry heavy bundles, with young, sad-faced children around them. They have all sorts of vehicles – covered wagons, hay carts, trucks, etc – all stacked high with their household possessions. And some have their farm animals with them. The cold bites into our bones when a turn on the ropes is interrupted by an all too necessary rest break. Snow continues on and off and it persistently seems to happen that our particular part of the long column always has its breaks in an exposed position. Dried raisins prove impossible to eat because they are frozen solid in a block. Our sledge ropes are getting shorter due to the breaks.

'We've done 16km on our first day – seems like much more! There has been illness along the way. Monday, 29 January is a poor night; very cold and shivery, little sleep. It is confirmed that the temperature was minus 25–26C. A lot of stuff had to be jettisoned in the snow on our first day out but we held on to our food. The little Rolex watch for my wife has hardly left my wrist since leaving Sagan; I'm determined to get it home safely.

'We proceed through bleak open country in snow showers. It is hard going and the rest breaks become unpleasantnesses of frozen sweat and we are glad to move off again. Monotonous long stretches of road seem never-ending and there are no friendly fir woods to give some shelter when the blizzard returns. Heads down ... eyes closed to slits ... mechanically watching the steps of the man in front to avoid bumping into his sledge if he stops ... Talking becomes less coherent and deteriorates into slurring and mouths and faces become frosted. The cessation of the scraping noises of the sledge runners when we halt makes the silence of the flat snowbound landscape seem eerie in contrast; the brooding lifelessness of the deserted white wastes is only broken when a dog barks at a distant farm, or when an unseen low-flying aircraft is heard above us in the thick snow clouds. Even the distant battle sounds are missing, as if to tell us that our chances of being overtaken by the Russian advances are fading. A "brew-up" in the lee of a haystack, huddling together, chewing frozen chunks of Spam ... A kindly cottager at her wayside door silently offering ersatz coffee, eagerly accepted as it is hot ... Drinks made with cold water turning into ice before they can be drunk ... Stories of dropouts in the deep snow banks.

'Our 10,000 "Kriegies" from Luft III will have become spread out by now into many long and scattered marching columns over a wide area which, mixed up as we are from time to time with the huge numbers of refugees, represent a sort of mass migration taking place through the snowbound lanes of Poland/East Germany – all struggling westwards.

'On hearing engine noises, we peer through the blizzard and discern an airfield on our left, where tractors are working on their difficult task of trying to keep a runway serviceable. Me 109s, a Me 410 and other types are recognizable on the deck. It is very bleak here under the slate sky. An aircraft comes over, flying westwards and is so low under the cloud base as to be recognized as a Ju 52. At Freiwaldau the snow has ceased and gangs of Luftwaffe types, including women, are busily engaged in clearing the roads of snow. A woman at a roadside house gives us some lovely hot soup when a rest break luckily halts us at her door; a "Goon" officer reprimands her but, amidst our loud cheers, she stands up to him and we give her a round of applause. We hear that some "Kriegies" left the column near the bleak airfield to try their luck at the old "Kriegies" dream of pinching an aircraft.'

'By the time the prisoners arrive at Spremberg on 2 February many of the "Kriegies" feet have become saturated in the slush and they are badly handicapped with diarrhoea, which means many urgent dashes into the snow, and it persists. Here and there a cottage door opens just as they pass; a feeble glimmer of light shows and the "Kriegies" gratefully hold out their mugs for hot soup. At one door an abusive cry comes from within: "*Terrorfliegers!*" Somebody perhaps bombed out somewhere …? There are no regular rest breaks as they straggle even more into little groups who just stop as they please to rest or melt snow for a "brew-up" and perhaps to nibble a biscuit or a bit of "Dogfood". There is much stumbling and tripping over. The numbers of abandoned sledges grow and many discarded personal possessions litter the wayside with them, but the "Kriegies" carry on pulling our sledges, either hoping things will change, or kidding themselves that it is still better to drag the complaining runners on the road surface than to offload everything on to their unwilling backs. "Kriegies" and guards are all in this together. An exhausted guard throws some of his heavy equipment away and it sinks into the snow; it is retrieved for him while he groans to himself and someone loads his rifle on to a comrade's bicycle. It is a confusing nightmare in the darkness that goes on and on and can have no end, with everybody in varying levels of trouble. Reality is suspended in a timeless, deserted world. Many are in trouble with their feet and various stomach disorders.

'Spremberg seems a brisk sort of place, a good thing to bring us nearer to normality after the dark nightmare. We turn into a German Army depot and are taken into big MT sheds without any formalities like counting and searching. Here we seem to be back in a real, inhabited world where uniformed soldiers go briskly about their jobs, in welcome contrast to the white frozen – and finally slushy – wilderness of our journey. The chance of welcome showers is enjoyed and a nice hot barley soup is laid on. And a bread ration is issued. A rumour of staying here tonight proves false and the night's march worsened many ailments. We are now briefly back to something like normal eating instead of snatching what bits of food we could under the shelter of hedges, etc. The little Rolex is going fine. As we are talking about those left behind at Muskau our old Luftwaffe guards come in to tell us it is now time to march to the train. We march the few kilometres in the dark and arrive at the railhead at 1700 hours but we are put out to find that the waiting train consists of cattle trucks. Strong protests by the SBO are met with the blunt answer that there is nothing else. Protests continue and there is a delay of 1½ hours, during which time we are issued with one USA Red Cross food parcel each. We begin to climb aboard at 1830 hours amidst jokes about the old well-known tag from the 1914–18 war: 'Forty hommes or eight chevaux' (horses). But it is worse than that; we are packed in tightly and there are nearer fifty in our truck, all squeezed in with our possessions in the darkness.

'The "Goons" dismiss our stronger protests as we realise that we are to be locked in right across Germany. We are told that the stale, suffocating air would clear alright when the train is in motion; our natural functions would be dealt with by letting us out at halts along the track and water would be supplied at the same time. The matter of food rations is dealt with vaguely and the question about being locked in during air raids is also shrugged off. We are told that *"Krieg ist Krieg"* ("War is war") and *"Ordnung ist Ordnung!"* ("Orders are Orders!") Doors close, the bolts slide home; we realise we are in for a different kind of unpleasant journey, locked in and tightly packed in the darkness. The train eventually moves off to loud ironic cheers; it is 2300 hours – a long time since boarding it at 1830 hours! We quickly get some organisation going to alleviate our conditions: fat-lamps, fuelled by "Goon" margarine, are lit and hung up to relieve the blackness and nails are knocked into the walls of the truck so that some of our kit can be hung up out of the way; and chinks are enlarged into peep-holes so that we can keep check of the route on our maps. The smoky gloom caused by the lamps is better than complete darkness. It is three hours before we are let out briefly for our urgent needs and to gulp in fresh air and stretch out cramped limbs that have been entangled with each other on the filthy truck floor. The air is very bad, despite the ventilation of the train's movement, because of the stops.

'The light of the fat-lamps is invaluable but their smoke and all the smells of sickness add up to a bad atmosphere in the truck and I am lucky to spend some time keeping watch at a look-out near the doors. We doze intermittently as proper sleep is impossible; people are restless and try to turn and twist amongst the mass of limbs. Loud shouts go up whenever the train stops and we are let out at two points during the night for urgent calls of nature; it is cold squatting at the trackside. One stop becomes long enough to scrounge some hot water from a kindly signalman to make coffee. Our search for a large can for a urinal in the truck is successful – and invaluable! The can is passed round regularly and is emptied through a hole. Stomachs and bowels are suffering and there is much vomiting to add to the mess and the stinks. There are rumours galore when we are out on the track, including reports of vanishings and yet more "Peace Moves".

'We travel westwards. The train slowly proceeds: Mecklenburg, Plessa and Falkenberg, through Wilden and the Elbe is crossed at Torgau, then Eilenburg. Conditions worsen in the truck as the day passes but despite all the stinks and discomfort some of the old RAF songs and ditties roll out at intervals and there are some light-hearted pranks at trackside gatherings when we are let out on 3 February. After many halts, shuntings and reversals, through Delitzsch and into the outskirts of Halle. More bombing noises are heard around here before we move off through Halle, but someone reports that an aircraft is seen to go down in flames. We trundle on in the second night in this stinking truck; the smells get worse as those afflicted with diarrhoea have to make use of empty Red Cross boxes. And the urinal can is constantly being passed round and emptied, but it is starting to leak. Our continuous shouts during our numerous halts are disregarded and it is during this second night in the nauseous truck that one begins to lose touch with reality. It becomes another sort of nightmare that is only relieved temporarily by dozing at intervals, only to rouse up with the sickening realisation of where we are. We are locked in for twelve hours with no water, we continue to breathe the same revolting air, we handle the bits of food we try to eat with filthy fingers and we cope as best we can with the incessant calls of nature. We crawl in long slow spells through Magdeburg, Brunswick and Hildesheim with confused feelings whenever air raid sirens or bombing sounds are heard; we can only hope and pray and keep our fingers crossed, right through such well-known target areas.

'It is daylight before we breathe fresh air again. The train jolts to a standstill as we run into Hannover at 0845 hours and the doors open. A bucket of water is hastily slopped inside to us but there is no chance to climb out because the train moves off again. But it draws to a halt in only a hundred yards for a proper stop and we are let out. We urinate and squat in full view of the Hanoverians who are walking along the footpath adjacent to the track, but our needs are very urgent after being locked in since last evening at Halle – and our senses about normal decorum have become rather blunted by now. It is cold and showery but any fresh air is wonderful after the excremental misery of the truck. We scrounge some water to wash with and to slake our thirsts and eat anything from our packs that comes to hand: bread, cheese, bully beef, biscuits, dried fruit, etc and drinks made from "Klim" milk powder. And another big can is found to replace our leaky one. This longer stop is used to clean up our filthy truck until the train departs. At Verden we are very glad to quit the train when it stops briefly. Water is obtained from a factory adjoining the railway line but not enough for our needs. A sign which says: "29 km to Bremen" reminds me of a previous life when that was a target back in 1942. We hear that our destination is a naval camp at Tarmstedt and the word "camp" suggests the old type of permanence that we somehow assumed we'd finished with. Barbed wire again after so much "freedom" in all our roughing it …?

'Another spell of reversing manoeuvres; more tedious stops and starts … With all the crawling, bumping and jolting, all the shuntings and the hold-ups of the last two nights and days in the hundreds of miles across the Third Reich, how has the driver of this overloaded train been coping?

'Rotenberg comes up and we leave the main line, branching off to Zeven where we get some welcome fresh air when we have to change to a funny old small-gauge railway for the last few miles. We trundle slowly past innumerable village halts and we finally pull up at Tarmstedt Ost at 1530 hours. We dash out for urgent reasons and have to relieve ourselves in sight of onlookers, as often before. It is now raining but it is a huge relief to move about in the fresh air. We slowly assemble outside the tiny station but it transpires that Marlag und Milag Nord doesn't know about us and it isn't ready. The rain sets in as we shoulder our possessions and march off slowly in ragged formation in the darkness and the wet murk. It is 3km along this muddy track. The familiar lighting system of a PoW camp is visible as we trudge on in heavier rain and it is dawning on us that the unaccustomed freedom which has accompanied (and compensated for) our hardships is coming to an end. While the prospects of more barbed wire are not entrancing, the thoughts of shelter offer some short-term consolation in our filthy and run-down condition, after the degradation of the cattle truck days and nights.

'The lights draw nearer and when we come to a standstill at 1800 hours when the head of our shambling lines arrives at the camp the sight of huts through the glare of the camp lights offers prospects of some warmth and shelter. And there is some cheer in the encouraging things that are passed down to us, about hot showers and food to look forward to. The perimeter lights show the relentless downpour as shining needles slanting down on our backs; we are completely soaked, kit and everything. The mud is churning up badly with the passing of many weary feet in the continuous rain, as we keep picking up our belongings out of the thick mud to shuffle on a bit at a time. At 2300 hours we are still well short of the gates. Some sit dejectedly on their kit and chain smoke as the waiting goes on. Talk has died away in the passing of the hours as many reach the limits of exhaustion. Those who just lie straight down in the mud cannot get any worse now ... they are beyond caring very much as blank numbness soaks up thought and feelings... Some can take no more and are carried by others up to the camp gates for prior admittance. Wandering searchlights swivel on us at intervals to illuminate the dreary scene of exhausted airmen willing themselves to last out. Our filth from the cattle truck now has thick mud plastered over everything. I have lost my companions in this saturated chaos which is strangely lit up by the harsh glare of the perimeter lights. Somebody's batch of personal papers is trampled into the mud at my feet as we move up another yard ... An exhausted guard is moaning until his officer comes along to tear a brutal strip off him.

'The final stage of the long journey across Germany is in keeping with its preceding low points; the snows and frosts that culminated in the degrading filth of the cattle truck are now matched by the saturated numbness as we wait to enter the timeless backwater of another camp. The suction power of the squelching mud is a slight reminder for me: a taste of what my brother had to endure in the Passchendaele swamps of 1917 ...?

'Here is no heroic end to our journey, no great dramatic action such as we imagined might possibly happen; it is an inglorious shambles as the driving rain and the trampled morass blot out our senses to rock bottom in six hours of waiting right at the end – the longest wait of all long waits in the thick mud outside the camp. Not for the first time on this trip comes a feeling about the suspension of reality ... It is midnight when my part of the disintegrated column finally arrives at the gates. We are first split into separate groups of ten for admittance and taken inside a hut for searching. More waiting while we shiver after stripping off most of our horribly messed up clothing, but at least we are out of the stinging rain. Our new "Goons" go through the motions of searching us and all our kit; it proves to be a perfunctory exercise, a waste of time; there is no problem about getting any verboten stuff through. But it is unhurried and takes up time while we stand and shiver. The camp compound was previously occupied by Merchant Navy ratings who had smashed it up on leaving. The huts are in a bad state with stoves and windows broken as well as the badly leaking roofs and there are no beds. The floors are of broken bricks, all very damp. And the big piles of rubbish everywhere resemble the mess we left behind at Luft III.'

The prisoners would spend a wretched two months at Tarmstadt lashed by rain and snow showers with fuel extremely scarce and little food available. By 25 February hunger led to many scavenging the communal kitchen refuse piles for any overlooked food; the daily numbers were growing. The arrival, on 1 March by seventeen trucks carrying 34,000 American food parcels, was a life-saver for many. By day and by night, large formations of Allied aircraft overhead helped boost morale. But on Monday, 19 March the 'Goons' finally insisted on all tins being emptied of food. That Friday though there was the welcome sight of Lancasters overhead again in the morning. At 15.30 the 'Goons' dumped parcel contents on the prisoners with all tins emptied out – the equivalent of one parcel per room for them to make the best they could of the horrible mess. That March the weather turned milder and big war advances increased speculation. Rumours ran thick and fast about the possibilities of moving. By early April there was so much talk and speculation, most began going through their belongings in case they had to pack and move again. If they were to march, where would they go this time? Their parcel stock stood at 6,402 so they would not leave empty-handed! On 8 April news from RN Intelligence leaked out that the 'Goons' were going to quit and leave the prisoners there. On Monday, 9 April it was announced that they were to march at 1700 hours.

'The Senior British Officer (Canadian Group Captain Larry Wray) addressed us. The policy was go-slow; delay as much as possible to help our forces to overtake us; don't obey unless forced to; we are to play for time. (Allied troops were said to be only about twenty miles away.) The "Goons" had said that escapers would be shot; the SBO had objected and had warned the Kommandant that he would be held responsible for our safety.

'We finally left on Tuesday, 10 April after a false start on the 9th for the forced march to the Elbe via Heeslingen, Bokel, Harsfeld and Gründoldendorf. The columns soon spread out into the ragged groups that were to feature in this march and a slow pace defied efforts by the "Goons" to speed us up. Gunfire was heard to the south. The pots and pans which we'd accumulated hung from our waists like many bells around us and there was quite a clanking noise as we walked. Some of the home-made vehicles wobbled and creaked. It was the sort of misty morning that promised a fine day for our first day out. We dodged into ditches once or twice when Allied air attacks threatened but we had no trouble; targets were shot up nearby but they seemed to know what they were doing. The mist lingered in places but a fine day promised.

'We passed through Kirchtimke, Osterkirche, then Ostertimke. Celandines and anemones a picture everywhere in this beautiful countryside; lovely meadows – just like April in England. I thought back to the start of the snow march in such different circumstances! It can't be very long this time, anyway … We heard that the "Goons" planned for 20km daily – what a hope! The scheduled halts of ten minutes per hour are being stretched right out. Badenstedt at 1410, heading NE towards Hamburg direction – presumably to skirt round that big city. Warm in the lovely sunshine. Home-made vehicles showed signs of wear, wobbling and breaking down, especially the hastily made boxes on wheels. The well-made jobs seemed OK and carried everything for their small groups who were able to saunter freely along and enjoy the welcome spring sunshine. Our efforts to "buy" something kept failing today so we plodded on.

'Zeven (14km) was reached at 1830. A signpost said: "Hamburg 77 km". We kept on for another few kilometres to Heeslingen at 1900 hours to stay the night in a field. I went out bartering for our mess and traded well in the neighbourhood for eggs and bread. We'd brought all the cigarettes we possessed with us, having learnt their value outside by now. While I was away the other four were fixing up our site for the night's stay, laying on straw, water and fuel for the fire to cook with. A good fire awaited my return and "Johnny" got on with his cooking, so we ate well.

'This night in the field was the first in a series of gigantic fairground atmospheres: fires blazing; pots sizzling; clothes drying. And curious villagers crowding round. And even a background of music from a gramophone to set it off. This was a new life and the freedom of it was very acceptable after our brief experience of more barbed wire.

'There was some water shortage at first but a farm pump supplied us. Plenty of wood for fuel and good supplies of straw for sleeping but the field was rather wet in places for bedding down on. A shooting incident occurred when "Duggie" Mathieson and another Rhodesian fighter pilot were shot and wounded while taking straw. The SBO protested to the Senior German Officer and an ambulance was soon summoned to take them to Zeven Hospital. The SGO was also reminded about the RN officers killed in air attacks behind us today. He conceded that we should scatter widely for cover in such cases – giving us more opportunities for further delays ...

'A chilly night set in; misty with heavy dew later. Sleep was intermittent with the cold and dampness, despite huddling into the straw. Everything became wet through in the mists. There was a scare in the night: an aircraft dropped a photo-flash in our field quite near to us; it was like daylight, then there was a loud bang later. There was gunfire to the south before dawn as I nestled into the straw and pulled the blanket over my head.'

During Wednesday, 11 April to 15 April the column of prisoners trekked towards the Elbe again. When the Kommandant said they were to cross the river to Pinneberg, to entrain there for Denmark, the SBO enquired: 'What's the great hurry?' The 'Kriegies' often had to scatter quickly into available cover for low-flying aircraft and pitch camp in fields and barter for food in the small villages and farms, the SBO insisting that 10–12km was the daily maximum for the 'Kriegies'. The columns were by now equipped with all manner of vehicles: handcarts, prams and wheelbarrows were in service, including some creaking wrecks that required attention to keep them going. Finally, on Monday, 16 April the 'Kriegies' crossed the south bank of the river at Granz west of Hamburg, a few miles east of where Leslie Sidwell had bailed out nearly three years before.

'When our turn came to climb into one of the two ferry-boats, our party embarked on the SS *Mozart* at 1330 hours. With the low cloud in our favour, we had been watching for air activity and it had been quiet. It was a quick and pleasant journey across the Elbe; it only took fifteen minutes. From the boat we thought we could see something of the well-known docks and submarine pens upstream towards Hamburg. It was rather like a holiday excursion trip on the SS *Mozart* as we were entertained on the crossing by a local cornet player who played merrily away as if without a care in the world on a conventional trip. His repertoire included *Lily Marlene* (our voices joined in with great gusto) and, appropriately enough, a snatch of Mozart. Our boat held about sixty bods plus all our gear and we made sure that all our varied types of vehicles accompanied us! Two ferry-boats worked non-stop and they took our complete columns over in 3–4 hours. We disembarked at Blankenese at 1345 hours with no problems at all about dangers from the air.

'Blankenese looked to be another delightful holiday place with balconied houses on narrow winding streets. We'd been told to reassemble in columns on top of the climb that faced us and our little groups straggled out from the landing stage to make our way slowly there. The weather had brightened up; it was now quite sunny, warm and dusty as we passed over the cobbles in the lower part of the place.

'This attractive little resort was on the side of a cliff rising above the Elbe, with narrow little roads winding up the steep green hills. Cafes with garden terraces gave fine river views; I called in one cafe and bought a welcome glass of beer for two cigarettes; it was lovely sitting and resting there in the sunshine. And I went into a post office and bought postcards and stamps for a few cigarettes; I wrote the cards and posted them home, wondering whether they might possibly arrive there ... With the war so obviously folding up, no eyebrows were raised anywhere we ventured now. Cigarettes were the all-purpose currency for whatever was needed, no matter how bizarre our appearance looked to be out of place in this delightful spot. Blankenese was another unreal bit of the war. Some air activity had resumed with the weather improvement but the general air here seemed to be out of the war-torn world which we knew about; it had a stylish air of serenity in the sunshine today – even though it must have known much about the big raids on nearby Hamburg ...

'After the slow climb up a long, cobbled, twisting road, we flopped down on the grass near the top of the steep hill. It was hot and dusty as we sat enjoying our rest in the sunshine, chatting away to any passers-by who stopped to talk. The local police tried to stop this but our derisive cries seemed to deter them from any action and they soon left us to it. Our guards had hardly been seen since leaving Cranz but they reappeared for us to continue our journey – when we were well rested and ready to move. Our spirits had been rather lower with the actual crossing of the mighty Elbe (regarded as a "barrier" to the Denmark idea) but they picked up in the sunshine – and we'd been thankful for a peaceful river crossing ...! We talked to wounded soldiers from a nearby hospital and I spoke to a Yugoslav called Michaelovitch (?) who worked in a local bakery; we reassured him when he asked about the war with a plaintive "When will it end?"

'I liked this very old fishing village and noted the name, Blankenese, as a place to revisit. But bartering here, like Cranz, wasn't as good as earlier on. Food seemed tighter and dearer but some deals were done after some persistence, though prices were high. The rate for a bottle of schnapps was 200 cigarettes or four bars of chocolate – rather dear.

'We re-formed as the other groupings joined us and we leisurely resumed our journey. The road out of Blankenese seemed a nice prosperous area. I thought how tranquil and out-of-the-war everything looked as we strolled past well-to-do houses with large well-tended gardens with people sitting out in deckchairs, just as on a peaceful sunny day at home, with sleek blackbirds scurrying across trim lawns. The sound of cuckoos calling 5km past Blankenese heightened thoughts of the English spring we were missing … Hard to realise that the war still went on elsewhere – or that, so near to a big city, it must have reached this peaceful spot. We only did a few more kilometres before packing in for the night at Sulldorf soon after 1700 hours. With news of the Russian attacks on Berlin itself, the final end of a crumbling Third Reich looks imminent – and the thoughts of trying to get us up into Denmark were treated as a joke. Sightings of Luftwaffe aircraft had become fewer all the way from Tarmstedt.'

The 'Kriegies' journey continued through the German countryside, to Ellerbeck and Pinneberg, Tangstedt and Elmenhorst, camping in fields at night. The Allies were 30km from Hamburg; Russians going hard for Berlin; and fighting in Nuremberg. On Thursday, 19 April, Allied fighters were right down on the deck over their field at 0500 hours and the 'Kriegies' heard that the British had occupied Lüneburg. Always tired, wet through and shivering after very rough nights, the 'Kriegies' passed through Neritz in showering weather and saw much bomb damage in Bad Oldesloe in the rain. On Monday, 23 April they had reached the valley of the River Trave.

'Masses of fruit blossom, many primroses and windflowers; blackthorn in flower and tulip trees look a picture. The river was crossed and it was onward to Trave, through Lokfeld and under the Hamburg–Lübeck autobahn, which happened to be quieter at the moment. Saw Red Cross vans going south which looked to be full of German soldiers. There were some grisly reminders all around the area of the autobahn: low-level rocket beat-ups with dead bodies and rough roadside graves. Reaching the main road to Lübeck, we passed through Stubbendorf and branched off to the left to Ratzbek, via Hamberge and Hansfelde to Poggenpohl only 4km from Lübeck.

'On Tuesday 24th April the "Kriegies" rose at 0930 in time to see about 200 RAF "heavies" bombing to the southwest. A beautiful morning lifted our spirits – warm and bright. RAF Typhoons attacked a target very close to our barn at 1030. There was much flak above our heads. We had news of the expected fall of Berlin to the Russians. More and more noticeable was the absence of Luftwaffe aircraft in the skies, which meant more attention was paid to the few of their new jet fighters said to be operating from the nearby autobahn because they have no aerodromes left. How are they rearmed and maintained? We saluted their guts in impossible circumstances that can only get worse ...

'On Wednesday much Allied air activity all around us as usual, much of it close by early on. The SBO announced in the evening that we're to stay on in Poggenpohl for two days; we would then retrace our steps for a few kilometres and stay put on an estate until the end. Loud cheers at this more definite news after all the uncertainties and the rumours, although it was hoped that we wouldn't finish up too near the autobahn – a hairy and noisy place. The German jets still operated from the autobahn, despite Allied attacks to stop them.

'On Saturday, 28 April we rose early at 0640, to get ready for our move to Trenthorst, about 20km south of Lübeck. Weather dull, and showery and we didn't hang about much with breakfasting. The SBO had some wagons laid on for our kit and our mess got our belongings loaded on OK, leaving just the light stuff in the pram. We were away by 0845 to retrace some of our steps through Hansfelde and Hamberge, near Rfitzbek and crossed under the Hamburg–Lübeck autobahn again and witnessed rocket attacks very close by that left more horrible sights of the fighter beat-ups. Grim sights indeed with blood and the remains of bodies scattered everywhere. Other earlier roadside messes had been roughly cleared up with steel helmets placed on top of hastily made grave sites. The whole of the autobahn area was a very ugly scene. After crossing the Trave at Wesenberg we arrived at Trenthorst at 1400 hours. We split up on approaching into two parties with the smaller party going to the Wulmenau part, only a few kilometres away. Trenthorst was part of a huge and very modern farming estate with huge, modern barn buildings with roomy haylofts and which were very well equipped, and big herds of pedigree cattle. And around us lovely countryside with lakes and woods. Our mess of five settled into a hayloft of one of the huge barns. Saw a few rats scuttling about at first but they vanished and were hardly seen again. Chicken for supper; it was wizard – voted the best one yet. Many bods set to work to construct thatched huts in the courtyard away from the barn buildings. We decided to sleep up in a hayloft for the present but to build our own hut if we should be here long. It was very surprising to see a YMCA van drive up this evening, bringing us more food parcels, pots and pans and even sports gear. The Canadians and Americans were soon out making use of the latter at baseball/softball practice, which was punctuated by heavy gunfire noises.

'On Monday, 30 April rumours passed round of Hitler's suicide attempt and news of Berlin falling. A big surprise at 1300 hours! Nine trucks rolled up containing some 7,200 Red Cross food parcels, plus more pots and pans – and an amplifier. We'd thought there would be no more food parcels, yet here they still come! This finally assured us that we shan't go short of food here; with nearly 2,000 of us split between Trenthorst and Wulmenau, it meant at least another three weeks on normal issue. Food has gradually been becoming a lessening priority for some time now. Next day, 1 May, local gunfire and a lot of air activity woke me up at 0930 after a fitful night's sleep. There were generous issues of food parcels this morning, following the recent arrivals and we drew American parcels for our mess so we were well off for food. The skies were full of Allied aircraft all through the day. The two German jets were still operating.

'HOME BY CHRISTMAS 1945?'

The SBO again warned us of the need to stay put here, to await the arrival of Allied troops, which can't be long now. The certainty of the imminent end of the war had been setting up a growing fever of excitement in us. After all the long stretched-out phases that kept extending the war, it was hard to grasp properly that it would finally end within a day or so ... The mind wandered ahead as never before: would there be interminable red tape delays in getting us home? How would our people know of our coming? How would everything work out ...? But some "Kriegies" were not content and wanted action; they journeyed much further afield in a growing mood of freedom as many sorts of "vehicles" were 'acquired' – bicycles, cars, horses ... I obtained an old bicycle. Gunfire had been nearing us by evening but still no signs of our troops. The gunfire went on into the early hours of Wednesday, when finally, firing seemed to be nearer. Little sleep after about 0300 – all anxious to get up and about as it was sensed that today would be THE DAY! But things quietened down after breakfast but at 1230 I heard that our other section at Wulmenau had been liberated – it was any moment for us now ...!

'We gathered expectantly and the big moment soon came when a single Bren-gun carrier ("Joan-Anne") belonging to the 11th Armoured Division, 21st Army Group drove up at 1255. The driver, a Londoner, was mobbed amidst scenes of unforgettable emotion; handshakes all round; tremendous jubilation; showery weather forgotten. Even some of our hardened old cynics from early "Kriegiedom" days let go of themselves in the joy of the big moment. They seemed to shed the mental veneers which had accumulated and helped them through the difficult times. One of them next to me shed tears unashamedly ... Scout cars soon followed to confirm that we are now officially liberated! Our status had changed in a flash: no longer are we PoWs; we are now ex-PoWs! Group Captain Wray took the official surrender of the "Goon" officers and guards who were still with us and formally took over the Trenthorst estates. Three cheers were heartily called for the king, followed by three tremendous cheers for the SBO; what a moment for this cheery Canadian who had done such a great job throughout the problems of the marches! He was an outstandingly popular man for his able handling of the "Goons". A Union Jack appeared and was hoisted over the courtyard. News came that Lübeck had fallen without any trouble.

'More guards had been disappearing since early morning and all of our remaining routines went out of the window with all the unusual things that went on around us: German troops and deserters coming in to surrender; weapons to be collected and stacked; guards with bad records to be rounded up and detained. The deserters were formed into groups with some of our guards and just sent off with orders to make their own way to the nearest PoW "cage" which awaited them. Some good-natured cheering accompanied them as they marched away, loaded up with their belongings. It was "For you the war is over" in reverse now. Some were sent off to their fate with a bit of sympathy; the tough ones, including SS types who had drifted in, were to be handled by our own troops. Sporadic bursts of gunfire around us provided a background to the happenings of today.

'On Thursday, 3 May as hopes of a quick departure gradually faded, some began to wander far afield: younger ones, unlike me, lacked urgent family ties to get home so they sought amusement; cars and motor bikes were taken for joy-riding until the petrol ran out and some set out to see if they could get home under their own steam. One group acquired a Mercedes car for that purpose and were not seen again. Complaints came from the vehicle owners and there was also trouble about incidents of crashes through driving on the wrong side of the roads. Tony Burcher was out all morning and he returned at midday – proudly riding a horse! Rumours circulated: we might move tomorrow, or even today, to an aerodrome to fly home. I had everything packed – I was ready to move and I didn't leave the site; I wasn't missing anything …'

Three days' later Leslie Sidwell and many of his fellow 'Kriegies' were flown from Diepholz to Brussels Evère aerodrome to a 'wizard welcome greeting, with a band playing martial airs and lashings of food and coffee and cigarettes served by WAAFs. It was a lovely day with hot sunshine – very fitting for our homecoming day. Next day Lancasters that were to fly the former prisoners of war home finally appeared and Sidwell climbed aboard one on 156 Squadron as if in a dream sequence and he had to pinch himself to realise they were actually flying home in their own Bomber Command. 'It was a memorable moment when the Lancaster pulled up at RAF Westcott and I was one of those who went down on the knees to kiss English earth after the absent years. I was reunited with my wife on VE Night, soon after 2100 hours, amongst a street full of excited people all clamouring around us in the tremendous jubilation of the occasion. Everybody was surprised that I was sunburnt and looked so well, if a bit lean. My condition was a bonus from the outdoor life at the end. Living off the land as we did, it had been my best period for food in Germany. It was the end of an adventurous period of my life; I had survived, I could not possibly have imagined any of it when I set out so light-heartedly from Ranulf Croft, Cheylesmore in Coventry, clutching my tatty little attaché case, from the home that was destined to be bombed only a few months later.'

Postscript

The Legend that is Colditz

There is today, a thriving prisoner of war museum at Castle Colditz (Schloss Colditz), a Renaissance castle in the town of Colditz near Leipzig, Dresden and Chemnitz in the state of Saxony in Germany, between the towns of Hartha and Grimma on a hill spur over the Zwickauer Mulde, a tributary of the Elbe. After the outbreak of the Second World War, the castle was converted into a high-security Prisoner of War camp for officers who had become security or escape risks or who were regarded as particularly dangerous *volksfeindlich*, or treasonous against the people. Since the castle is situated on a rocky outcropping above the Mulde, the Germans believed it to be an ideal site for a high-security prison.

The larger outer court in front of the Kommandantur (commander's offices) had only two exits and housed a large German garrison. The prisoners lived in an adjacent courtyard in a 90ft (27m) tall building. Outside, the flat terraces that surrounded the prisoners' accommodation were watched constantly by armed sentries and surrounded by barbed wire. The prison was named Oflag IV-C (officer prison camp 4C) and was operated by the Wehrmacht. The first prisoners arrived in November 1939; they were 140 Polish officers from the September campaign who were regarded as escape risks. However, later most of them were transferred to other Oflags.

In October 1940 three Canadians – Donald Middleton, a Hampden pilot shot down on 12 April 1940; Keith Milne, a Whitley pilot who was born at Khedive, Saskatchewan, and had joined the RCAF in 1936 before transferring to the RAF; and Flight Lieutenant

THE LEGEND THAT IS COLDITZ

Howard Douglas 'Hank' Wardle, became the first RAF prisoners at Colditz.[1] In November, they were joined by the 'Laufen Six', who on 5 September 1940 had managed to get away from Oflag VIIC, Laufen Castle near Salzburg, through a tunnel. These were Captain Harry Elliott of the Irish Guards; Captain Rupert Barry (later Sir Rupert Barry); Captain Patrick R. Reid, who was captured with his Royal Army Service Corps unit, near Cassel on 27 May 1940; Captain Richard Herbert Howe MBE MC; Lieutenant Peter Allan of the Queen's Own Cameron Highlanders; and Captain Kenneth Lockwood, commanding a company of the 1st/6th Battalion of the Queen's Royal Regiment. After marching with his unit to Belgium, he was captured in the retreat to Dunkirk in May 1940. Having been recaptured, all six arrived at Colditz on 10 November, where they were soon joined by a handful of British Army officers and later by Belgian officers.

By Christmas 1940 there were sixty Polish officers, twelve Belgians, fifty French, and thirty British, a total of no more than 200 with their orderlies. The camp was home to prisoners of war from many different countries, including Poland, France, Belgium, the Netherlands, and Canada. On 24 July 1941, sixty-eight Dutch officers arrived, members of the Dutch East Indies Army, who had refused to sign a declaration that they would take no part in the war against Germany. Afterwards a number of would-be-escapees would borrow Dutch greatcoats as their disguise. When the Wehrmacht invaded the Netherlands, they were short on material for uniforms, so they confiscated anything available. The coats in Dutch field grey in particular remained unchanged in colour, since it was similar to the tone already in use by the Germans, so

---

1. Wardle, a Canadian who like Milne joined the RAF just before the war, was flying a Fairey Battle when he was shot down near Kreilsheim, Germany, on 20 April 1940. Wardle bailed out and was captured soon after landing but Sergeant Edward Davidson and AC1 Albert Bailey were killed. Wardle was first taken to Crailsheim and then Dulag Luft before transfer to Oflag IXA (Spangenberg).

these greatcoats would be nearly identical with very minor alterations. In February 1941, 200 French officers arrived. A number of the French demanded that French Jewish officers be segregated from them and the camp commander obliged; they were moved to the attics. By the end of July 1941, there were more than 500 officers: over 250 French, 150 Polish, 50 British and Commonwealth, 2 Yugoslavian and the 68 Dutch. In May 1943, the Wehrmacht High Command decided that Colditz should house only Americans and Commonwealth. In June the Dutch were moved out, followed shortly thereafter by the Poles and Belgians. The final French group left on 12 July 1943. By the end of July there were a few Free French officers, and 228 Commonwealth officers including Britons, Canadians, Australians, New Zealanders, South Africans, Irish, and one Indian.

Although Colditz was considered a high-security prison, it had one of the greatest records of successful escape attempts, probably due to the general nature of the prisoners that were sent there. Previously most had attempted escape from other prisons and were transferred to Colditz because the castle was thought to be escape-proof. Notable among the *prominente* (German for 'celebrities') and the more notable inmates, were: Lieutenant Colonel David Stirling, founder of the Special Air Service (SAS); Captain Charles Upham VC*, 20th Battalion, the only fighting soldier to be awarded the Victoria Cross twice; Colonel William Schaefer, who graduated from the US Military Academy at West Point, Class of 1924; General Tadeusz Bór-Komorowski, Head of Polish Underground Army; General Jean Flavigny, notable tank Commander from the Battle of France; legless RAF ace Group Captain Douglas Bader; Captain Micky Burn, No. 2 Commando, journalist and writer; Lieutenant Charles, 51st (Highland) Division, 3rd Marquess of Linlithgow; and 2nd Lieutenant Desmond Llewelyn, Royal Welch Fusiliers, later known as the actor who played 'Q' in seventeen James Bond films.

Lieutenant Airey Middleton Sheffield Neave, Royal Artillery (later Lieutenant Colonel and Conservative MP) the first British officer to escape from Colditz Castle, was wounded during the defence of Calais and captured on 26 May 1940. After months in a hospital in Lille and still suffering from his wounds, Neave was sent to Oflag IXA (Spangenberg) until in March 1941 he was moved to Stalag XXA near Thorn in Poland, where he managed to escape with Norman Forbes, a fellow prisoner in April 1941. They were captured near Iłów while trying to enter Soviet-controlled Poland and were briefly in the hands of the Gestapo before they were sent to Colditz that May. For his first escape attempt from Colditz on 28 August Neave disguised himself as a German NCO but he failed to get out of the main gate as his hastily contrived German uniform (made from a Polish army tunic and cap painted with scenery paint) was rendered bright green under the prison searchlights. On 5 January 1942, again disguised as a German officer but this time with Dutch Lieutenant Toni Luteyn, they made a quick exit from a theatrical production using the trap door beneath the stage. By train and on foot they travelled to Leipzig and Ulm and finally reached the border to Switzerland near Singen via France, Spain and Gibraltar, in just four days. It was not until 14 April that Neave was suddenly summoned to Geneva to meet a mysterious man at the station. Over drinks, the man explained that Neave was to escape over the Swiss border the next day with Captain Hugh Austin Woollatt, late of the 2nd Battalion, Lancashire Fusiliers, who was captured with his carrier platoon at the L'Escaut Canal on 22 May 1940. Early next morning Neave and Woollatt were taken to a small cemetery where the border was pointed out to them. They were to cross the wire and stand by a signpost to Annemasse, where they would be collected. The arrangements worked perfectly and the two men were delivered safely to Louis Nouveau and the Pat O'Leary organisation in Marseille.

Woollatt and Neave arrived at Louis Nouveau's on 16 April where (according to Neave's book *They Have Their Exits*) they stayed for a week. On about 23 April they were taken to Toulouse, where they stayed another week at the Hotel de Paris before being taken to Perpignan. They (with others) were taken across the Pyrenees and delivered to the British Consulate in Barcelona courtesy of the Ponzan-Vidal organisation. On 12 May 1942, shortly after his return to England, Neave was decorated with the Military Cross. Neave was recruited as an intelligence officer for MI9, supporting underground escape organisations, such as the Pat O'Leary Line and Comet Line in occupied Europe, with equipment, agents, and money; assisting downed Allied airmen and other Allied military personnel to evade and escape capture by the Germans.[2]

Squadron Leader Brian Paddon was shot down flying a Bristol Blenheim on 40 Squadron during an attack at St-Valéry-en-Caux on 6 June 1940 during the Battle of France. After passing through the interrogation and transit camp of Dulag Luft, he was first sent to Oflag IX-A/H at Spangenberg, before shortly afterwards leaving for Stalag Luft I at Barth. He arrived there on 12 July 1940, where he became the Senior British Officer. After several escape attempts from various camps, he was sent to Colditz, arriving there on 14 May 1941 with three other officers, including Airey Neave. After several more attempts to escape, on 11 June 1942, Paddon was sent to a court martial at Stalag XX-A for insulting a German officer during one of his previous escape attempts. However, he managed to escape from his cell, and with the aid of other British prisoners of war, left the camp with a work party, slipped away and travelled to Danzig. He stowed away on a Swedish ship and successfully reached neutral Sweden on 18 June. He returned to the UK on 6 August 1942. He was awarded the DSO and promoted to group captain. He was also awarded the DFC.

---

2. On 30 March 1979 Airey Neave DSO OBE MC TD, member of Parliament for Abingdon since 30 June 1953 and appointed Shadow Secretary of State for Northern Ireland in February 1975, lost both legs in the explosion of a car bomb detonated by the IRA as he drove out of the Palace of Westminster car park. He died of his wounds at Westminster Hospital an hour after being rescued from the wreckage. He was 63 years old.

THE LEGEND THAT IS COLDITZ

Squadron Leader Peter David Tunstall holds the record for the most time spent by an Allied PoW in solitary confinement. Tunstall piloted Hampden bombers on operations over France during and after the British retreat to Dunkirk. He was captured on the night of 26–27 August 1940, when, due to a wireless failure, his aircraft became lost and crash-landed on the Dutch coast. When a German officer reminded him that his war was over, Tunstall responded: 'It damn well is not.' As far as he was concerned, a different type of war had started. His first duty was to escape, the second was to be 'as big a bloody nuisance as possible to the enemy'. He was initially sent to a PoW camp in Poland. After trying to escape dressed as a German NCO he was transferred to Spangenberg Castle. It was during this incarceration that Tunstall, along with Eustace Newborn and Flying Officer Dominic Bruce, came up with the escape plan known as 'the Swiss Commission'. The escape attempt has gone down as one of the most audacious of the war. Using uniforms found in the castle and suits made from uniforms, the three PoWs simply walked out of the camp during an inspection by the Swiss Red Cross. They spent ten days at large before being recaptured. In another escape, Bruce – known as the 'medium-sized man' – hid in one of the 3ft-square tea chests given to prisoners to stow personal belongings. Guards carried the chest to an attic, where Bruce broke out and then used a rope to escape through a window. He got as far as the port of Gdansk, 400 miles away, before he was recaptured while trying to board a Swedish freighter. He was returned to Colditz, where he spent the next eight months in solitary confinement. 'I kept trying because it was fun,' he once said of his unsuccessful escape attempts. 'It gave you a feeling like winning the football pools or hitting the jackpot. And, most importantly of all, I knew it got up the Germans' noses.' Once he left behind a message for his captors that read: 'The air in Colditz no longer pleases me. Goodbye!'

It has been argued that Bruce and Tunstall were the original innovators of the wooden horse escape technique. In March 1942 the Germans transferred them to Colditz (Bruce having been caught attempting to hijack a German aircraft), where they began digging an escape route with a wooden horse tunnel from inside the gymnasium. The horse was placed roughly 4ft from the wall that separated the gym from the moat. The digging was a very slow process as it required the removal of spoil, bricks and stone work, and was aided by other prisoners distracting the guards. Later they were joined by a syndicate who were promised a second go if they escaped undiscovered. But when Bruce and Tunstall noted the slow progress, they left the digging to the other team. The tunnel almost reached completion but unfortunately the diggers were caught when a guard become suspicious at the large stones that were accumulating outside the gym. The guard then called a search and found the tunnel.

At Colditz Tunstall and Bruce refined their skills in the art of 'goon baiting'. By 1941 Bruce had been 9 Squadron's Navigation and Bombing Leader. A notorious prankster with a wicked sense of humour, on the bomb run over Berlin in a Wellington he persuaded the pilot to descend to 500ft. Bruce climbed down into the now empty bomb bay, hand cranked the doors open, sat on the bomb rack and threw a lit distress flare out of the 'Wimpy'. When asked later why, he answered, 'Because I've always wanted to see the Unter den Linden lit up at night.' He has been described as 'the most ingenious escaper' of the Second World War. In all he made seventeen attempts at escaping from PoW camps and he was awarded the Military Cross.

Tunstall derived most pride from a system he devised to convey information back to London. Coded messages were written on tracing paper and concealed in letters and photographs that the PoWs sent to their relatives, who then passed them on to MI9, the Military Intelligence Directorate at the War Office.

Pierre Mairesse-Lebrun, a French Army cavalry captain who served in the 4th Regiment, Chasseurs de l'Afrique, was captured during the fall of France. Before arriving at Colditz he had already escaped twice from camps and had reached Switzerland on the first occasion without realising; drifting back to the German side and being arrested by a patrol. He made his first escape from Colditz on 9 June 1941 by climbing into the rafters of an open-sided pavilion in the middle of the park used for exercise. Fellow PoWs had created a series of innocent-looking diversions to enable Lebrun to make the move without being seen by the guards. He was able to hide himself away until after the exercise party had left the park and was not detected by the dogs sent in for a final check of the area. Mairesse-Lebrun walked the 6 miles to Grossbothen to catch a train to Leipzig. All was going well until he tried to pay for his ticket. The old blue 100-mark note was out of date as it was from 1924 during the reign of King Wilhelm II. Mairesse-Lebrun was taken to the stationmaster's office and detained there before being returned to Colditz.

Mairesse-Lebrun escaped successfully on 2 July 1941. After a walk in the park all PoWs gathered to be counted and be escorted back to the main castle. At this moment all guards, who stood around the park fences, also returned to the park entrance, leaving the back fences unguarded. Lebrun and Lieutenant Pierre Odry, despite persistent abdominal pain with a possible grumbling appendix/appendicitis, used this opportunity to leave the group and together they ran to the fence at the backside of the park. Odry cupped hands and catapulted Mairesse-Lebrun over the fence, who then ran in a zigzag towards the park wall and scaled it. The German guards were so stunned that they did nothing initially; when they recovered, they started shooting without success. Still in his sports clothes, Lebrun hid in a field, stole a bicycle and via Vichy France reached Switzerland in just eight days. In December 1941 Lebrun went to Spain, where he was arrested. He tried to escape again but fractured his spine, paralysing his legs.[3]

After Mairesse-Lebrun's escape from the park prisoners in solitary confinement took their exercise on the north-west terrace. On 11 May

---

3. Odry later escaped while returning from Elsterhorst hospital on 14 October 1941 and made a successful home run.

1943 six prisoners were in solitary confinement. They were taken out into the terrace for an hour every day to get fresh air. To this end they were led through the door on the night. After Flight Lieutenant Donald Sutherland Thom[4] had passed through the door, he suddenly leapt over the terrace's balustrade and grabbed hold of the crossbars in the windows of the guard room. He dropped to the bars of the lower window, which he held for a moment before dropping to the ground. As the guards opened fire on him, he climbed over two barbed-wire fences and then jumped down into the park. He ran into the woods before being stopped by coils of wire and being apprehended. In August 1941 Thom and Lieutenant John R. 'Bertie' Boustead, a thin, 6ft Seaforth Highlander, tried to escape from the park dressed in sports gear like members of the Hitler Youth. But they came across a German sergeant, who gave them a good dressing down because they had failed to salute him properly. The game was up when they were unable to answer his questions. That same month, on 15 August, two Dutch naval lieutenants, Etienne Henri 'Hans' Larive MWO, DSC* and Francis Steinmetz hid inside a shaft they had discovered in the park. Their absence initially went unnoticed by the Germans because during roll call that evening they were replaced by two dummies. Under the cover of night, Larive and Steinmetz climbed out of the shaft and escaped, becoming the first Dutch prisoners to do so. By skilfully making the screwed-down manhole cover look as if it were still intact, they enabled the route to be used again in September when their fellow countrymen, Major Cornelis Giebel and 2nd Lieutenant Oscar Drijber, escaped. The shaft was finally exposed when a British and a Polish officer were seen climbing into it by guards.

Imprisoned officers were allowed to use the inner courtyard for a few hours during the day. Weather permitting, they could stroll around, talk to each other and even hold and attend language classes.

---

4. Thom was piloting a Hurricane of 1 Squadron when he was shot down by AA on 25 May 1940.

THE LEGEND THAT IS COLDITZ

The German guards summoned all the prisoners to roll call every day regardless of their nationality. If it transpired that someone was missing, the PoWs were counted again and again and their names called out until the missing person was identified. The courtyard was also used for numerous volleyball, football and stoolball matches. The version of stoolball played was a rather vicious form of rugby dreamed up by British prisoners. Two stools were placed at opposite ends of the yard. Points were scored by getting past the goalkeeper and touching the stool of the opposing team. 'Two sides, consisting of any number of players, and often as many as thirty a side. There was a half time when everybody was too tired to continue.'[5]

Over a period of eight months starting in 1941, a long, intricate tunnel was dug beneath the chapel. The French builders used an old shaft in the tower clock in which the clock weights had once been suspended. The French quarters were located near the clock and the shaft led down to the basement. The prisoners began digging their own shaft in the wine cellar, breaking through the Romanesque foundations of the chapel. Their tunnel then ascended and wound its way beneath the chapel floor from west to east. The aim was to reach ground level outside on the terrace east of the castle. When the tunnel was discovered by guards on 16 January 1942, a section 44m long had already been completed. Just a few more metres and the French officers would have achieved their objective. The tunnel was filled in again by the Germans. The shaft was reopened bit by bit between 1989 and 2012. Nearly all the tunnel can now be viewed again in the wine cellar and the chapel. The French officers included Lieutenants R. Madin, J. Paille and Bernard Cazaumayou. At least six other PoWs were involved but their names are unknown.

In May 1941, Polish Lieutenants Miki Surmanowicz and Mietek Chmiel were discovered in the locked attic of the theatre building.

---

5. As described by Pat Reid in his book *The Colditz Story.*

They were placed in solitary confinement in the cellar – from where they launched another escape attempt. They picked the locks of their cells and entered the courtyard, where Polish PoWs lowered a rope and hoisted Surmanowicz and Chmiel up onto a narrow ledge. They gingerly made their way to the guardhouse (now the building housing the Escape Museum) before climbing down a rope from the gable window in the attic. After a while the guards were alarmed by the sound of shoes scraping against the wall and apprehended the would-be escapees. Pat Reid assisted in many escape attempts, some successful, until April 1942, when he was replaced as Escape Officer by Captain 'Dick' Howe. He wrote about Surmanowicz in *The Colditz Story*, saying: 'The fire that burnt in his soul showed only in his eyes, which glowed with fanatical ardour,' and that he was the 'most daredevil Polish officer at Colditz'. Surmanowicz taught Reid how to pick locks, and being a skilled mechanic, he made more than fifty compasses to help other PoWs in their escape attempts.

The first 'celebrity prisoner', 24-year-old journalist Giles Samuel Bertram Romilly, was imprisoned at Colditz in May 1940, having been captured in Narvik in Norway while working for the *Daily Express*. Romilly was also a nephew of Winston Churchill's wife, Clementine. Adolf Hitler himself had specified that Romilly was to be treated with the utmost care and he was the first prisoner of the war to be classified by the Germans as a 'Prominenter' – a well-connected PoW who was therefore a potential hostage. Romilly used this position to his advantage and caused trouble by issuing complaints at every conceivable annoyance. In particular, he took offence to the noise created by the boots of his guard outside his door, which he said prevented him from sleeping. Following a visit from the Red Cross, a red carpet was placed outside his door to dull the sound. When French and Belgian prisoners were being moved to Lübeck in July 1943, Romilly hid in a transport crate and reached Colditz railway station along with the PoWs' baggage. The crates were weighed on scales (now on display in the museum), but after

Romilly's crate had been weighed, it was turned upside down. When he climbed out, Romilly was arrested by a guard. He did successfully escape, however, with two Dutch officers, in April 1945, while the Prominente were being moved to Oflag VII-D, Tittmoning Castle, when all three men abseiled down the castle walls.

On 5 April 1943, 31-year-old Flight Lieutenant John William 'Jack' Best, a pilot whose aircraft ran out of fuel off the coast of Greece in 1941 and was captured, and 30-year-old Captain Edward Michael Harvey, a naval officer, were missing at roll call. In fact, the two Englishmen had merely tricked the Germans into believing that they had escaped and were instead hiding day and night in the castle. Having dug a tunnel under the pulpit in the chapel, they eventually expanded it into a hiding place where they hid for 352 days. These 'ghost' prisoners emerged during roll call to cover for prisoners who really had escaped. Best attempted escape several times but was recaptured. When eventually Harvey was caught just outside the castle walls, the German High Command in Berlin refused to believe the story of the 'Ghosts' and insisted that, after escaping the previous year, they must have returned to Colditz of their own accord. Oberstleutnant Gerhard Prawitt, the camp commandant indignantly refuted the suggestion saying, 'What do they think this place is; a damned hotel, where people come and go as they please!'

About midnight on 2 September 1943 the figure of a grandiosely moustachioed Stabs Feldwebel (staff sergeant) purporting to be Fritz Rothenberger, whom the prisoners had nicknamed 'Franz Josef', appeared at the eastern gate with two sentries. Claiming the camp had received an air-raid warning, he relieved the two sentries on duty at the gate early, replacing them with his own. For reasons he could not explain later, the second relieved sentry asked for Franz Josef's pass. It seemed to be in order, but 'Franz Josef' did not know the password when asked. The sentry pressed his warning bell. A German corporal appeared and demanded 'Franz Josef's revolver. A scuffle apparently ensued, and the corporal shot 'Franz Josef'. 'Good God,' cried one of the sentries. 'You've shot our sergeant major.'

But no: it was 25-year-old Lieutenant Albert Michael Sinclair RAF, whose red hair and audacity had earned him the title among the Germans of 'Der Rote Fuchs' – 'the Red Fox'.[6] Sinclair survived and went on to attempt two other escapes. In January 1944, Best escaped from the castle with Lieutenant Michael Sinclair. This 'sixty-second escape' was preceded by five months of painstaking preparation. Sinclair, and Best, used the short period before the searchlights were turned on to climb down a rope from the windows of the prisoners' quarters to the west terrace, from where they made their way to the town. They were recaptured near the Dutch border in Rheine.[7] Shortly afterwards, Mike Harvey and Flight Lieutenant Vincent 'Bush' Parker, a Spitfire pilot who had been shot down in the English Channel on 15 August 1940, descended from the theatre building and hid in the basement, but they were discovered when they came out.

After four hours in the water, Parker was picked up by an E-boat and held in various PoW camps, where he was continuously involved in escape attempts. He was particularly interested in magic and sleight of hand, and for a time he had been an assistant to a magician called 'the Great Levante', from whom he learned various methods of escapology.

---

6. Educated at Winchester College, Sinclair played for the college cricket XI at Lords. He went on to study History and Modern Languages at Trinity College, Cambridge. Later, this linguistic ability and knowledge was to prove invaluable. Commissioned into the 2nd Battalion, The King's Royal Rifle Corps, in July 1939, he was captured in northern France and sent to Stalag XXI-D (Poznań) in Poland.

7. The two failed attempts by Best and Harvey to escape revealed that they had managed to conceal themselves undiscovered in the castle for almost a year. (The hiding place of the 'ghost' prisoners can be seen today in the castle chapel). On 25 September 1944, without anyone knowing his plans, Sinclair suddenly leapt over the fence while on the exercise walk in the park. Perhaps he thought he could get through the main wall 150 yards downhill, where a stream flowed beneath it, but a grid covered the opening. Sentries shot him dead and the Germans buried him in the Colditz military cemetery with full honours.

Sent eventually to Colditz, in spring 1943, 'Bush' Parker was involved in his sixth tunnel escape attempt, having previously dug two at Dulag Luft (Oberursel), two at Stalag Luft I and one at Stalag Luft III. As well as making at least two escape attempts himself, he was involved in most of the other schemes because of his uncanny ability to pick even the hardest lock. He was able to get the other inmates into parts of the castle that the Germans thought was totally inaccessible.[8]

However, Harvey and Parker were not the first British PoWs at the camp, for they received a jubilant welcome from three officers of the Royal Air Force – not to mention 150 Poles. Pat Reid described this moment in his book *The Colditz Story*. '[The courtyard] was an unspeakably grisly place, made no less so by the pallid faces, which we noticed peering at us through bars. There was not a sound in the courtyard. It was if we were entering some ghostly ruin. Footsteps echoed and the German words of command seemed distorted out of reality. I had reached the stage of commending my soul to the Almighty when the faces behind the bars suddenly took on life; eyes shone, teeth flashed from behind unkempt beards and words passed backwards into the inner depths: 'Anglicy! Anglicy!' Heads crowded each other out behind tiny barred windows … From every other window that we could see there were jostling heads, laughing and cheering … We breathed again. We were among friends. They were Polish officers.'

---

8. Vincent 'Bush' Parker was born Vincent Wheatley on 11 February in Chester-le-Street. When Vincent's mother died suddenly at the age of 26, he was formally adopted by Lydia's sister Edith, who was married to John Parker and hence his name changed to Vincent Parker. Vincent's new family then emigrated to a new life in Australia. However, upon arrival it was found that the house and place of work for John Parker had been destroyed a few days before by a typhoon. John managed to obtain temporary work on the railways, but eventually the family settled in Purono, North Queensland, when Edith became station mistress. Only eight months after being released from Colditz, Vincent was killed during flight training on the Hawker Tempest V when he crashed to his death in a field not far from his airbase. See *'Bush' Parker: An Australian Battle of Britain Pilot in Colditz* (2007) by Colin Burgess.

Escape Statistics

Between 1941 and 1944, about 300 attempts were made to break out of Colditz and sixteen officers managed to escape, with a further fifteen escaping from outside the castle. After a first escape attempt from a prison camp in occupied Poland, Lieutenant Alain Le Ray, a keen alpinist in the French mountain infantry when wounded and captured by the Germans in June 1940, was transferred to Oflag IV-C. There he became the first PoW to successfully escape from Colditz Castle, on 12 April 1941. After hiding in a cellar of a house that stood along the park path, Le Ray climbed over the park fence and disappeared. He eventually made it safely to Switzerland. Three more French escapes were then followed by Hans Larive and Francis Steinmetz from the Netherlands, who fled by hiding in the well in the exercise park. In August 1941, Lieutenant Kroner became the only Polish officer to break out. The first British 'home run' was Airey Neave on 5 January 1942. Three months later, Belgian Captain Louis Rémy followed suit. The final successful escape took place in May 1944 when four Britons (Harry Elliot, Flight Lieutenant Francis 'Errol' Flinn, James Barnett and Micky Wynn[9]) feigned illness and escaped from a hospital.[10]

---

9. Robert Charles Michael Vaughan Wynn, 7th Baron Newborough, DSC (24 April 1917–11 October 1998) was a British peer and Royal Naval Volunteer Reserve officer who played a decisive role during the St-Nazaire raid in 1942, in which he commanded a Motor Torpedo Boat. Captured after his boat had to be abandoned, he was sent to Colditz after an escape attempt.
10. Indian RAMC Captain Birendra Nath Mazumdar MD was the only Indian in Colditz. He went on a hunger strike to have himself transferred into an Indian-only camp. His wish was granted three weeks later and he escaped from that camp to France and reached Switzerland in 1944 with the aid of the French Resistance.

THE LEGEND THAT IS COLDITZ

The PoWs viewed the attempts to escape by different nationalities with sporting rivalry:

	Successes	Failures
France	12	12
Great Britain	11	109
Holland	7	17
Poland	1	17
Belgium	1	

Successful Escapes

> 11.4.1941 Lieutenant Alain Le Ray – First PoW ever to escape from Colditz. He hid in a terraced house in the park during a game of football.
>
> 31.5.1941 Lieutenant René Collin – Hid in the rafters of the summer house in the park during exercise until dark and slipped away. Made it back to France.
>
> 2.7.1941 Lieutenant Pierre Marie Jean-Baptiste Mairesse-Lebrun – From the park. He reached Switzerland in eight days on a stolen bicycle.
>
> 8.7.1941 Lieutenant Tatischeff[11] – From Schutzenhaus prison building about half a mile from the castle.
>
> 15.8.1941 Lieutenants Etienne Henri 'Hans' Larive and Franz Steinmetz – Hid under a manhole cover in the exercise enclosure, emerged after nightfall, took a train to Gottmadingen, and reached Switzerland in three days.
>
> 20.8.1941 Polish Lieutenant Kroner – Transferred to Koningswartha Hospital, where he jumped out of a window.

---

11. Lieutenant Tatischeff was a French White Russian.

> 19.9.1941 Major Cornelis Giebel and Lieutenant Oscar Drijber – From the well in the park using the same method as Steinmetz.
>
> 25.9.1941 Lieutenant André Boucheron – From a military hospital. Then after his arrest, from a prison cell in Düsseldorf.
>
> 4.10.1941 Lieutenant Pierre Odry – While returning from Elsterhorst hospital.
>
> 17.12.1941 Lieutenants Jacques Durand-Hornus, Guy de Frondeville and Jacques Prot – While visiting the dentist in the town.
>
> 5.1.1942 Lieutenant Airey Neave and Lieutenant Abraham Pierre Tony Luteijn – From the room beneath the theatre stage.
>
> 26.4.1942 Captain Louis Rémy – Escaped from Gnaschwitz military hospital. His three companions were captured, but he reached Algeciras by boat, and later Britain.
>
> 11.6.1942 Squadron Leader Brian Paddon – Escaped to Sweden via Danzig from a cell in Thorn, where he had been sent for court martial.
>
> 25.6.1942 Lieutenant Raymond Bouillez – Sent for court martial in Stuttgart, jumped train but found unconscious next to tracks, sent to hospital and escaped from there.
>
> 9.9.1942 Flight Lieutenants Hedley Fowler and Damiaen J. van Doorninck – From Stabs Feldwebel (Staff Sgt) Gebhardt's office.

Flight Lieutenant Hedley Neville 'Bill' Fowler, a Hurricane pilot, was shot down on 15 May 1940 near Fumay, just over the Belgian border. He was captured the next day by a German armoured unit and driven to Dulag Luft at Oberursel. On 5 June Fowler and nineteen other officers was sent to Oflag IIA (Prenzlau), a Polish camp near Stettin. On 5 July Fowler was transferred to Stalag

Luft I (Barth) on the Baltic coast. Following his first escape on 5 November, when he got as far as the docks at Sassnitz in an attempt to stow away on a boat to Sweden, he was sent to Oflag IVC at Colditz on 1 December 1941. Fowler joined Lieutenant Geoffrey Wardle RN, Captain 'Lulu' Lawton and three Dutch officers: Damiaen Joan van Doorninck,[12] 2nd Lieutenant H. G. Donkers and Lieutenant Bates, in a scheme to dig a tunnel from the Stabsfeldwebel's office to a clothing store. They planned to enter the store at night and leave in disguise the following morning. Van Doorninck and Donkers would dress as a German officer and Donkers as a German NCO because they were both fluent in German. The other four were to dress as Polish prisoners. Early on the morning of 9 September 1942, Donkers and van Doorninck and the other four as a Polish work party duly marched out of Colditz to the nearby woods, where they destroyed their uniforms and donned civilian clothes. Then they split into three Anglo-Dutch pairs. Wardle, Donkers, Lawton and Bates were captured within 5 miles of Colditz. Fowler and Van Doorninck, meanwhile, headed for Switzerland via Stuttgart. They walked the 31km south to Penig, where they caught a train to Plauen and then later that evening, another train to Stuttgart, where they stayed overnight at a hotel. Next day they went on to Tuttlingen and walked the final 25 or so kilometres to the Swiss border, crossing near Ramsen in the early hours of 13 September. After a few days of questioning by the Swiss, the two escapers were sent to Berne, where they reported to their respective legations.

On the night of 14–15 October 1942, Pat Reid, along with Major Ronald Littledale, Lieutenant Commander William L. Stephens

---

12. In May 1940 he was aide de camp to the Dutch supreme commander, General Henri Winkelman. He refused to give his word of honour not to harm German interest and became a PoW.

RNVR, and Flight Lieutenant 'Hank' Wardle,[13] cut through the bars on a window in the prisoners' kitchen and climbed out onto the flat roof of the German kitchen, which led to the outer courtyard, then through the carpenter's store and down three levels of the old moat to a road which led out of the camp. Most of the route could not be reconnoitred in advance since it was brightly lit and easily seen by the German sentries. Distraction of the guards by other prisoners allowed the escapers to enter the kitchen and then they broke their way through the various barriers using tools either acquired or made in the camp. At five o'clock on the morning of 15 October the four escapers were outside the castle walls, at which point they split into two pairs. They entered a storage cellar under the Kommandantur (Commandant's HQ), crawled out through a narrow air shaft leading to the dry moat, and exited through the park. They split into pairs, with Reid and Wardle disguised as Flemish workmen travelling by train to Tuttlingen, near the Swiss border, via Zwickau and Munich. They crossed the border on the evening of 18 October. Stephens and Littledale also travelled to Tuttlingen by train, via Chemnitz,

---

13. Lieutenant Commander William L. Stephens RNVR was commanding HMML 192 when it was sunk at Saint Nazaire on 28 March 1942. Stephens and his crew were captured immediately and along with the other prisoners from St-Nazaire, sent to Stalag 133 at Rennes. In April, Stephens was sent to the Naval PoW camp of Milag Nord (for Merchant Seaman) and then to Marlag (for Royal Naval personnel) at Westertimke near Bremen. On 25 June he was moved to a camp that was still under construction at Bremervorde and on 24 July to Stalag VIIIB at Lamsdorf. On 1 September Stephens was moved to Oflag IVC at Colditz Castle. Major Ronald B. Littledale was captured at Calais on 26 May 1940. He was a prisoner at Stalag VIIC (Laufen) from June 1940 to March 1941, when he was moved to Stalag XXID (Posen). Following two escapes, one from Posen in May 1941 (he was recaptured on 17 November) and the second in January 1942 from the train back from Vienna where he had been held for six weeks following his first escape, he was sent to Colditz in July 1942.

Nuremberg and Stuttgart, then followed Reid and Wardle across the border in the early hours of 20 October.[14]

Ronald Littledale was the first of his group of four Colditz escapers to get back to England. He left Switzerland on 25 January 1943 with Hedley Fowler. Fowler left Gibraltar by air for Hendon on 27 March and Littledale left Lisbon by air for Whitchurch (Bristol) on 24 May 1943.[15] For security reasons, Bill Fowler was unable to divulge the details of his escape. When his father asked him how he did it, he simply replied, 'I dug a hole'. For his escape, Fowler was awarded a Military Cross in 1943 and by then he had been promoted to squadron leader. He was killed on active service, testing a Hawker Typhoon on 26 March 1944. He was 27 years old. Howard Wardle left Switzerland on 9 December 1943. After various false starts he finally crossed the Pyrenees with a party of Dutchmen on about 18 December and left Gibraltar by air for Whitchurch on 5 February 1944. William Stephens left Switzerland on 5 June 1944 with RAF evader Sergeant Edwin Worsdale and journeyed across France. In Toulouse they were joined by Flight Lieutenant Adolphe Duchesne RCAF and the three men crossed the Pyrenees that month. Stephens and Worsdale left Gibraltar by air for Whitchurch on 10 July 1944.

One escape scheme at Colditz even included a glider, the 'Colditz Cock', that was built and kept in a remote portion of the castle's attic during the winter of 1944–45. The glider was never used, as the camp

---

14. Reid remained in Switzerland until after the end of the war, serving as an Assistant Military Attaché in Bern from 9 March 1943 until early 1946. Reid went on to write multiple works on the living conditions and various escape attempts at Colditz from 1940 to 1945: *The Colditz Story* and *The Latter Days at Colditz*. In the early 1970s, he served as a technical consultant for a BBC television series featuring David McCallum, Edward Hardwicke and Robert Wagner that focused on life at Colditz. Major Pat Reid MBE MC died on 22 May 1990.
15. Lieutenant Colonel Littledale was commanding the 2nd Battalion, King's Royal Rifles when he was killed in action on 1 September 1944; aged 42.

was liberated not long after its completion. However, the glider was then brought down from the hidden workshop to the attic below and assembled for the prisoners to see. It was at this time that the only known photograph of it was taken. For some time after the war the glider was regarded as either a myth or tall story, as there was no solid proof that it had existed and Colditz was then in the Soviet Occupation Zone. Bill Goldfinch, however, took home the drawings he had made when designing the glider and when the single photograph finally surfaced, the story was taken seriously.[16]

During 1999, a full-sized replica of the glider was commissioned by Channel 4 Television in the UK and was built by Southdown Aviation Ltd at Lasham airfield, closely following Goldfinch's drawings. Watched by several of the former prisoners of war who worked on the original, it was test flown at RAF Odiham during 2000. The escape plan could have worked. In 2012, Channel 4 commissioned a team of engineers and carpenters to build another full-sized replica of the glider at Colditz Castle, and launch it (unmanned) from the same roof as had been planned for the original. The radio-controlled replica made it safely across the river and landed in a meadow 180m below. In the 1990s a quarter-scale model arrived at Colditz Castle. A full-sized replica and an exhibition about the glider can now be visited in the attic.

On 23 August 1944 Colditz received its first Americans: 49-year-old Colonel Florimund Joseph DuSossoit Duke of the Office of Strategic Services (OSS) – the oldest American paratrooper of the war; Captain Guy Nunn, and Alfred Suarez. On 15 March all three counter-intelligence operatives had parachuted into Hungary near the Yugoslav border in Operation 'Sparrow' after the prime minister of Hungary dispatched an emissary to OSS Bern to establish

---

16. Although the 'Colditz Cock' never flew, the concept was fictionalised, depicting a successful flight and escape, in the 1971 TV movie *The Birdmen* starring Doug McClure, Chuck Connors, René Auberjonois, and Richard Basehart.

THE LEGEND THAT IS COLDITZ

a confidential line of communication with the United States. The Hungarians were seeking an end to their relationship with the Nazis and hoped Washington would guarantee their sovereignty in the face of a Soviet takeover of their country. Their cover story was that they were part of a military mission heading for Tito's partisans but their plane was hit by flak and they were forced to bail out over Hungary. However, the Gestapo uncovered elements of the mission and three German armoured divisions were immediately dispatched toward Budapest. All three operatives were captured and spent 396 days in captivity at Colditz.[17]

On 19 January 1945 six French generals – Lieutenant-General Jean Adolphe Louis Robert Flavigny; Major Generals Gustave Marie Maurice Mesny, Louis Léon Marie André Buisson and Arsène Marie Paul Vauthier and Brigadier Generals Albert Joseph Daine, and René Jacques Mortemart de Boisse – were brought from the camp at Königstein to Colditz Castle. On 5 February Polish General Tadeusz Bór-Komorowski, deputy commander of the Armia Krajowa (home army) and responsible for the Warsaw Uprising, arrived with his entourage. In March 1945, 1,200 French prisoners were brought to Colditz, with 600 more being imprisoned in the town below. During the last days at Colditz, many of its prominent or high-ranking prisoners were transferred to Laufen by order of Himmler. But in April 1945 troops of the US 1st Army entered the town of Colditz and, after a two-day fight, captured the castle on 16 April 1945. In May, the Soviet occupation of Colditz began. According to the agreement at the Yalta Conference it became a part of East Germany. The government turned Colditz Castle into a prison for local criminals. Later, the castle was a home for the aged and nursing home, as well as a hospital and psychiatric clinic. For many years after the war, forgotten hiding places and tunnels were found by

---

17. *Operatives, Spies, and Saboteurs: The Unknown Story of the Men and Women of World War Two's OSS* by Patrick K. O'Donnell (Free Press, 2004).

repairmen, including a radio room established by the French PoWs, which was then 'lost' again only to be rediscovered twenty years later.

During 2006 and 2007, the castle underwent a significant amount of refurbishment and restoration, which was paid for by the state of Saxony. The castle walls were repainted to recreate their appearance prior to the war. With renovations largely completed, the castle now includes a museum and guided tours show some of the escape tunnels built by prisoners of the Oflag during the war. The chapel has been restored to its pre-war decoration, with glass panels inserted in the flagstone flooring to reveal an escape tunnel dug by French escapees. The outer courtyard and former German Kommandantur have been converted into a youth hostel/hotel and the Gesellschaft Schloss Colditz e.V. (the Colditz Castle Historical Society), founded during 1996, has its offices in a portion of the administration building in the front castle court.

Index

Abernethy, Sergeant James Alexander Stephen, 1–2
Anabitarte, Tomás, 23
Armée Belge Secrete (ABS), x

Beamont, Roland, 115
Beobide, Florentino Goïcoechea, 23
Brettell, Flight Lieutenant Edward Gordon DFC, 104
Brickhill, Flight Lieutenant Paul Chester Jerome, 116
Bruce, Flying Officer Dominic, 171–2
Bruneau, Sergeant Joseph Arthur Angus, 22
Buckley, Lieutenant Commander James Brian DSC, 117, 119–21
Burton, Flying Officer Harry, viii–ix
Bushell, Squadron Leader, Roger, 118–21, 124, 127, 129–30, 136

Carter, Flying Officer DFC* RCAF, 45–64
Carter, Janine, 54–5, 58, 63–4
Clark, Lieutenant Colonel Albert Patton Jr., 109
Coache 'Madame Raymonde, 24–5
Codner, Second Lieutenant Richard Michael Clinton MC, 37–44, 145
Colditz Castle 120, 166–8
Colditz Cock, 185-186
Comet Line Escape (Flight Sergeant Stanley Munns) 76–93
Comet Line, xi–xii, 18, 20, 22, 25–6, 76–93
Craske, Warrant Officer Basil Sidney, 73–4
Cullignon, Maurice, 19

Day, 'Wing Commander Harry Melville Arbuthnot (Wings)', 117, 119–21, 137
De Jongh, Andrée Eugénie Adrienne, 20–5, 76, 87–8

De Jongh, Frédéric, xi, 20–1, 24, 76
Demany, Fernand, ix
Dewé Walthère, xi–xii
Doolittle Raid, 110
Dulag Luft Interrogation centre, Oberursel, viii, 2, 36–7, 41, 69, 70–2, 115, 117, 119, 170, 179, 182
Dumon, Andrée, ('Nadine') (Dédée), 20–1

Escape, The Great, 103–40
Evans, Flight Sergeant Bernard DFM, 20, 22, 24

Flockhart, Warrant Officer Cyril Bruce 'Paddy', 70–1

Goïcoechea, Florentino, 25–6
Goldie, Private James M.L., 24
Goodchild, Warrant Officer Kenneth Albert, 65–70
Grant, Cy, 113–14
Great Escape, The, 103–40
Grimson, Sergeant George, 71, 73–4

Hamburg, 28
Harsh, Flying Officer George Rutherford RCAF, 111–13
Hartnell Beavis, Squadron Leader John DFC, 116–17, 124–7

Heydekrug (Stalag Luft VI), 65–75
Heydrich, Reinhard, 120
Hillebrand, Karl, 4–9, 11

Kacenelenbeigen, Simon, 3
Kellett, Group Captain Richard DFC AFC, 42
Kinnan, Henry Wallace 'Wally', 114

Lamason, Squadron Leader Philip John DFC* RNZAF, 108–109
Lamsdorf, Stalag Luft VIIIB, 2–3
Leblanc, Flight Sergeant Charles Emile, 20–1
LeRay, Lieutenant Alain, 180–81

MacFarlane, Private William, 22, 24–6
Mairesse-Lebrun, Pierre, 172–3
Massey, Group Captain Herbert Martin, 121, 137
Moors, Gertrude, Maria Hubertina, 18
Mudgett, Major David 'Tokyo' Jones, 109–10
Munns, Flight Sergeant Stanley, 76–93

Neave, Airey, DSO OBE MC TD, 169–70, 180, 182

INDEX

Oakington, 28

Pack, Joseph Thomas 'Joe', 12–19, 21, 24–7
Paddon, Squadron Leader Brian, 170, 182
Parker, 'Bush', 178–9
Parnell, Sergeant Geoff, 65
Pat O'Leary Line, x–xi
Philpot, Oliver MC DFC, 40–3
Pire, Lieutenant General Jules-Joseph, x
Plunkett, Flight Lieutenant Desmond Lancelot, 124–5
Potter, Sergeant Alan Frank RNZAF, 2

Ravensbrück, 21
Redgrave, Squadron Leader Mark Evelyn, 1–2
Reid, Captain Patrick R., 167, 175–6, 178–9, 183–5
Réseau, Clarence Réseau, xii
Rofé, Cyril, 1–11

Sagan, 36, 72, 109
Sage, Major Jerry M., 110–11
Schaw, Warrant Officer Frederick Arthur RNZAF, 112
Scheidhauer, Souse Lieutenant Bernard W.M., 129, 136

Schoenmecker, Paul, 19
Sidwell, Pilot Officer Leslie Raymond, 28–44, 141–65
Spivey, Colonel Delmar Taft, 110
Stalag Luft IIIE, Kirchhain mass escape, 73
Steinhauer, George, RCAF, 16
St-Jean-de-Luz, 22–3

'Tante Go' or 'Auntie Go') Elvire De Greef, 22–3
Tuck, Robert Stanford, 113

von Lindeiner, Oberst Friedrich Wilhelm Gustav, 105, 108, 135

Watson, Pilot Officer John Henry RCAF, 20, 22
West, Sergeant Thomas Robert Augustus, 25–6
Williams, Flight Lieutenant Eric, 37–8, 40, 42–4, 145
Wilson, Pilot Officer Thomas William Spencer, 39
Wooden Horse Escape, the, vi, 39, 42–4, 145, 171–2

Zafouk, Pilot Officer Jaroslav 'Jack', 120
Zawodny, Sergeant Marian Henryck, 22, 24